THE IRISH BRANDY HOUSES OF
EIGHTEENTH-CENTURY FRANCE

The Irish Brandy Houses
of Eighteenth-Century France

L.M. Cullen

THE LILLIPUT PRESS
DUBLIN

First published 2000 by
THE LILLIPUT PRESS LTD
62-63 Sitric Road, Arbour Hill,
Dublin 7, Ireland.
www.lilliputpress.ie

A CIP record for this title is available from
The British Library.

ISBN 1 901866 40 8

Set in 11 on 14.5 Sabon by Sheila Stephenson
Printed in Ireland by ColourBooks, Baldoyle, Dublin

Contents

Illustrations between pages 116 and 117

Illustrations

Preface

Irishmen were prominent in the trade of Spain and France in the eighteenth century; Irish names still survive in streets, trading houses and chateaux. Lawton, Barton and Johnston are hallowed names in Bordeaux, a Quin has been one of the administrators of the port, and wine chateaux carry the names Lynch, Kirwan, MacCarthy and Boyd. In brandy, the Irish connection was particularly strong. Two Cognac houses descend from Irish families, and three others – Martell, Hine and Augier – had many Irish associations.

This book follows on from an earlier work, *The Brandy Trade under the Ancien Régime*, published by Cambridge University Press in 1998. That book dealt with production and trade. This book concerns primarily the brandy families of Cognac, Jarnac, Bordeaux and La Rochelle. Much has been left out for reasons of space. An account of the impact of the inflation on the brandy trade under Law's monetary experiments in 1720 has been left aside, and the story of the Irish experiences in Cognac and Bordeaux under the Revolution has been greatly compressed. Although much attention has been given to the house of Martell, which, though not Irish, had a large role in the Irish brandy trade, full justice has not been done to Louis-Gabriel Lallemand and Théodore Martell, in their day very remarkable men, the latter also the moving force in creating the Hennessy–Martell matrimonial alliance of 1795. I hope to return to these subjects on another occasion.

Since this research began more than twenty-three years ago, the landscape of the modern cognac trade has changed almost beyond recognition. The custody, and in many cases the physical location of the records, has inevitably changed also, though a researcher can not but retain nostalgic memories of the Hennessy records under the care of the sommelier of the house, the genial and hospitable Louis Bertin. Over time the quest for information led to many locations beyond the expected ones, to the Archives de la Guerre in Paris; to Vannes, Jerez, and (fruitlessly) Bath; and the Hennessy records themselves prompted an interest in Edmund Burke, childhood friend of Richard Hennessy.

The obligations accumulated in the course of a protracted research project are too many to list. Some are set out in the 1998 volume. Two in particular have to be restated, both to descendants of the surviving Irish houses who may may be relieved as much as pleased that the book has been completed. Alain Braastad, descendant of James Delamain, provided unfailing encouragement, much hospitality and advice on a wide range of issues: without him the inadequacies of this book would be even greater. Maurice Richard Hennessy, like his ancestor custodian of the Irish market, has likewise provided unstinted assistance and support.

The Hennessy archives in their completeness and in their content of both business and personal correspondence are virtually a unique collection of business records. Madame Marie-Gabriel Jouannet, the Hennessy archivist, and Mlle Danièle Rousseau in Martell have often had their time taken up, and my gratitude to them is great. I am thankful to M. Gérard de Ramefort, former managing director of Otard, M. Jacques de Varenne of Augier *frères*, M. Bernard Hine, Madame Evelyne Chapeau Woodrow (who pioneered the excellent order of the Martell records), Mr Arthur Moran of Matheson Ormsby Prentice, Mr D. Doyle of Killavullin, Co. Cork, Mr Paul Weber, Mr Gerry Lyne of the National Library of Ireland, and Professors Thomas Bartlett and Kevin Whelan.

For permission to reproduce illustrations, I am indebted to M. Hennessy, M. Braastad, Madame Noël Sauzey, Dr Jean-Louis Plisson, M. Christian Vernou, M. Hine, the Musée de Cognac, and the Musée de la Marine, Paris. I acknowledge also the permission of Cambridge University Press to reproduce the map, and the skill of Matthew Stout in preparing it.

The Arts and Social Science Research Fund, the Provost's Development Fund and the Grace Lawless Lee Fund of Trinity College, and the CNRS–Forbairt exchange agreement provided material support towards the research in France. Periods as a *directeur d'études associé* at the Centre de Recherches Historiques, Ecole des Hautes Etudes en Sciences Sociales, Paris; Visiting Fellow in All Souls College, Oxford; and Visiting Professor in the University of Strathclyde, helped to make possible the pursuit of some of the background issues in Franco–Irish and Franco–British trade and payments of the period.

Finally, publication has been made possible by generous financial support from Hennessy Cognac, the Provost's Development Fund and the Grace Lawless Lee Fund.

L.M. Cullen
January 2000

Glossary

anker: In French *ancre*, a small measure used by smugglers, about 12 to 16 gallons, English or Irish measure.

barrique: In English, barrel. In La Rochelle a measure containing 27 *veltes* (or 54 gallons), in Bordeaux 32 *veltes* (or 64 gallons).

Charente: Denotes both the river and the region, though in French as the region was divided from revolutionary times into two *départements* with Charente in their title, the region is referred to in the plural as the 'Charentes'. The term was also used to signify the tiny port of Charente which grew up on the tidal limit of the river at Tonnay. Though rarely so described at the time, it is now usually referred to as 'Tonnay-Charente' to avoid ambiguity and confusion with Tonnay-Boutonne.

gallon: In England the gallon measure was slightly larger than the so-called Irish one (the measures were unified at the English standard in the wake of the Act of Union). The gallon measure in England was 231 cubic inches, while the Irish measure was 217.6 cubic inches. In other words an Irish gallon was approximately 94 per cent of an English gallon. It is never clear in contemporary French correspondence which gallon was in mind in correspondents' letters. In the text of this book a gallon is to be assumed to be English capacity unless otherwise designated or implied.

généralité: Administrative district superintended by an *intendant*. It usually embraced several historic provinces, and was the basic unit for the compilation of the statistics of the *balance du commerce*. As such each généralité contained several 'bureaux' (in British customs parlance 'creeks').

livre: French money of account. Foreign exchange between Ireland and France was usually done through Irish houses in London. The par rate, based on the combined par in the Anglo-Irish and Franco-British exchanges, was approximately 23 livres to an Irish pound.

négociant: Merchant who received or drew credit instruments in the form of drafts and bills of exchange. The older term *marchand* was disappearing from use, and was increasingly confined to lower grades of merchant.

pièce: A large measure, the largest used in shipping brandy, generally the equivalent of 81 *veltes* or three barriques. In Bordeaux the *pièce* was a measure of 50 *veltes*.

puncheon: In French, *tierçon*. A measure amounting to two barriques. The puncheon was the barrel most commonly used in actual shipments.

rectification: Enhancing the alcoholic strength of brandy, usually by a further distillation.

tierçon: French for puncheon.

velte: Or *verge*. Widely used as a measure of content, the equivalent of two (English) gallons. Hence it contained 8 *pintes*.

In general, measures are given in *ancien régime* units, rather than as in modern French practice, converted into metric equivalents. The use of *ancien régime* measures reduces the ambiguities of processing uncertain or variable measures, and, more importantly, remains a more convenient mode of comparison for historical purposes with figures as quoted in both older and modern sources in English, where metric usage is still little used in historical monographs.

Quotations are given verbatim, in their often faulty English or French. Given the high incidence of errors and archaisms in the originals, I have used [*sic*] as sparingly as possible.

For the conversion of the Republican calendar into the Gregorian calendar, I have followed M. Lyons, *France under the Directory* (Cambridge, 1995), appendix I, pp. 239–40.

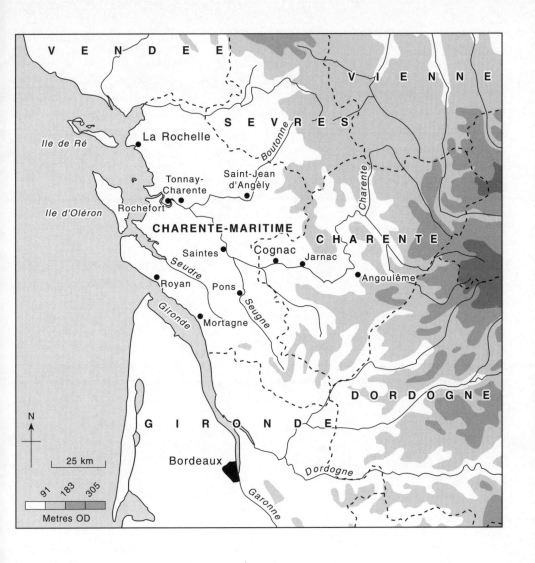

The Charente region and environs

I

The rise of the brandy trade

THE EMERGENCE OF BRANDY

The seventeenth and eighteenth centuries were an age of transformation in trade. A degree of abundance began to emerge in western Europe, and after 1741 famine had largely disappeared. The quality of food improved, and exotic products were increasingly available. Growing cities became prime centres of consumption, drawing on internal and international supply routes alike. London proved pre-eminent in Europe because England's gentry, the richest by virtue of the inegalitarian distribution of wealth in England, spent much of their income and leisure in London. Where spirits were concerned, they took over the role formerly played by the Dutch, who had been the driving force in international demand for spirits.

Trade and production in alcoholic beverages changed inevitably as part of the overall transformation of agriculture on both sides of the Atlantic. As surplus arose from a more productive cereal agriculture and from the soaring output of the new sugar plantations in the West Indies, a rising proportion of output could be converted into alcohol. At the outset of the period, the quality of beverages from grape and grain was undistinguished. Beer was often made from inferior cereals. Spirits were little consumed, and rum was as yet unknown. In Ireland spirits were made, like the indigenous ale, from oats, an unsatisfactory raw material for brewing (which was itself a preliminary stage in distilling). Moreover, much of the later stages of a pass through the still,

1

containing an inferior liquid in which alcohol strength was low and noxious substances numerous, was allowed to join the earlier stages in the receptacle which gathered the outflow: the product was at worst a killer if consumed in quantity, at best unpleasant and often necessarily sweetened by additives.

Wine went off quickly and was usually consumed well within the year; beer, even shorter-lived, was consumed within days; spirits were hastily made just ahead of demand. A paradox, but a rational one, was that apart from regions rich in barley, densely populated and consuming a more professionally made though still short-lived beer, red wine was surprisingly prevalent as a beverage of the colder, wetter and more thinly populated parts of northern Europe for all who could afford it. For centuries a large inflow of wine characterized the exchanges between northern and southern Europe and though this wine was itself indifferent, it was better as a beverage than the crude beers in most of northern Europe.

Because wine turned, sometimes in as little as a few months, to a vinegar-like substance, some preferred a white wine made from late-ripening grapes with a high sugar content that protected the product on long voyages. Typically, it could be drunk a year or more after being loaded aboard, whereas other wines were by then often undrinkable. Poor wine, no less than ale, could make soldiers ill, and as late as the 1770s the Irishman Thomas Sutton, a major figure in financing East Indian voyages from France, regarded the keeping quality of red wine as grossly inferior.[1] As long sea voyages became common, the poor-keeping red wines were consumed first, the sweet white wines during the later stages. Even when spirits had begun to take the place of wine on the return voyage on French ships for the ordinary crew members, wine remained the preferred drink of officers. The white wine was an expensive product, a circumstance which limited its foreign markets to well-off customers or to fleets like the Dutch which were the best of their age. Its high cost made it easier for brandy to take its place, except among conservative, influential and status-conscious drinkers such as the officers on French vessels. Sutton preferred rum to other spirits for his vessels.

After 1600 the wine trade, as one of the longest established of Europe's trades, grew slowly as the comparatively good statistics of the period show.[2] In peacetime and even in wartime, when provenances (the ports of origin) rather than quantities were falsified, wine statistics are fairly reliable. In the eighteenth century wine exports from Bordeaux rose only moderately, once consumption in the booming French colonies is excluded, despite the city's swelling colonial market and its place as one of the three or four most important ports of Europe. Likewise, coastal shipments, which are a guide to consumption in the north of France, increased relatively little.

While new centres of wine exports emerged, they did not alter the overall level of consumption decisively. If port wine from Portugal expanded, Canary and Spanish wine, comparable products, fared badly. A large proportion of the increased output in Languedoc went into new spirit demand, not into the existing wine trade. A more serious threat to wine's place in the global consumption of alcohol came from new products rather than from new centres of wine production. The emergence of factory-type processing activity, both in food products like sugar and in beverages such as beer and spirits, set the pattern. The expansion of gin production in Holland was decisive in elaborating techniques for a new scale of spirit production and in promoting tastes. In beer, the Flemish Lowlands and at a later date London provided the models for a larger scale of production and above all a keeping quality which widened the market in geographical extent: London could dominate the Dublin market of the middle decades of the century, and the real growth of Dublin brewing dated only from the 1770s.[3]

A revolution in beverages is part of the story of the century. Beer was transformed from a near-domestic production (made on the premises by the alehouse keeper) into a factory product, with a longer life and of better quality. In wine, more care was taken with the identification of the best growths, fermentation and after-care: the classic Médocs and burgundies began to emerge. For other than the top customers paying high prices, and indeed even for them after poor vintages, imported Spanish wine was mixed with the often thin Bordeaux wine; the conflict of interest between shippers and growers on this score, already evident by the 1740s, was to remain through the century. *Coupage* – blending – with the stronger imported wines added colour and strength. Complaints about Bordeaux wines on the score of these deficiencies had been the main ones from Dublin importers (who imported far more claret than Londoners did, though little of the quite small total quantity of Margaux and Lafite of which rich Londoners were the main consumers). Another solution, as in port and sherry, was to fortify wines with spirit.

These changes in wine seem to have occurred within the period 1680–1720. Significantly, they occurred in the context of external markets, where the unavoidable delays in transport ensured that poor quality was most in evidence, and the changes were increasingly promoted and even directed by foreigners: in Bordeaux, Irish and Germans; in Iberia, principally Englishmen in Oporto and Irishmen in Seville and Cadiz. In the Canaries the English colony of the seventeenth century was replaced by a largely Irish one of the eighteenth century.[4] Thus a wide range of products emerged: the classic wines expensively and carefully made; the common Bordeaux strengthened with Spanish wine after weak vintages; and port, Madeira and sherry in their new form of fortified wines. In the same years brandy exports from France rose and the decisive superior quality of cognac was for the first time unambiguously recognized, and somewhat more quickly abroad than in France itself.* Gin, in London and even earlier in Holland, was the first true factory-made spirit. Rum, already widely available in the West Indies, began in the 1720s to reach Ireland and England in commercial quantities. In other words, we now had the whole range of products and manufacturing techniques of modern wine and spirits.

TRADE AND PRODUCTION IN SPIRITS

Spirits encountered two problems. The first was that some abundance of wine or grain was necessary. Even casual abundance was not of itself sufficient, because the grapes used for table wines did not produce good brandy, and successful distilling required a thin acidic wine; in the case of beer, barley (increasingly rejected as a bread flour as food standards rose) was grown expressly as a raw material for

---

*Brandy from near the town of Cognac traded under the designation 'cognac', and increasingly as 'champagne'; from somewhat farther afield, it came to be marketed under the rather ironic term of 'best cognac'. That in turn differentiated it from brandy from still more distant districts, which traded simply as 'eau de vie'.

brewing on ground that would otherwise have grown food crops of wheat. In the best circumstances six units of wine made one unit of brandy; likewise a grain-distillation industry required an advanced agriculture or ready imports of quantities of the desired cereals. Availability of specialist grapes not suitable for table wines was indispensable (and became realistic only as a market began to emerge), and in the case of whiskey, the distilling industry, especially inland, could not prosper without a switch of land to barley growing, in other words from food crops to beverage crops. The second problem was the need for the expert production necessary to ensure adequate knowledge of techniques and a willingness to eschew time-saving and material-saving methods that produced an abundant but defective and even dangerous spirit.

The latter consideration makes it necessary to set out some description of distillation processes. Brandy is produced by the distillation of wine. As the alcohols contained in wine have a lower boiling point than water, the volatile alcoholic elements separate easily from the liquid, leaving less volatile elements, some of them noxious, behind. In distillation the fire must be maintained evenly: if the heat becomes excessive, the whole liquid boils over, and desired and undesired elements alike simultaneously ascend through the neck or head of the still, and down through the cooling worm or serpentine into the basin intended to receive the alcohol. A single distillation of wine does not produce a palatable product, and a further distillation of the distillate (sometimes even a third one) is necessary to produce a satisfactory product. In the second distillation, today known as the *bonne chauffe*, the proportion of alcohol in the flow progressively declined to a point where spirit in the flow was a declining fraction of a watery and noxious residue. The first stage of the flow was known in the eighteenth century variously as *première* or *bonne et forte eau de vie* – the *coeur* of modern language. The later stage in the flow, down to the point where there was more aqueous residue than alcohol in the flow, was known as *seconde*. The spirit as marketed in the seventeenth and eighteenth centuries contained both *première* and *seconde*. However, in the most advanced districts and among the most skilful distillers a process of retaining only the *première* or *coeur* was beginning to emerge, producing a finer and more palatable product which was closer to modern cognac than the typical brandy of the early eighteenth century. It was recognized even in the seventeenth century that recourse to further distillation (i.e. a third or fourth distillation) would result in even stronger brandy. With the aim of producing a better quality and a higher strength, distillers consciously selected the early flow from the still. A factor influencing quality and strength alike was that when the first distillate was returned to the still for a second distillation, the still was topped up with distillate (high in degrees of alcohol), rather than wine (low in alcohol). This would be highly inconvenient for a distiller working in a confined space with one or even two stills, and hence the best brandy making was done by the larger distillers with several stills, and came to characterize the regions where they predominated. Stills had a capacity of a mere 60 to 80 gallons, and the scale of production was measured by the number of stills, not by their capacity.

An added problem with spirits was that the estimation of strength was erratic. It was first measured simply by observation or crude empirical tests of the volatility of the liquid. By the 1760s the pioneering hydrometer was in widespread use in Dublin (following the example of London). It was introduced to the Charente from Dublin and by the Irish traders of the early 1760s, eager to buy brandy at the right strength. However, *éprouvettes* of any kind were slow to become known in Paris in commercial and scientific circles alike, and Richard Hennessy's relative Pat Nagle wrote from Paris to him in frustration in 1766 that 'after all the enquiries I could make as well of grocers as brandy sellors and four members of the Academy of Sciences I could not succed, all whom told me there was no such thing'.[5]

Early commercial distillation was pioneered in Holland. However, despite Holland's easy access to a supply of grain, brandy was necessary to supplement the supply of grain-based spirits as demand increased in the second half of the seventeenth century. By way of contrast, in much poorer countries, such as Ireland, imported spirits, not domestic output, provided the basis of the sustained expansion in spirit consumption. In Holland, Europe's central grain market, gin found itself at a disadvantage if bad harvests pushed up gin prices. Only from the 1720s was grain supply universally reliable enough to make possible a stable gin industry. Dutch techniques and taste had already migrated to England, and created a new industry which soared in the 1730s, when grain was cheap. In France, a Paris market for spirits, satisfied with brandy, was developing at the same time; it accelerated greatly in the extraordinarily favourable vintages and low prices of the late 1720s and 1730s. The sale of spirits at street corners in Paris to artisans on their way to work in the morning in the 1720s is not much different from the excesses of Hogarthian London, and the pace of spirit development was dictated by urban demand. Export markets and French inland markets were now for the first time in serious competition with one another for the available supply of brandy, and in years of poor vintages when prices rose, the spirit consumer in the north of France, with no alternative spirit to turn to, inevitably outbid the foreign buyers.

In England, with its high import duties and an abundant cereal agriculture, home-distilled spirits satisfied the new demand. In Ireland, with a defective cereal supply, the situation differed from England, and from Holland with its international grain market. In 1665 imports amounted to 65,638 gallons, the equivalent of 1200 La Rochelle barriques. They were already a subject of adverse comment as a novel form of luxury expenditure by 1670,[6] and held their own subsequently. With a short-lived boom in Irish purchasing power in 1697 at the end of a seven-year European war, spirit imports soared in unprecedented fashion to 271,796 gallons in 1701. Before 1731 spirits imports were more than twice the level of domestic spirit production, but this was to change, as was sensed by Samuel Madden in 1738 when he declared that 'our distillers make excellent spirits, from our own grain of aqua vitae, which are as palatable and vastly cheaper, and more wholesome, and do also furnish us with an usquebaugh, which no nation can come up to'.[7] By 1753 W. Henry, alarmed by the spread in the consumption of whiskey, noted the impact of domestic production on French brandy.[8] In the 1750s home output satisfied half of consumption, though a decade later a combination of soaring demand and poor harvests reduced this proportion.

A dramatic crisis, which occurred in Ireland in the wake of bad harvests in the second half of the 1750s, continued into the early 1760s as, because of war, the supply of rum faltered. Brandy exports from France to Holland, which in the preceding decade had become negligible, immediately jumped as neutral Holland served in wartime as an entrepôt base for Ireland. At their peak in 1761 the exports from La Rochelle to 'Holland' were 17,800 barriques; if we strip from this figure English imports of brandy of 1910 tons (or 7640 barriques) as recorded in English trade statistics, the balance of 10,000 barriques would crudely approximate to Irish imports. This would be 507,600 Irish gallons of brandy, very close to the Irish customs returns for spirit imports, which in the four years ending March 1763 averaged 500,000 gallons. The end of war itself did not halt the growth of the trade. A stronger demand for spirits combined with some delay in the response of the rum trade and a recurrence of poor domestic harvests in the mid-1760s meant that up to and including the year ended March 1768 brandy imports were to run at a level just above or below 700,000 gallons (approximately 12,000 barriques).[9]

Given the modest Irish business with La Rochelle in the past, the fact that Irish buyers congregated there and in its hinterland in the 1750s and 1760s reflected the dominant place that Cognac now held in export brandy trade on the Atlantic coast. This, though certainly not the first boom in Irish brandy imports, was the first real one from La Rochelle and its hinterland. Good French vintages in 1759–61, a temporary halt in Irish distillation (in the wake of harvest failure) and a shortfall in rum were the factors behind it.

THE ECONOMIC SIGNIFICANCE OF BRANDY BUSINESS

The place of brandy in what can be described as a consumer revolution has been underestimated as a result of a tendency to see it as a product of excess wine (a French parallel, though of a different kind, to various Irish and Scottish whiskey-myths). If seen as a phenomenon of excess, it can be represented, and has been so seen, as a consequence of chronic wine surplus, and hence less as a sign of development than of growing crisis. In reality, it was part of a phenomenon of changing tastes and products in a complex and unprecedented framework of choice. Brandy supplemented gin; in time, brandy lost some markets, notably the Dutch; on the other hand other markets arose, including a quality one in England (to supplement the gin and rum consumed by other classes in society), less qual-ity-conscious markets in Ireland and northern Europe, and large mar-kets in northern France (a metropolitan one in Paris and a more diffuse one in towns and countryside farther north).

Hence brandy relied on stable markets in Paris and London and on more transient or fluctuating outlets such as Ireland. After poor vintages, Paris was forced to outbid other customers; in good years, when Paris did not need to pay high prices, foreigners came back in force as buyers. As foreign demand fluctuated widely, influenced by the availability and prices of rum and whiskey, Paris became the backbone of the French brandy trade. One consequence has been that because exports (readily documented in statistics of foreign trade) fre-quently collapsed, brandy has been regarded as an erratic trade (because statistics of the soaring inland trade do not exist). There was a contrast also between the rich London merchants buying rather fixed quantities regularly and with a degree of price-resistance, and the Irish importers who entered and disappeared. In contrast to the London importers, who were wholesalers dealing directly with retail-ers and larger consumers, the Irish importers were less stable opera-tors, selling speculatively rather than wholesaling, and hence apt to fail if they miscalculated. In 1774 Lallemand, the effective manager of the Martell house, observed to his London correspondents in regard to the solvency of the Irish houses that 'nous ne pouvons con-damner votre circonspection vis-à-vis des maisons irlandaises en général ...'.[10] The Irish operators were squeezed on one side by the pressures from Paris buyers in bad years to bid up the price, on the other side by the fact that Irish consumers could buy spirits elsewhere in a Dublin market which had a far larger import content in relation to total supply than the London market.

A progressive separation of brandy-making regions from wine-exporting ones took place; this was inevitable, as brandy required a distinctive vine unsuitable for table wine. Thus brandy was not a product brought into existence by an unsaleable glut of wine. Brandy production along the Loire was at first promoted by proximity to Paris and by a foreign market in Nantes (largely in the hands of Irish-men who into the 1730s sold their beef and butter there more than in Bordeaux). Farther south, Cognac did well; as Bordeaux's brandy distilling contracted, Cognac's hinterland developed a specialized trade in several markets: Paris and the north of France via inland and coastal routes, and foreign markets via riverine and coastal outlets in and adjacent to the Saintonge province. Competing demands even pushed prices up. La Rochelle as a region (or *généralité*) grew stronger (even if La Rochelle, the port, was progressively marginalized to the benefit of the houses and small ports in its hinterland); the brandy trade also helped to strengthen Bordeaux as a foreign-exchange market; and brandy bills, sold in Bordeaux by Cognac houses to acquire cash and constituting the largest single block of first-class bills of exchange on London, arbitraged the London exchange rates in Bordeaux and Paris.

IRISH BRANDY HOUSES

In other words, brandy prospered. Foreign trade was dominated by a handful of houses largely of foreign origin. Two modern houses surviving to this day are Irish in origin: Hennessy, itself one of the two giants of the modern industry, and Delamain, a small house that makes one of the world's most famous cognacs. Other Irish houses that made an appearance in the region, though deaths meant that they never made a permanent stake, were Bellew, Galwey, Geoghegan and Saule.

The story of the Irish stake in the Charente in and after the 1760s revolves around three names – Delamain, Hennessy, Saule – with the addition in the 1780s of a Delamain nephew, Turner. As Martell Lallemand, the most successful house of the second half of the century, had also originally been an outsider, the question arises as to why foreigners at large played such a central part. If Otard is treated as a house of foreign origin (an issue which raises tantalizing questions), the three dominant houses of the first half of the nineteenth century had foreign origins.

Outside settlement was concentrated in two periods, the first around 1720, when the Channel Island houses of Martell and Le Mesurier and the Londoner John Baker appeared; the second, the years 1760–6. In this second period, settlement was prompted largely by Dublin interests who wanted to extend their involvement into buying in the Cognac region itself, and by Irish interests in Bordeaux, who felt that the Irish demand for cognac could be satisfied by a transit trade through Bordeaux. In Bordeaux the Irish colony, second only to the Hamburg colony in numbers and wealth, had grown in both the 1720s and in the 1740s/1750s as a consequence of the rising exchange of Irish beef and butter for Bordeaux wines. By the early 1750s a Galwey house, in other words a house with a connection to a family of the same name in Bordeaux, had made a short-lived appearance in Cognac, and the revival of a great design for settlement in the region by the Bordeaux Galweys occurred in the 1760s. For the remainder of the century, close links existed between Bordeaux and Cognac largely through the region's Irishmen: they both sought to ship cognac through Bordeaux to Ireland (because shipping was more numerous there) and promoted a more commercialized distilling within the port of Bordeaux itself. As such they are a key element in the movement of men, capital and skills which was an essential factor in the conversion of the southwest of France from two separate economic regions into a single and richer economic entity.

BRANDY SMUGGLING

Brandy was itself divided into two components: a quality one (first evident in Amsterdam but more powerfully represented by London's unique dominance from the 1720s of the aged champagne brandy from Cognac town and its immediate hinterland), and a lower grade taken in part by Holland, but also by Ireland and by Hamburg. As brandy duties overseas were high, once consumption grew it was clear that the market for the lower grades could be tapped by brandy supplied by smugglers. Nantes represented this market in its origins; as many as forty vessels each carried a hundred puncheons of brandy to Ireland in the 1730s, in other words some 400,000 gallons (of which roughly half was on the account of smugglers).[11] The Isle of Man supplied the same market and drew variously on Nantes up to the 1730s, and in later days on Charente, Bordeaux and Spain. Once the Isle of Man was closed, business opened up for direct shipment from Dunkirk, Roscoff and Guernsey. A pattern emerged in the business in later decades: Dunkirk and Boulogne concentrated on the English clandestine market (though Dunkirk had an Irish custom of consequence in the 1760s and 1770s), while Roscoff and Guernsey supplied the Irish and Scottish market. Thus, there were two segments in the trade: one a regrouped business in an extended and fluctuating pattern along the coast from Roscoff to Bordeaux that catered for the Irish and Scottish market, the other the concentrated activity which emerged in Boulogne and Dunkirk. From the 1760s this smuggling enjoyed systematic support in French official policy, including explicit toleration in wartime. In 1776, when a decline in smuggling in Roscoff was attributed to the zeal of the parish priest in compelling cooks to refuse to cook meat on Fridays and Saturdays for English mariners, Turgot the *contrôleur général* or minister of finance intervened.[12] When a shortage of spirits resulted from grain failure and a closure of distilleries in 1782–5, Irish smugglers, who of course continued to visit Roscoff, also appeared in Bordeaux.

The Scottish houses of the Isle of Man and the Ayrshire coast were a central component of the brandy business on the western coasts of both the Irish and British markets, and they migrated variously to Guernsey, Roscoff and Dunkirk after 1765. By 1789 Guernsey greatly overshadowed Dunkirk in supplying the Irish market (as the British business crowded out other activity there), and even Roscoff despite its few advantages proved surprisingly resilient. Smaller to start with, the trade in smuggled brandy to England had become the largest segment of spirits business in the 1780s, with a huge turnover conducted through Boulogne and Dunkirk. Smuggling was not itself the central element of brandy business at large, but it is necessary to look at it both because legend – incorrectly – sees smuggling as a basic feature of the rise of brandy consumption and because the Irish smuggling presence was at times a significant element in international brandy trade, though never so in the business of Cognac itself.

The 1780s were a strange Indian summer of activity in the southwest of France in smuggling brandy to Ireland. Trade at large between Ireland and France was in decline from the end of the American war. Supplies of beef from America were beginning to replace the Irish beef sent in transit via French ports which had been the backbone of the Irish trade, and new taxes imposed in Ireland on French wine during hostilities had encouraged a switch from French to Portuguese and Spanish wine. A large traffic in legal brandy in the early 1780s flourished only as long as Irish harvests were bad. By contrast brandy smuggling from the south-west of France actually expanded in the remainder of the 1780s: suspected smuggling sailings from Bordeaux rose to 22 in 1788 and to 29 in 1789, and while smugglers intending to load directly for the Irish market had very rarely if ever visited the Charente itself, they made an appearance there in 1784–7. While the usually small smuggling craft vessels also took other contraband aboard (especially tobacco) in Bordeaux, brandy was consistently an item, and sometimes the sole cargo. In the second half of the 1780s they dominated the brandy trade in the port itself. Smuggling was by nature highly speculative, with activity swinging from intervals of hectic buying from the port-based distillers to long ones of inaction. The busy bouts of activity served to keep alive the illusory hope that the brandy business in Bordeaux might become a secure trade. That false hope explains why the Irish distiller Andoe worked through the 1780s and lingered until war broke out in 1793; why Hennessy had offers from others of joining him, if he could hold on, when he ran into difficulties in 1787; and why some Irishmen with the capital which Hennessy lacked entered afresh into distilling in the port as late as 1789.

2

Brandy smuggling

SMUGGLING DEMAND AND TRADE

The parson's brandy and the squire's cellar are part of popular historical fiction. The best brandy, however, was not smuggled, and the growth of smuggling itself depended on a widening consumer market for spirits and on cheap and competitive products to satisfy it. In the short term, both ends of the trade prospered at the same time. Intermittent bouts of public or administrative concern about smuggling have created a false impression of its extent: the evidence has been assembled in modern accounts, disregarding chronology and contemporary administrative concerns, into a proof of the ubiquity and persistence of the practices, as if all the smuggling centres flourished simultaneously. The reality was that in a highly speculative and cost-conscious activity the supply routes and channels of distribution were never constant: individual supply centres abroad and points of distribution were unstable and often short-lived.

Smuggled brandy tapped social levels below those supplied by the legally imported product. At this end of the market, given its lower prices, it also had a better prospect of competing with rum. Hence smuggled brandy both played a part in supporting the spread of spirit drinking and in maintaining a niche for brandy in the wider spirit consumption that was becoming a feature of the 1720s and 1730s. If, for instance, Irish legal imports contracted in the 1730s, the Irish market for contraband brandy, both direct and roundabout through the Isle of Man, held up. Brandy from Nantes was important in the Irish smuggling trade in the 1720s and 1730s, as well as in legal trade at the time.[1] Some business lingered on in later decades in Nantes for the Isle of Man, managed through the hands of the Nantes branch of the Galwey family. When the British authorities in 1765 decreed the closure of the island to trade in commodities which on the neighbouring Irish and British shores were high-duty goods, this business came to Nantes. The Parks, Irishmen working in the Isle of Man for a partnership directed by the Bordeaux Irish house of Black, settled after 1765 as an independent enterprise briefly in Nantes and then transferred to Roscoff. The Galweys conducted some business with Ireland. They sold some brandy to the O'Connells of Derrynane, for instance in 1766; and when an Irish army officer Warren was involved in redeveloping the island of Bellisle off the coast of Brittany for the Acadians, i.e. Frenchmen who had left Canada, they briefly used it as an entrepôt centre for supplying Irish smugglers.[2] The partnership of Baker & Bryhan was the sole Cognac house with a regular Isle of Man trade. Further afield in Bordeaux, the Irish firm of Black had a branch house in the island as early as the 1740s which remained active until that business was suppressed in 1765.[3] When Spanish brandy made its appearance in growing quantity, in 1760 the merchant house of Brock in Guernsey quoted a price for Spanish brandy to the County Kerry smuggling business of the O'Connells, who had formerly drawn their brandy from Nantes.[4]

RUM, THE ISLE OF MAN AND DUNKIRK

With the easing of the supply of rum in the wake of the ending of the Seven Years War, and soaring brandy prices in France, rum became the main staple of spirit smuggling. Peace in European waters made it feasible to re-export rum, with a refund of the duties paid on first entry, to the Continent from either Ireland or Scotland with the explicit intention of selling it there to the smugglers for the Irish and Scottish markets. Such rum dominated spirit business on the Ayrshire coast, for instance, and smugglers warehoused the spirit at Guernsey and Dunkirk.[5] When the Isle of Man's fiscal independence was terminated in 1765 by the British government's purchase of its fiscal privileges from the Duke of Atholl, owner of the island, Dunkirk, long the forwarding station for quality cognac for London, for a time became the main repository of all spirits destined for the smuggling market, supplemented by Guernsey and from 1769 by Roscoff.

Relatively little brandy from the Charente region reached the Isle of Man, the smugglers' preferred mart of mid-century, and even more rarely did smugglers actually load supplies in the Charente for direct dispatch to their home districts. An exceptional order was that from the Bantry house of Robert Young in 1767: he had been recommended to Delamain by a correspondent, Robert Hutchins, described as a mutual friend. The vessel was to be cleared for Bantry though with liberty to touch other points on the Irish coast; its charter party and bill of lading were to specify Bergen, and care was to be taken to ensure that incriminating papers were not on board.[6] Young's fleeting contact with Cognac coincided with brandy orders by the O'Connells to a Nantes house in 1766 and 1767. Both ventures, coming close on the closure of the Isle of Man in 1765, reflect a hasty exploration of alternative supply channels. Even if the contacts with Charente were fleeting, the highly speculative character of the business meant that smugglers could make a reappearance in Charente: in October 1774, for instance, Delamain was loading a vessel skippered by a member of a well-known Rush smuggling family, John Oram.[7] The soaring brandy prices at this time in France soon killed off business with French suppliers. Rum became central to the business. Imported from America to Scotland or Ireland, it was re-exported to Guernsey or Dunkirk for shipment back. When business in smuggled spirits rose, it ate into the existing legitimate channels of supply. This explains too why a Dublin brandy dealer complained to Hennessy in 1774 that 'the private traders have hurted our trade here very much'.[8]

When Robert Young had ordered his brandy in 1767 it was supplied in barriques, not in the ankers standard in the smuggling trade. What this implied was that the ankers or small barrels preferred by smugglers were not to hand, and that Young had to make do with the smallest size of barrels regularly available in the Charente. Illegal in Irish customs law, ankers were not encouraged by the revenue authorities in France either, though not prohibited. However, if notice was given, there was no problem in making such barrels, and once smuggling visits could be taken for granted, their availability eased. The problem was that smugglers, involved in highly speculative operations switching often at short notice from one source of supply to another, usually arrived with little notice, or even without any advance advice of an order. As early as November 1773, however, Hennessy assured a Dublin man that there was no difficulty in shipping in twelve gallon casks.[9] In 1774 a merchant, Luke Cassin, bringing in brandy in a legal fashion, became interested in smuggling in the face of competition from the 'private traders'. In August he wrote to Hennessy that 'I have been informed that you shipped some time ago a parcel of brandy in small casks. Let me know in your next is casks to be got in a week notice. If there was I would order you to ship me a parcel.'[10] In the brandy boom in the early 1780s, smugglers still arrived at short notice, occasionally even with specie to settle their account. In the case of one small vessel which came out to Cognac regularly in 1784 and 1785 casks seem to have been brought out from Dublin. Saule commended the smugglers: 'you've done well to send out the small casks which will be a great saving as all the unusual made casks cost very dear'.[11]

In the 1770s, there were for smugglers two major spirit marts, Guernsey and Dunkirk. Guernsey may have finally fared better than Dunkirk, which was the more speculative centre. When the Hutchins of Ballylicky finally gave up business in 1778, for instance, Guernsey was their centre of supply.[12] Moreover in 1778, on the advent of war, Dunkirk's business was transferred to the neutral port of Flushing. The wartime increase in duties was a catalyst of future business once war was over; higher duties meant both a rise in smuggling and a relative shift from the good-quality cognac to the cheaper brandies of other provenance. The fact that the brandy trade in Dunkirk in 1783 was 'almost at a stand' was merely a first reaction to new anti-smuggling laws in England.[13] English demand, hitherto smaller than Irish or Scottish demand for smuggled spirits, quickly became the dominant smuggling custom in Dunkirk, and activity expanded in Boulogne as well.[14] Business always peaked in winter and spring months when the supply of new brandy was highest. In the summer, 'the smuggling boats are mostly laid up ... by reason of the short nights'.[15] Contemporary accounts are impressive in their estimates of the volume of business.[16] A mixed quality of brandy was prepared under the name of cognac but was 'fit only for the smugglers'.[17] Provided it was strong and well-coloured, 'it will do for the common sale here and the ... old [brandy] ... may do for the London market, if there should be a demand from thence for it'.[18] In 1789 the total quantities of spirits for England from Dunkirk and Boulogne made a total of 26,897 barriques (1,452,579 gallons).[19] This activity alone accounted for about a quarter of spirit exports from France.

BRANDY SMUGGLERS IN BORDEAUX AND CHARENTE

Bad years or shortages created wider circuits of demand, and custom overflowed from the more regular channels to Bordeaux and Charente. Thus Bordeaux, especially for smugglers, experienced an upturn in late 1782 and even more decisively in 1783. In the autumn of 1783 the second of two bad Irish harvests guaranteed a demand for brandy. Even before the outcome of the second harvest was clear, distilling in Ireland had been halted to eke out food supplies. In October a Dublin merchant noted that brandy had been in good demand for four months 'owing to the stop put to our distilling'.[20] Much of this business went into the hands of the smugglers or 'private traders'. Hennessy usually distilled for the Bordeaux shippers, but in such an upsurge he distilled to the direct order of Irish importers and even of the masters of vessels. In this period most, perhaps all, of Hennessy's customers at peak times were smugglers: 'we are as yet the principal consumers. Irish smugglers daily arriving but little or no orders for the trade'.[21] A month earlier in October 1784, there was 'no Irish demands except for smugglers'.[22] In the same month he commented that the smugglers who avoided the duties of 4s.1d. a gallon must make 'a fine hit of it'. Direct sales by Hennessy to smugglers were supplemented by orders put in his way by other Bordeaux houses who had smuggling customers:

> There are now three smugglers loading here. We shipped yesterday 100 (eight velte to nine velte) ankers on one to address of Messrs Johnston. Cassin has one to John Galwey and we are to load with brandy.[23]

An added factor in widening Irish demand was the new Irish revenue laws, intended to prevent wholesale evasion by smaller distillers, which required stills to be of a minimum capacity of 1000 gallons.[24] In the wake of a better harvest in Ireland in 1784, brandy – legally imported brandy – was selling at 12 per cent loss in October.[25] On the other hand the smugglers had actually benefited from the new Irish laws. Their purpose had been to cut out small producers who were suspected – and with reason – of defrauding the revenue. A growing clandestine market then developed which was satisfied either from underground distilling in Ireland or in the short term from smuggled spirits. A consequence was that while business with smugglers turned down from a peak in 1784, it continued fitfully for the remainder of the decade. In January 1785 Hennessy noted that 'the smugglers fall in from time to time'. At that stage he had loaded one vessel and was awaiting another.[26] At the end of the same year Théodore Martell in Bordeaux reported to his brothers' house in Cognac that 'il parait y en avoir beaucoup d'ordres pour l'Irlande; ce sont au moins les maisons établies ici de cette isle, qui en font les emplétes les plus conséquentes.'[27] In February 1786 Hennessy loaded above 3500 small casks of brandy on board five smuggling vessels which came in at one go.[28] On the other hand, a year later calls for Ireland were but 'very trifling'.[29] Yet within a month Hennessy was loading four smuggling vessels, and a smuggling captain assured Hennessy that, as two revenue vessels were laid up, there were no doubts about their expected success.[30]

Legal imports themselves soared to 540,686 gallons in the year ended March 1784 (a level previously exceeded only in 1761/2 and again in the mid-1760s) and were still 411,549 gallons the following year. Smugglers are easily identified by the small size of their vessels or by declarations for false destinations in Norway or the Faroe Islands. Smuggling was still relatively limited in 1783: only eleven Irish vessels declared for Norway or North Faroe, and their varied Irish provenance suggested little concentrated organization in the business.[31] For the busy year of 1784 the *congés* or exit permits do not survive for Bordeaux. In 1785, smuggling masters from the specialist port of Rush were much in evidence. Of thirteen *congés* for Norway granted in 1785, five of them were for members of known Rush masters, Patrick Harford, Matthew Hore, Jacques Rickard (twice), and Laurence Sweetman. At the end of 1785, business was uncommonly hectic. Hennessy reported that they had orders for three hundred *pièces*: 'our fifteen stills for those 12 days past are going day and night as hard as we can drive them'.[32] In October 1785, he remarked casually 'that I have been very busy these some days past making up cargoes for two Rush-men'.[33] Though we have no *congés* for 1786, one of the masters supplied by Hennessy in 1786 was a Sheridan from Rush. In 1787, for which the *congés* exist, four of the masters of twenty-two suspected smuggling voyages were Peter Conor, Patrick Harford, Patrick Connoly and Richard Oram. Among the vessels in this year was the *Washington* of Drogheda, Thomas Weldon master. A year later John and James Murphy are recorded as master for three of four voyages on the same vessel, and this John Murphy was very probably the Rush smuggling master of the name destined to reach fame in the late 1790s.[34] The following year, 1788, was also an active year with twenty-nine sailings declared for smuggling destinations. A Rush–Drogheda axis accounted for no fewer than fourteen of the sailings, showing how as business in Bordeaux continued, men with interests on the north Dublin coast increasingly dominated it: Joseph Grumley, Richard Hore, Patrick Hore, Patrick Macken, John Oram, James Cullen (two sailings), Sam Disney and Nicholas Keane, as well as Weldon and the Murphys who between them captained four voyages of the *Washington*.[35]

The fact that rectifying capacity in Bordeaux was at times stretched to the limit made it inevitable that on such occasions Irish vessels, smuggling and legitimate alike, would appear on the Charente. As early as June 1783 Martell wrote to Cassin of their appearance.[36] With Irish duties raised in 1784,[37] business spilled over from the Garonne to Charente. Saule handled some five cargoes in 1784–6. Martell benefited even more extensively. In 1786 three Rush men made their appearance in Charente: Patrick Macken, Jacques Cullen, and, in March, Richard Hore, untypically in a large vessel, the *Good Intent* of one hundred tons; in 1787 on two occasions Patrick Harford arrived.[38] Luke Cassin, another regular customer of Bordeaux houses, ordered large quantities of brandy from Martell Lallemand in 1784, 1785 and 1786. The absence of other and more regular Irish traders suggests that much of this brandy foun d its way into clandestine trade; that probability is supported by the fact that Martell letters to and from the Rush smuggling house of John Hore were sent c/o Cassin. In April 1786 Cassin wrote on behalf of Hore, who was absent at the time, complaining of the quality of brandy received from the Martell house and saying that dissatisfaction was responsible for Hore switching an order to the house of Ranson & Delamain.[39] Cassin was a *rara avis*, a substantial merchant with a foot in both the legal and clandestine markets.

John Hore himself was a small but competent merchant in Rush, proprietor of one of a group of houses, of which better known ones were Sheridan and McCabe. Rush men, as owners and masters of smuggling vessels, had a high profile on the Irish Sea coasts of Scotland, England and Ireland alike.[40] They had ties with Dublin merchants and were the executive front for traders in Dublin such as Cassin, who had discreet money in smuggling activity. There were others. At the outset Hore had suggested to Martell Lallemand that they should reimburse themselves through Val Tallon, a minor house, or Val & Mal O'Connor, a major Dublin business. The Tallons had a long-standing interest in the brandy trade, and their first contacts with Hennessy date back to around 1772. Tallon had also dealt in brandy with Geoghegan in Bordeaux on a regular basis. On the information of his friend Thomas Knight, who was related to Tallon, Hennessy reported to Saule that Tallon 'did pretty largely in it with Geoghegan before he parted for London, and I believe ever since, as his [*i.e. Geoghegan's*] house still keeps up here. His clerk had been telling me these six months that he expects his [*i.e. Tallon's*] arrival immediately'. In 1784, Hennessy intimated to Saule the hopes of a Bordeaux friend that orders for Charente would come from Tallon.[41]

The bulk of Martell Lallemand's business with smugglers came from a single house, that of Hore, who maintained contacts with Martell in the remainder of the decade. All their business came to Martell with the exception of a shipment in 1785, when Cassin had introduced Hore, dissatisfied at the quality of the last Martell consignment, to Delamain by a letter delivered by a smuggling master, James Sweetman. The cargo was finally shipped off on 22 November.[42]

JOHN SAULE AND ROBERT WHITE: A CASE HISTORY

Martell Lallemand and the two Irish houses of Saule and Delamain were the Charente houses with dealings with smugglers. However, except for custom from one concern in 1784–5, Saule provided little brandy for smugglers, and Delamain, with a sole shipment (in 1785), even less. Unfortunately for Saule, his only sustained business was with a small combine which continued beyond the boom in 1784 into the more uncertain Irish market of 1785. In Bordeaux, smugglers were sent away empty unless they had a confirmed credit on a London house. Saule, however, was trusting beyond the more seasoned practice of Bordeaux, assuring one of the parties concerned in the venture that 'the *Hamilton* should have had the like fate this voyage, had she been set by any person else but you.'[43] The Irish house of Tallon, known to both Saule and his friend Hennessy, had an interest in the first shipment by this vessel and this led Saule to grant credit subsequently.

Robert White was the organizing 'genius' in the small combine with which Saule dealt. White's methods not only impressed Saule, but had drawn some appreciative comment from Martell Lallemand. Saule's commissions were brought his way by the accident of the son of the Irish merchant Val Tallon having spent two years in Saule's house in the early 1780s.[44] The securing of his orders was copper-fastened by the fact that Tallon had apparently already been doing some business in Bordeaux in brandy in the early 1780s (no doubt in the context of the Dublin smuggling interest), and that Richard Hennessy had played a part in recommending him to give orders to Saule.[45] Thomas Knight, a close friend of Hennessy, was a brother-in-law of Tallon, and thus White's commissions in Charente depended less on commercial contacts than on numerous personal ties.

The business that came Saule's way consisted of four cargoes handled by White, and a further cargo which constituted the major financial grief of Saule's few remaining years of life. Tallon himself had a stake in the first four cargoes. The first order was on a vessel named the *Hamilton*, with Robert White as supercargo. The cargo was shipped in September 1784 and later letters confirmed its safe arrival and the success of the venture.[46] A second voyage by the *Hamilton* was executed later, and a report in February 1785 suggested that this trip proved successful.[47] The vessel later executed a third voyage which was completed by June.[48] The master of the vessel in April 1785 seems to have been John Oram, as three semi-literate letters from him in Charente to Saule survive. The vessel then executed its fourth voyage, which proved to be the first of the voyages to present problems.

The travails of this voyage amply illustrate the difficulties and risks in smuggling. The vessel came out with some goods, apparently textiles, for sale. These were themselves prohibited goods. Under close surveillance by the French customs, who had already seized what had been put ashore, the smugglers were unable to dispose of the balance of the venture, and decided to sail, as soon as the brandy was put aboard, for Lorient and attempt to sell the goods there. The vessel departed from Charente, kept under observation on its way down the river by a customs boat.[49] White succeeded in selling the goods in Lorient and the proceeds were put aboard in nankeen tea, a venture which, like the textiles on the way out, was unauthorized by the principals.[50]

Further adventures occurred off the Irish coast. The vessel (whose voyage had been protracted by the unscheduled visit to Lorient) began to let in water, and it had to enter Wexford where it came under the scrutiny of the revenue officers. As bulk had not been broken (which would signify that some of the cargo had already been run ashore), the first optimistic report back to Cognac was that the vessel would not be detained.[51] However, no doubt on instructions from Dublin, the vessel was declared a seizure, and Hennessy was able to report the progress of the subsequent saga in news from Rush smuggling masters arriving in Bordeaux.[52] One of them told Hennessy that 'White is at law for his vessel and cargo but seems doubtful of his success, though no fair prize'.[53] However, he won, a legal consequence of the very terms of revenue law: if White's destination was Norway, and bulk had not been broken on the Irish coast, the revenue case, however strong the circumstantial evidence, was not of itself compelling. A successful outcome meant that an emboldened White could attempt a fifth venture. Out of this fateful voyage, Saule emerged with considerable personal losses from his sales on credit to its organizers.[54]

THE ROLE OF THE SMUGGLING TRADE

The smuggling peaks were the 1760s, when both cheap rum and a boom in demand expanded the spirit trade, and the 1780s, when concentrated business from Dunkirk and Boulogne for the English market drove the volume to new heights. In the 1760s the business was primarily dominated by Scottish houses in Dunkirk, large *comptoirs* created in the

1760s. After 1765 they diversified into Guernsey and Roscoff. They were specialist concerns, supplying spirits to small partnerships on the Irish and Scottish coasts. The latter in turn collected debts from the small fry and remitted the proceeds in bills on established houses in London. The Dunkirk houses were in time supplemented by other houses like Rosenmeyer & Flore in the Faroe Islands, Carteret Priaulx in Guernsey, who came to the fore in the 1780s, and, after 1815, houses in centres such as Flushing.[55] Elsewhere, activity was either short-lived or small-scale or, as in Bordeaux and Charente, fitful, responding to the stimuli of circumstances, whether bad harvests or, as in Ireland in the early 1780s, regulation of the domestic spirit trade.

Smuggling in itself was a substantial activity, well organized, and con-ducted by interests in trade and shipping which stood on the margins of legal business. However, while it was important for particular houses and particular ports, it was in the end a secondary feature of trade at large. Legal trade was more important, and while smuggling might on occasion exceed legal traffic in the turnover in individual commodities in some markets, its success depended invariably on transient features of shortage, taxation or regulation. Hence it was fluid and its activity short-lived. Moreover, illegal trade in spirits reflected some of the char-acteristics of all trade in spirits. Spirits were to a degree interchangeable, especially given the comparatively novel phenomenon of mass spirit con-sumption itself. The only stable markets for brandy were Paris, inland and lacking a grain-based rival, and London, with its readiness to pay a premium for quality. In Scotland and Ireland in particular, the fact that expanding domestic production could replace imported spirits in what was the hitherto somewhat limited and upper-class market for spirits in the Lowlands or in Munster, put a ceiling to the smugglers' market, and boded ill for the spirit smuggler's welfare.[56] The tapping of a popular market in London or the south-east of England might have provided a novel boost to Dunkirk and Boulogne in the 1780s; the supplier of the Scottish and Irish markets in that decade, however, faced competition from grain-based spirits, both legal and, especially in the older centres of production in Ireland, illegal. In those markets the classic age of spirit smuggling came to an end, despite the high wartime taxation of the 1790s and 1800s. Only in tobacco, which faced no domestic rivals, did smuggling for a while after 1815 enjoy a resurgence.

3

Domestic, foreign and Irish merchants of the brandy regions

FAMILY CONNECTIONS AMONG COGNAC MERCHANTS

Many legends have accumulated around the story of brandy. One is that the product was created by Dutch merchants who spread out from La Rochelle, a major port in 1600, into the interior to convert surplus wine into brandy. However, outside the ports, as in Ireland, the Dutch were significant as manufacturers bringing in advanced techniques, not primarily as traders.[1] The inland nucleus of the trade rested in the hands of local houses, French and almost exclusively Huguenot. Two of these stand out. The first is the Augiers, though the claim of foundation in 1643 and of being the oldest house in the region does not stand up well. All that can be said with certainty is that an Augier was already in the brandy business in the 1680s. The oldest house surviving into the eighteenth century belonged to the Ransons. They were among the merchants mentioned in a dispute over a somewhat unreal projected brandy monopoly in 1604; they were Augier's closest business connections in the Cognac region itself in the 1680s; and through the marriage of a daughter of Isaac Ranson of Jarnac in 1762 to the Irishman James Delamain, the partnership of Ranson & Delamain, for a time in the 1760s probably the largest house in Cognac/Jarnac, came into existence.

A pattern of young men going abroad, especially to Holland, to learn trade or to settle as merchants, was well established in the south-west of France at the end of the seventeenth century and in the early decades of the eighteenth.[2] A small group of families, closely connected, already intermarried or soon to become so, can be found at this time along the Charente: Augier, Richard, Guérinet, Brunet, Lallemand. To this circle should be added a wider circle of business associates including, among others, Riget and Ranson. With Amsterdam and La Rochelle ties, it was this group that in the first two decades of the eighteenth century effectively broke the dependence on La Rochelle houses and created the direct link between houses in the little ports of Tonnay-Charente, Cognac and Jarnac, and foreign centres. The growing control of brandy business by this grouping was enhanced by a supporting circle of Gasts, Lallemands, Augiers and Dardillouzes as shipping agents at Charente for their friends and connections upstream.

The basic strength of the trade in the eighteenth century was a local coterie of five or six long-standing families in the central districts who absorbed the two most successful foreign arrivals, Martell and Delamain. Lallemand, brother-in-law of the first Martell, was the presiding genius of the Martell house in mid-century. Isaac Ranson gave Delamain his inland or Paris trade, which made it possible for him to avoid the unexpected collapse or near collapse of all the new Irish houses, within a few years of their arrival in the boom of the early 1760s. Several other native houses came to the fore at various times, such as Régnier with ties in La Rochelle and married locally (into the influential Dardillouzes), the Arbouins of Pons, and later the Otards and Dupuys who advanced from the role of buyers to that of *négociant*. Among outside arrivals, Martell and Delamain stand apart because of their early marriage into local families.

La Rochelle had dominated the region originally to the point that only in the early eighteenth century did cognac houses begin to become independent of commissions received from that port. La Rochelle was at one time the largest Atlantic port of France; its Irish colony went back to the 1630s and was a large one to the end of the century. By that time, its largest business house was the Irish one of Butler, which then gradually passed from trade to patrician status. Though the port was in decline by 1700, foreigners still tended to think of it first for a long time after. Thus the Englishman Jean Baker

settled as a brandy merchant in La Rochelle before transferring to
Cognac at the outset of the 1730s. Geoghegan, the first Irish brandy
house, was established at La Rochelle in 1739, and a later house, that
of Antoine Galwey, tried at the outset of the 1760s to combine both
worlds, residing in La Rochelle but passing on commissions for direct
shipment to Ireland from Rochefort and Tonnay-Charente. Sometime
around 1750 Daniel Galwey was the first Irishman to settle in the
town of Cognac itself. Six Irish merchants settled in the region in the
1760s, of whom only one (Antoine Galwey) chose to reside in La
Rochelle. The nephew of one of the merchants of the 1760s, John
Saule, did enter into a partnership in general trade there, but in 1776
moved to Cognac as a brandy merchant.

Tonnay-Charente had emerged in the seventeenth century on the
last great tidal meander of the river Charente as an informal port for
transferring brandy from the river barges to coastal craft for La
Rochelle. In the rising brandy trade of the early eighteenth century, it
was also frequented by coastal craft for the north of France and by
larger vessels from foreign countries. Its acquisition of a foreign trade
was made easier by the fact that the estuary of the Charente was well
to the south of La Rochelle itself; direct shipment from Tonnay
reduced costs both directly, by avoiding transshipment, and indirectly,
by avoiding transit duties from the province of Saintonge to Aunis
(though export duties had of course to be paid at both destinations,
and were in fact lower in the Aunis than in Saintonge). In contrast to
other masters, masters of Irish vessels insisted on loading several
miles downstream on the stretch of water at the naval arsenal of
Rochefort (itself conveniently just within the frontiers of Saintonge).
The reason was that they brought beef for the French navy, and were
unwilling to involve themselves in the labour of having to manoeuvre
upstream twice in the waters of the Charente. In other words, brandy
had to be carried downstream to them, though in the final decades of
the eighteenth century some Irish vessels did go directly upstream.
Rochefort, however, had no brandy factors of its own, and the formalities of loading and customs alike were usually looked after by the
houses in Tonnay-Charente. No Irish houses opened in Rochefort,
and even the few who first halted or thought of staying in Tonnay
lost little time in moving to Cognac town itself.

The Dardillouze house was unique in handling the business of houses lacking kinsmen of their own in Tonnay-Charente, and thus it became agent in the 1760s for the newcomers and rivals of Martell Lallemand in the region, such as Delamain and Hennessy. The Augiers always had kin in Charente, and the Martells relied on kin through the house of Gast, Lallemand & Co. The sole Charente house with an overseas trade, of which some records survive, is that of the very well connected Léon Régnier, who opened business there in 1719. A Dardillouze son had married a daughter of Léon Régnier in 1759.[3] One of Léon Régnier's letter books and an invoice book survive in Hennessy's archives. The reason that they unexpectedly lie among the Hennessy papers is probably that they came to them through the Dardillouzes, who did so much business for the Hennessy house.

Overall, there was no monopoly tendency in trade, and the benefits of its expansion were ultimately diffused over several thousand distillers in the *généralité* and an intricate and diffuse network of merchants, jobbers and local traders. That also helps to explain how in such a tightly-knit society the most important individual houses from the 1720s onwards could have been consistently foreign, whether Martell, Delamain, or the Hennessys who became a major house in the 1790s. The lack of a closed shop also meant that distillers and local brandy buyers in time became *négociants*. The first outstanding instance is the Otard family in the 1790s, but other houses like Rémy-Martin and Biscuit in the nineteenth century had similar origins. The growth of outside interests in the region bunched in two periods, the 1710s and 1720s, and the 1750s and 1760s. The English market and the remarkable role of the Guernsey interest in its growth prompted the appearance of outsiders in the first period; an abrupt expansion of Irish demand, which made Ireland fleetingly the main foreign customer, accounted for the arrival of Irishmen in the latter period.

A key factor in ultimate success in business, where an expertise in local buying was essential, was local marriage. Jean Martell's survival was due to his successive Brunet and Lallemand marriages, and Delamain's Ranson marriage in 1762 gave him access to a Paris trade which saved his business when the Irish trade contracted. Antoine

Galwey's settlement in La Rochelle was due in part to his marriage into the Butler family, an Irish family already more than a century in the port. Saule's improved fortunes were owing in part to his marriage to Victoire Bernard in 1778, and a partner in the later Hennessy house, Samuel Turner, a nephew of Delamain, drew some of his strength from a local marriage in 1787. The apotheosis of this pattern was the marriage in 1795 of James Hennessy to a Martell daughter. The greatest challenge of all to categorize is the house of Otard in 1796. To what extent was the Otard family foreign in its origins? The family had obscure Jacobite ties, which were greatly embroidered in later times, but its marriages were local ones over a century, and its successful partnership of 1796 was of course an alliance with the forceful and rising local family of Dupuy. The only other foreigners to make a permanent mark in the region depended on marriages. Thomas Hine was a clerk in Delamain's house in the early 1790s, and his entry into partnership depended on Delamain's dispute with his sons, and on marriage to a Delamain. The Exshaw who entered the brandy trade shortly after 1800 was the son of a daughter of the Dublin branch of the Bordeaux Nairac family, and he first settled in Bordeaux.

JEAN MARTELL AND THE GUERNSEY INTEREST

The story of outside intrusion into Cognac starts with Jean Martell from the Channel Islands, whose move to Cognac in 1718 had been prompted by the upsurge in the Guernsey business. Guernsey merchants sought to bypass merchants in the ports and deal with suppliers in the interior and specifically in Cognac, whose rising star had already given brandy produced within a radius of nine or ten miles of the town its growing repute. Guernsey's long wartime boom from 1689 to 1713 had greatly increased its commodity business: the profits converted its shipowning families, privateers in wartime, into established mercantile houses. The main thrust of this business had been in prize wine, which created the contacts and knowledge for a more orthodox trade in peacetime. As for brandy, very much a subsidiary traffic in international business, the initiative seems to have come from younger men needing to establish themselves, rather than from senior members of the same families in more established trades. The essential backing for the brandy business rested on an older and established Guernsey figure, Laurent Martin. It was Martin who had set up Martell in business, who encouraged him to go to Cognac, and towards whom Martell retained a sense of indebtedness.

Young men in Guernsey also had links with relatives in London, where their more established compatriots had already acquired a prominent place in business.[4] The brandy trade, smaller and more novel than the wine trade, was the refuge of lesser houses, a pattern incidentally repeated in the Dublin brandy boom of the 1760s. Thus Nicholas Dobrée, a partner in the Guernsey venture, had an apparently older and more established brother William in London. Another London merchant, William Lefebvre, was a nephew of Dobrée, and was brother-in-law to Jean Bonamy,[5] who was a member of the circle backing Martell.

Two things influenced the early fortunes of Martell. The first was that the London houses attached more importance to wine than brandy. After almost a quarter century of war from 1689 to 1713, during which English houses left France, there was (the Irish houses in London apart) no business group in England with first-hand knowledge of the French trade other than the Guernsey men. Their extensive business in wartime prize wine and brandy, originating in their successful privateering, was behind their newly-created financial base in London. After the wars, given the absence of an English business community in France, they sought to turn their wartime interest into a durable peacetime trade. Brandy was, for the bigger houses, a secondary activity to wine, left to lesser houses or young relatives. That brings us to the second factor: as specialized brandy making in Nantes and Cognac replaced the inferior brandy of Bordeaux, the brandy buying of the Guernsey men shifted from Bordeaux to more northerly ports. This explains both why Martell was dispatched from Guernsey to Cognac, and also how, in a second move in 1723, Martell went to Bordeaux as the partner of a peripatetic figure, Fiott, to help cater for the wine trade, which was booming at the time. Their surviving 1724–5 letter book is one of a business mainly in wine and enjoying an enlarged correspondence with at least ten

Guernsey houses. Fiott and Martell were buying Margaux at 350 livres per barrel: in other words they had dealings at the top end of the London market (Haut Brion and Margaux). Wine was consigned directly to Elisha Dobrée in London. The brandy business in Cognac was handled on his behalf by his fellow Channel Islander, Le Mesurier. The partnership with Fiottt ended in 1725, apparently as a result of a falling out among the circle of Guernsey men who provided the custom for the business. Martell lingered on in Bordeaux, and his marriage to a Brunet in 1726 explains why, when bankruptcy overtook him later in the year, he was able to return to Cognac and re-enter the brandy business.

The wine business brought Martell into relations with Ireland: he was buying for Jean Brunet of Dublin at the outset of 1725.[6] Brunet had a brother Henry in Cognac (who also did a small trade in brandy with Dublin), and some of the funds for the wine purchases for Ireland in Bordeaux came through Cognac.[7] These links may explain how Martell was drawn into the Brunet circuit. The Brunet marriage became the first stage in integrating him into the region, and his wife's mother was a Lallemand. After his wife's death, his second marriage in 1737 was to Rachel Lallemand, a first cousin of his wife.[8] The marriage brought his wife's powerful and overbearing brother, Louis-Gabriel Lallemand, at the time described as a student, into the ambit of the house, making possible its later success and converting an expatriate business into a thoroughly indigenous presence steeped in local values and, beyond business, deaf to the external world and ideas.

Dissatisfaction in London in the mid-1720s, at first directed significantly more to Bordeaux wine than to cognac, led to recrimination between the Guernsey interest and Fiott in Bordeaux. It was accompanied by a belief that the intermediary layer of Guernsey men could be replaced. In December 1725 Augier had advised Martell that something of the sort was in prospect.[9] As early as February 1725 Bucknell of Portsmouth had been in touch with the Cognac house of Augier: he inquired benevolently about Martell, which suggests that in England the blame was placed on the Guernsey circuit itself rather than on Martell.[10] Bad vintages in 1725 and 1726 which sent brandy prices soaring accelerated the tensions in the trade at large. In the summer and early autumn of 1726 the export trade had virtually folded up, and little foreign business was done. As in another period of heavy Paris demand and high prices in 1766–7, London wholesale buyers made few allowances for difficulties overseas and blamed their suppliers for problems of price, supply and regularity of dispatch. The idea took shape of Dunkirk replacing Guernsey as the staging point for supplies of brandy to England, and of the transfer of the conduct of the trade from Guernsey houses in London into the hands of English brandy importers. In other words crisis encouraged brandy merchants to switch from a passive role as buyers in London into the active one of importers on their own account. Martell's own bankruptcy in 1726 can only have confirmed doubts about the value of the old route, and the house of Augier stood to gain. Augier already had an order from Bucknell of Portsmouth in the spring of 1726, which he described as his first (i.e. first English) order for a long time,[11] and he was in correspondence with Elisha Dobrée of London on the subject of a trade through Dunkirk in August 1727.[12] He engaged in a flurry of correspondence with London in the autumn of 1727. He made his contacts with James Hatch in London at this time and his invoices in 1728 show a respectable volume of business with Hatch and with other London houses.

The trade for Britain and Ireland remained small in volume for the decades of the 1730s, 1740s and early 1750s (though the London trade itself purchased the bulk of the prime brandy from the immediate vicinity of the town of Cognac itself). This low level of activity reflected in part the existence of alternative products (in Ireland rum, a novel product of the period, and in England gin from a booming industry), in part a recurrence of bad vintages in 1739–41 and, more paralysingly, in 1745–51, which brought Paris buyers into the Cognac area to make good the loss of the vines and hence of brandy along the Loire. A static London trade was shared mainly between two houses, Augier and Martell, each doing a rather modest amount of business of 1000 to 2000 barriques a year, with the Martell house surviving better than Augier's in the long run. In a small and difficult market, Martell's business itself was not very large, as the letter book for 1753 shows; however, that was also the year in which Martell died and his place was taken by his brother-in-law Louis-Gabriel Lallemand, the powerful figure who had personal experience of residence in Ireland and England in 1742. The transition in 1753 resulted in Martell's overhauling Augier's in the London market, and as the best-established house it inevitably handled the bulk of the new Irish custom when Dublin turned to Cognac in 1756.

THE IRISH HOUSES AND THEIR BORDEAUX TIES

If Martell or, as it became, Veuve Martell, Lallemand & Co., now dominated the market, they were bound to be challenged in turn by Irish houses, who sought to capture some of the benefits the house enjoyed of what promised to be a durable trade. Walter Geoghegan was an established brandy merchant in La Rochelle from his arrival in 1739 until his failure in 1755;[13] it is not clear whether the Stephen Geoghegan of the 1770s, who settled in the hinterland, was an immediate relative. The first Irish house to appear in Cognac itself was that of Daniel Galwey.[14] It started at a bad time, in or before the early 1750s, and it is hardly surprising that, in the wake of the virtual collapse of the export trade, it went bankrupt by 1753. Irish houses did not reappear until the brandy boom after the mid-1750s began to alter prospects. And even then, the accidents of death – four in 1766–8 – were less decisive than the instability of Irish demand in reducing the new influx. The only Irish house (Delamain) that thrived after the 1760s, did so on the basis of its Paris business; Richard Hennessy thought of leaving Cognac on several occasions in the 1770s, finally moving to Bordeaux in 1776, and the Irish interest in brandy centred more on Bordeaux than on Cognac for the next decade.

The pattern of the Irish market was that if there was boom in Ireland, direct shipments from Tonnay-Charente were worthwhile; if not it was simpler to ship from Mortagne or Rochefort to Bordeaux, where 60 to 100 ships called every year. By 1766, in the wake of a decade of boom in demand, there were as many as ten Dublin vessels at a time in the Charente. On the other hand through the exchange of Irish beef and butter for red wine (on which Irish tariffs were far lower than English, which for political reasons favoured Portuguese wines), Irish business with Bordeaux had grown to vast proportions and the Irish merchants along with Hamburg ones were the largest foreign communities in the port. By the end of 1767 Delamain was regularly dispatching brandy to Bordeaux for his reduced Irish clientele, and Hennessy too increasingly relied on this route in 1771 and 1772. In 1773, on the other hand, with some rise in Dublin demand three different Irish vessels made six trips in all to Rochefort according to Delamain invoices, and the only consignment to Bordeaux was in January. Again in 1774, there were in Delamain's records seven consignments to Dublin, and only two invoices for Bordeaux. In 1775, however, the Rochefort or Mortagne route for Bordeaux was active again. With an upsurge in Irish demand in 1776 only one consignment seems to have gone by Bordeaux, and that from Rochefort, not from Mortagne. The trade to Ireland was also supplemented by the rectification in Bordeaux of inferior brandies. Overall, in the 1770s, apart from a boom in direct shipments in 1773–4 and in 1775–6, the bulk of brandy for Dublin went through Rochefort or Mortagne to Bordeaux. Delamain observed in December 1778 that 'it is now near two years since we have had in this river a ship for your city nor do we hear of any coming …'.[15]

The outbreak of war in mid-1778 ensured that this state of affairs would continue indefinitely. As Irish vessels masked as neutrals, sailing from Bordeaux,[16] made possible the conduct of a fairly normal volume of trade, the alternative of direct shipment to Ireland ceased to be a practical possibility in any circumstances. Delamain acquired a warehouse in Mortagne. While brandy purchased in Mortagne had usually been cheaper than in Cognac, it now came up to Cognac price levels and even exceeded them, especially in the winter months. After 1783 Mortagne quickly lost importance as a staging point for good-quality brandy for Ireland. Resumption of some direct shipments to Ireland, combined with the peacetime ease of coastal shipment from the Charente to Bordeaux, seems to have resulted in Delamain running down stocks in the warehouse.[17] In the end Delamain ceded his interest in the warehouse to Hennessy and Boyd, though with a proviso that he could use it for any business of his own as well. Their business was quite different, a gathering of brandies, often weak ones from far afield, which were carried to Bordeaux and redistilled there. The warehouse at Mortagne was an adjunct to a new Royan busi-

ness, itself supplemented by rectification in Bordeaux. All this distilling business depended largely on orders from Irish houses in the port.
Even major Bordeaux general houses like MacCarthy *frères* or Coppingers took a consistent interest in brandy, though for them it was
sent around from Rochefort to Bordeaux rather than from Mortagne,
and arose from their association with prestigious Dublin clients and
a demand for a higher quality.

The advent in 1774 of the Irish house of Andoe heralded a new
phase in Bordeaux brandy business. So did Théodore Martell's settling in Bordeaux at much the same time; and his partnership in 1775
with Stephen Geoghegan, who moved from Pons to Bordeaux, was
intended to procure brandy for his trade. Ties between Bordeaux and
the larger Cognac region now became more numerous; the Irish
house of Gernon in Bordeaux was allied with the Broussards of Pons
from 1781, for instance, and members of the Augier and Otard families settled in Bordeaux in the 1780s. Théodore Martell was a man
ahead of his time: speculative and imaginative, he was able, given the
Paris demand for bills on the famously solvent brandy houses of
London, to consolidate a close connection with the politically powerful Paris banking house of Necker and his associates. A contemporary described Martell as lively and brilliant with a conversation
'remplie de sarcasmes mordants'.[18] His character comes across in his
letters of 1795 to James Hennessy. Théodore Martell's standing in
Bordeaux and the usefulness that it offered even for a thrusting house
like Hennessy & Turner in time led to business alliance between the
two houses and the Hennessy–Martell marriage of 1795.

CHANGING STATUS OF BRANDY MERCHANTS

Beginning in the 1770s, brandy families acquired a more exalted
status, supported by larger turnover and greater profits. The houses
of the Martell and Delamain families are the finest eighteenth-century mercantile residences in the towns of Cognac and Jarnac respectively. Richard Hennessy lived modestly in rented accommodation
and only under the Revolution did the family become property
buyers. The purchase of La Billarderie in the 1790s was, however,

more than a property purchase; it was an expression of status. They might have sought to house themselves grandly, as Delamain did, on land at the water's edge, or, like Martell, at the end of the built-up waterfront. They did not, in part because their predecessor Saule lacked resources and lived in rented quarters, and in part because in the wake of the good fortune that attended their return in 1788 all land overlooking the quays was already exploited. James Delamain, perhaps first, and in 1789 Etienne Augier as deputy to the States General, set the fashion in portrait painting. The two Martells, Jean (the younger) and Frédéric-Gabriel, together with their wives, also had their portraits painted in their heady ascendancy in the 1780s. Other families lacked portraits, until in the early 1790s Richard Hennessy's position as a lieutenant of the Cognac National Guard prompted one. One was made later for his more successful son, James, but none survives for the son's equally successful partner, Samuel Turner.

A new folly, that of gentrification, was overtaking merchants. Even Richard Hennessy, modest in his business circumstances at the time, was already worried about his son's Irish brogue in the late 1780s. The Hennessy acquisition of a rural seat was a declaration of a new social elevation. No doubt, there was some lingering thought of their gentry background in Ireland and of a return to rural surroundings in keeping with gentry status. Richard's son, James Hennessy, the most prosaic and hardheaded of men, referred to the family genealogy on one occasion, and in London speculated on the family's relatives there. The acquisition of La Billarderie, occurring at the time when Hennessy & Turner was the most prosperous house in Cognac, was the first stage in the creation of the Hennessy stake in property and status: if business required the constant attendance of James in Cognac, the father, now uninvolved in daily business, had it as his residence. No successful merchant could afford to remain long away from the counting house. Martell and Delamain were the first to house themselves in more princely dwellings, even if overlooking the quays, and later residences were, if sometimes in easy reach of the quays, firmly out of sight of them. The allurements of public office, first mayoralty (for Turner and then Otard) and later parliamentary seats (as for James Hennessy in 1824), beckoned as well.

The building of substantial town houses or the acquisition of a country residence reflected the new-found social prestige of the brandy families. Most dramatic of all in its rapidity was the business success of Otard & Dupuy, who in the decade from 1796 rose to a par with the Martells and Hennessys. Somewhat more slowly than for other families, though more splendidly, their status was reflected in stone as well as in other ways: the magnificent house of Jean Dupuy (brother of Léon) around 1840, now the municipal museum, and around the same date for Léon Otard, son of Jean-Baptiste-Antoine Otard, a house in a large parkland, today the Hôtel de Ville.[19] Rising status seems also to have been accompanied, in the case of the Otards, by a new and public emphasis on their origins.

STATUS AND ORIGINS: THE CASE OF THE OTARDS

Otard (sometimes referred to as De la Grange) was already a seller of brandy in the 1750s. Though they crop up in business and an Otard dined on occasion in the circle of the Hennessys, they were not intimates of the Irish circle as one might expect if they were either conscious of or cultivated their supposed origins in the British Isles. Prominent in the social life of the town and its hinterland, an Otard was secretary of the Cognac Masonic lodge in both 1747 and 1761.[20] It may have been the masonic association rather than either Jacobite or British ties that brought them into the circle of the Hennessys. The business role of the family derived from the Bruneaud side, who early on moved into Bordeaux, where they already had or acquired a business. Thus, when the Otard family were involved in a law suit in Bordeaux in 1767, Otard and his wife stayed with the Bruneauds.[21] At this time the Bruneauds were among the most active Bordeaux correspondents of Lallemand (though reference to Otard himself in the letter book of 1766–7 was very rare). The Bruneaud family can be traced again in 1788, when one of the Otard brothers was in Bordeaux. That Otard was not a regular resident in Bordeaux at that time is suggested by the fact that Saule wrote to him c/o Bruneaud *frères*. Otard already had property in Bordeaux, as Hennessy apparently was at that time renting a warehouse from him for a second year.[22]

The Otards did seem to regard their background as noble, something suggested by Guillaume Otard's comments as early as 1757 when his pursuit of a bride ran into difficulties: 'je vois avec douleur qu'on cherche à me perdre à vos yeux; ma fortune est, en effet, peu importante, mais on ne pourrait sans injustice contester la force et la hauteur de ma naissance'.[23] This theme of social insecurity echoed in the 1790s in the words of the young Jean-Baptiste-Antoine Otard himself. The witnesses to Jacques Otard's marriage in 1704 were all French and the sum of money mentioned in the contract small. The Otard genealogy, incorporating a 'notice historique et chronologique' prepared by the genealogist De Valls, son-in-law to what appears to be the last of the court genealogist D'Hozier family (1764–1846), and thus dating probably to the early decades of the nineteenth century, stresses with some abandon a Scottish antecedence and their association in France with the Jacobite court. It is astonishing but revealing that Ursule Oglethorpe, married to a Bruneaud of Libourne, whose daughter married Jacques Otard de la Grange of Périgord in 1704, does not feature in the account by De Valls. The Oglethorpe connection alone and the fact that there is a portrait of James II – probably a late-made copy – in the house today provide, the genealogy itself apart, the sole prima facie evidence of a Scottish connection.[24]

The vagueness of their claims – and the absence of the Otards from the genealogy in Scotland of the Keiths from whom they claimed descent – hints at a problem glossed over by the commissioned French professional genealogist. On balance it seems likely that Jacques Otard was not born at Saint-Germain-en-Laye, the later court of the exiled Stuarts, as the genealogy holds, and that if he was of Keith ancestry he was a son or grandson of Robert Keith, a mercenary officer of the mid-seventeenth century in an alliance which for whatever reason was not recognized and which accounts for the fact that the family name Keith did not decend to them. The Cognac Otards became the business equals of the older established houses, and Jean-Baptiste-Antoine Otard was mayor from 1804 to 1824 and deputy for the Charente from 1821 to 1824. Socially well-connected marriages followed. It is tempting to conclude, given the absence of contemporary supporting documentation of their Scottish ancestry, that they embroidered a slight claim to Scottish ancestry, glossing over the absence of the family name Keith and bolstering either a real or fictitious Scottish connection by exploiting the coincidence of De La Grange as a fief name in both Scotland and France and making play with the place name Dunottard in Scotland. If De La Grange was turned into a Scottish family name, an equally logical and more necessary step, given the absence of persuasive evidence, was to turn the family name Otard into a Scottish name. Otard itself is neither an obvious French or Scottish name (though written by Lallemand as 'Otard', it was written by Hennessy as 'Ottar', which suggests that the Otards pronounced it with a silent 'd', and that French was the first and perhaps the only language of the family in the eighteenth century).[25] Late in the nineteenth century, possibly for the first time on the occasion of the printing in 1882 of the earlier De Valls genealogy, it was rendered as an even more improbable O'Tard.[26] If the Otards (who were known socially to the Hennessys) were English-speaking and especially if they were conscious of a Jacobite connection, they should have assumed a positive place in the social life of the intense little Irish milieu: they obtrude mainly in the accounting records and rarely in the voluminous social correspondence. The question also remains whether the portrait of James II is simply a later acquisition or a copy of a portrait of the monarch to embellish the Scottish link.

Whatever the realities, the contrast is striking between the total absence of British associations in the mid-eighteenth century and the self-conscious advertising of an Otard Scottish and Jacobite background at a later date. Not wholly different circumstances arose in the case of the Hennessys, at much the same time. In their case it concerned army service rather than genealogy. In becoming a Restoration parliamentarian for the Charente, James Hennessy faced accusations by his opponents in 1824 that he was a mere foreigner, which would have deprived him of his seat. It was in this context that a document of 1757 falsely certifying that his father, Richard, had served ten years in the military (which certification automatically conferred citizenship) became relevant. (See chapter 5 for an account of the circumstances under which the certification was granted.) In reality, Richard's military service began in 1748 (when he was serving as an *homme de troupe* and awaiting a commission) and ended in 1752 or

1753. Either by accident or by design, the ten-year certification was used in support of the claim that Richard's service had begun at least ten years prior to 1753, and thus that he had fought at the great battle of Fontenoy in 1745.

4

The Irish challenge to Martell, Lallemand & Co. in the 1760s

The influx into the brandy trade in the 1760s was an Irish one. Anthony Galwey and James Delamain set the pattern, with Delamain first in the field. Delamain's Huguenot ancestry creates a deceptive link. His family had first come to England in the retinue of the French consort of Charles I in 1624. James Delamain was a nephew of Henry Delamain, the potter whose porcelain factory in Dublin made a name for itself in the 1750s.[1] In a letter in 1784 he stated that he had been in the brandy business upwards of twenty-five years. In April 1757 he was granted a passport in Bordeaux for his return journey to Ireland.[2] This journey marked the end of a stay in Blois to improve his French. He was also familiar with Tours, where he believed the French to be 'as pure as at Blois', and in 1768 he advised Delap on pensioning a son there.[3]

We can only guess that he set out for Bordeaux in 1757 (probably at the end of his Blois stay) with a career in the wine trade in mind. His Huguenot ancestry was not of special help to him in the region, as his ancestors had come from Normandy. However, the Ransons were intermarried with a Thomas family, according to the *contrôle des actes* for Jarnac, and if this family was that of the late Thomas Thomas of London, much involved in the foreign exchange transactions of the Irish trade, Delamain could well have had letters of introduction which would explain not only why he halted in the region but why in Jarnac rather than in Cognac. At this stage contact with Ranson did not result in any immediate business. In a letter at a much later date Delamain referred to himself as 'the writer who did some business in the wine branch in Dublin'.[4] From Blois he may have visited the south-west as a neophyte wine merchant. His key contact might well have been with the Delaps, a prominent Irish Presbyterian family, destined to be for many years his closest Bordeaux connection.

With rum scarce and bad harvests reducing whiskey distilling, brandy, a trade less dominated by established houses, may have offered better opportunity for a young man than the wine trade. On the evidence of the sole surviving journal, beginning in October 1758, of Isaac Ranson's business, a consignment of brandy is recorded under 14 August 1759 as shipped on joint account with Robert Nevin in Dublin.[5] The fact that in the preceding ten months, when Delamain must have been in Dublin, there had been no orders from there, suggests that this was a first venture by Ranson. Subsequent entries of later consignments refer only to brandy to Nevin, not to a joint order, which suggests that the shipment in August 1759 was a special or trial order. It may well be that Ranson, looking for a wider market, turned to the services of Delamain, who in turn, as an underemployed young merchant attempting to build up a business in wine (a charmed and capital-intensive commerce hard to break into), would have been only too ready to undertake brandy business.

Delamain was still in Dublin in September 1760, but he was in Rochefort the following month, eager to bring the captain of the vessel he had travelled on to Jarnac 'pour lui oter l'occasion de conférer avec les négociants d'ici, qui sont toujours au guet. D'ailleurs le plus de politesses que nous lui ferons, le mieux il sera disposé à nous rendre service par la suite.'[6] In other words, it was necessary to whisk the captain away before the established Cognac merchants offered him their services. Delamain described the cargo that the vessel was to take back as a 'premier envoi'. From the tone of the letter, Delamain, young man though he was, was far from a passive collaborator. From as early as October 1762 the Ranson–Delamain partnership was already seen as a successful one, and Delamain's father in Dublin was working forcefully on brandy importers in Dublin in his favour.

The Ransons were the oldest trading family in Jarnac or Cognac, but in contrast to the 1730s when a member of the family was a merchant in the brandy trade in Amsterdam,[7] no member of the family was living abroad in the late 1750s. In the 1758–61 journal their business consisted in part of the acquisition of brandy for the Augiers and Lallemands in Cognac and of wine for the Augiers, in part a substantial trade in brandy to Paris. Isaac Ranson also dealt in flax-seed, and in 1757 he seems to have supplied lead to the naval dockyard in Rochefort, judging by references thirty years later to 'effects royaux' as payment which were still in Delamain's possession.[8] Whatever the circumstances, Delamain retained a profound sense of obligation to Ranson, and after Ranson died in 1782 the business continued to be conducted under the style of Ranson & Delamain.[9] A formal partnership was signed only in April 1769 on the basis of a sharing of the profits. The agreement referred to the preceding eight and a half years, thus confirming the absence of a formal agreement, and also indirectly establishing that Delamain's return in October 1760 was the effective beginning of his permanent residence in Jarnac. It was followed by marriage with Marie, Ranson's sole daughter. The contract was dated 1 November 1762, and the ceremony took place on 24 November.[10]

The house had as many correspondents in Paris as it had abroad in the late 1760s. In turn when foreign trade grew more difficult, dependence on Paris increasingly reasserted itself. Delamain's foreign contacts were almost exclusively in Dublin: in March 1767, as far as London was concerned, 'we are only sorry the business we do in your city is so inconsiderable as to be hardly worth my friends' while'.[11] Lallemand, the driving force in the Martell house, thought Delamain 'un brave homme', noting that 'I wont tell you may guess Messrs Delamain and Ranson acted wisely wanting each other'.[12] By December 1762 he was forced to admit to McDermott, his 'oldest acquaintance' in Dublin, from whom he sought support, that 'Ranson & Delamain have got the better of us. Pray tell ingeniously if they owe it to the quality of the goods or their protectors.'[13]

The impact of the Delamain presence in the region, the first har-
binger of challenge, was reinforced by Galwey's venture ordering
from La Rochelle. Antoine Galwey first appeared in France in Saintes
in 1756 to learn French. His status was reflected in his later marriage
to a La Rochelle lady: her father was a Colonel Labadie, her dowry
was very substantial and her mother, 'the proud, the haughty Miss
Butler formerly',[14] was one of the La Rochelle Butlers, who had eventually forsaken their long-held position as the city's leading business
family for a more aristocratic lifestyle. His regular ordering from La
Rochelle through the Broussards in Cognac for direct shipment from
the Charente was in place by mid-1763. The virtual absence of orders
to Martell Lallemand from Anthony McDermott after 1763 reveals
that McDermott's circle was buying from others, including Galwey.

Yet the activity of Galwey and Delamain engendered little of the
emotional concern that others occasioned for Lallemand. Galwey,
though both an outsider and a Catholic, relied on existing Protestant
families in Cognac to buy for him. Delamain was still less an outsider,
as his marriage to Ranson's daughter made him effectively a partner
in an existing business. Saule & Jennings, on the other hand, were
quite a different matter. They were total outsiders; they also represented an outward thrust by Dublin importers to monopolize the
business on the French side. In contrast to the Galweys (from a Munster background) and even to Delamain (despite his close associations
with Dublin Catholics), Saule & Jennings, counting on the backing
of the articulate Catholic merchants in the Catholic Committee in
Dublin, intended to dictate conditions at the buying end, and to
replace the local intermediaries or *négociants* by direct contact with
brandy makers.

News of Saule's intent in 1766 to move from Tonnay-Charente to
Cognac, the true buying centre, alarmed Lallemand. Though an outsider, Jennings, not simply content to use the new hydrometer, strove
to have a standard settled for the brandy shipped (by which he meant
measurement by instrument rather than the hit-or-miss empirical
'proof') but, in Lallemand's words 'we doubt of his success therein,
and believe that everyone should be allowed to do his best for his
friends' interest'.[15] As an erratic quality was on Lallemand's own
admission one of the problems in the trade and dissatisfaction had

promoted upheaval, he was on the defensive. The reference hints at the first appearance of the hydrometer in the region and Lallemand's less than enthusiastic first reaction to the new instrument (though he was realist enough to adopt it, and rather quickly).

Saule's forceful expansion of his business in 1766 coincided with soaring prices for brandy on the Charente and emerging price resistance in Dublin. That in turn led in 1767 to a falling market and heavy losses for speculators. Death was even more effective than disastrous speculation in removing Martell Lallemand's most serious rivals: Jennings died in late 1766 and Saule in September 1768. Death also carried away Antoine Galwey prematurely, in 1767, so that the two most serious Irish Catholic houses melted away. There were two other arrivals, Luke Bellew and Richard Hennessy. Both were ex-army officers, counting on a network of relatives to guarantee their success. However, after a fleeing appearance in Charente in 1765, Bellew died in 1767 in Britain while setting up a rather ambitious trade network. That left Richard Hennessy, apart from Delamain, as the sole Irish survivor in business in 1768. A nephew of Saule's, John Saule, could find a place in Cognac only in 1776.

DISCONTENT WITH MARTELL LALLEMAND & CO.

Trade with Dublin at first created a demand for English-speaking clerks in Cognac. More dramatically, a prospect in 1762 of peace, which would mean a resumption of direct trade, set in motion the creation of the Dublin brandy 'clubs' each with its own shipping, often with a relative as master. Combined with a surge in Dublin demand, this led to a search for new buying agents in the Cognac region and even a readiness to guarantee custom for Irishmen prepared to settle there. The growing discontent with the services of the buying houses in Cognac repeated the saga of the 1725–6 London discontent with the then-dominant Guernsey circuit. Its aim was to replace with new hands Martell Lallemand (or, to give it its full style, Veuve Martell, Lallemand & Co.), which had monopolized the growing wartime dispatch of brandy for Ireland via neutral Rotterdam.

The brandy import trade required relatively little capital to set up. Established business houses set up brothers or in-laws in the trade. Others set up their own sons. Thomas Egan sought the good will of Martell Lallemand for his son Barney, who opened house in Dublin.[16] In the brandy business at large Catholics were more numerous than Protestants. Hence it escaped the traditional ties and prejudices of the business world, especially characteristic of the wine trade, and seemed to leave ample scope for both the young and for those not belonging to the established church, like Delamain, who enjoyed surprisingly good relations with Catholics, to make a mark. Lallemand, the Cognac man with the closest knowledge of the foreign market, wrote to a Dublin importer in 1762: 'We believe there's too many hands in the brandy trade with you and maybe your's [*i.e. your custom*] is lessened and discouraged by it. We know of such another time but it did not last. The new clubs were soon blown up and the old traders had again their turn.'[17] The Martell Lallemand custom was reduced to orders from some of the longer-established houses such as Mathew Stritch. Stritch, faced with competition from new houses in Dublin, agreed a closer association with Martell Lallemand in 1767: Lallemand would write fortnightly to Stritch and large orders would be settled in paper at long usance, which Martell Lallemand would discount in London.[18]

As always in a boom, buyers ran into problems in price, quality or speed of dispatch. An alleged decline in quality or strength was a persistent complaint. As measuring instruments became commonplace in London and Dublin at this time, the barrage of complaints may simply have reflected a new-found sophistication in the appraisal of alcohol in both cities.[19] For London the problem was not as acute as for Dublin because for forty years it had been customary to add spirit to cognac brandy to bring it up to a higher London standard, though even there, as Lallemand's letters show, complaints occurred. Given the fact that brandy for Dublin was at the basic market strength, once the Irish importers began to use the hydrometer, complaints about variation in strength multiplied. The harassed agents, faced with a barrage of complaints from importers in their new-found sophistication, attributed the defect to a decline in quality, a circumstance outside their control, rather than to the variations in strength at the margin, which would involve an admission of the hit-and-miss character of the traditional proof.[20] As the dominant supplier of the Dublin market, Martell Lallemand bore the brunt of the recriminations from Dublin.

Delamain, familiar from the outset with the new hydrometer, had an initial advantage over Lallemand, who judged his brandy on empirical tests. However, Lallemand was quick to adopt the new instrument, and henceforth quoted the strength of brandy as measured in degrees read on the hydrometer. Even so, Delamain's advantage appeared to persist.[21] By June 1766 Lallemand admitted to his most steadfast and trusted Dublin correspondent, that 'we cant match with Ranson & Delamain. We must not hope to ever do it, and we rather choose to stand idle than to lose by what we do …'.[22] Ranson & Delamain alone of the shippers overseas had a Paris trade in which the tradition of dispatching brandy at a strength well above market strength was already established for over twenty years. The challenge was a real one and Martell Lallemand lost ground over the period from 1762 to 1767. As if this was not bad enough, Martell Lallemand's hold on the London trade declined in 1766 and 1767. As they were better established in the London trade, high prices and a decline in quality were factors less likely to take their toll there. In January 1767 in the Leeds trade Lallemand was writing that 'we are surprised that your neighbour receives stronger spirits from Messrs Augier than what we have sent you'.[23] For London the decisive factor was less quality than delays in shipping from Charente. What cost Lallemand the custom of London houses, and that of the important house of Steele in particular, was the sheer difficulty in getting supplies as the Irish trade soared: vessels took a long time to load (in part because of a bottleneck in coopering), and, most damaging of all, brandy for some houses got to market later than brandy for rivals.[24] With a loss of confidence in Martell's on this score, orders were now much more divided among Cognac houses as a form of insurance of supply, and Lallemand lamented that 'the widow Martell & Lallemand are nowadays good for nothing, because they are no more in fashion'.[25] Augier in particular was a local beneficiary of these trends in 1766 and 1767.[26]

THE PEAK OF THE CHALLENGE: LAURENCE SAULE'S
EXPANSION IN 1766–7

For Lallemand, the advent of the house of Saule & Jennings was quite a different matter from competition by Galwey, or by Delamain in partnership with an existing house: their business had not disrupted established ties between shippers and sellers. Galwey's buying was in the hands of the Broussards and Augiers, and as recently as 1762 the Martells had become linked with the Augiers by the marriage of a daughter to Etienne Augier of Tonnay-Charente.

Dr Edward Jennings was one of the handful of merchants present at the meeting in the Globe Tavern in 1757 which had founded the Catholic Committee.[27] Laurence Saule achieved some notoriety in 1759 in having a very public profile in Dublin in resistance to a case of proselytization of a young lady to the established church.[28] He declared at that time his intention of emigrating (a rather ritualistic declaration of rich Catholics, patterned on the long-standing place of the threat in mercantilist logic or special pleading), but he was in no hurry to do so, and migrated finally only when peace returned to Europe, and in the midst of a brandy boom. As a member of this milieu, Saule would obviously be deemed to be rich, and the later prominence of the house of Davys & Jennings, which on Saule's departure took over his premises in Fishamble Street,[29] seems to confirm the resources on which Saule could call. In departing Saule not only gave powers of attorney to Davys & Jennings to recover debts for him but left 'all my books and papers not taken with me in the old shop house in the back closet up one pair of stairs'.[30]

The earliest reference to the house is in a letter of 15 August 1763 to Lallemand's Dublin correspondent Mathew Stritch. Jennings had arrived in Charente at this stage. Lallemand expressed his surprise that:

> Gentlemen of great property beloved in Dublin and settled there can think of settling at Charente or even in any place in this country. I am sure I should incline to the reverse if I was in good circumstance enough to bear it.[31]

Lallemand in this letter and in others to Dublin correspondents publicly put a brave face on circumstances. To Christopher Boyle, in
referring to 'your countryman Mr Saule', he expressed the view in
September that 'his friends shall find it hard to enable him to outdo
young Delamain and the widow Martell & Lallemand how[ever]
much [or] little his property, was it as large as the Duke of Bedford'.[32]
To merchants elsewhere he expressed alarm more explicitly. To Van
Yzendorn in Holland, who in the course of the Seven Years War had
handled much of the Irish trade from Cognac, he reported:

> We have a new house in Charente by an Irish gentleman come over
> from Dublin [who] will have most of the business from that place,
> being as most of the importers there are now, a Roman and Ranson
> & Delamain as well as us are presbyterians. However we are resolved
> to make no abjuration of our faith. Messrs Clancy our good friends
> are already turned to them and their ship the *Thomas*, captain James
> Clancy, is coming to that gentleman consigned ... His name is Lau-
> rence Saule, a grocer and much esteemed there we are informed
> besides a good property which won't be needless here.[33]

Ranson & Delamain had already taken over the custom of the Clan-
cys from Martell Lallemand, and the transfer of some or all of it into
Saule's hands was all the more significant as his first consignment for
them, as Lallemand feared, came to a rising market.[34] By October he
admitted to Van Yzendorn that 'what you observe about religion and
trade is very right; however the new house in Charente has got many
of our correspondents on her side'.[35]

As late as 23 November, Lallemand had not yet seen Laurence
Saule in person.[36] By that time Saule had executed a master stroke in
negotiating with success for all the supplies of the house of Gourg of
Saint Jean d'Angély. Lallemand's fear (and his unpleasant personality)
is reflected in the fact that, while his guarded comments to Dublin
houses were respectful, his epithet for Saule in letters to French correspondents was less so – 'mylord Saule' – and revealed real appre-
hension. Jennings, a medical doctor, was almost invariably referred to
sarcastically as 'le docteur' rather than by name. Lallemand's only
consolation was to dwell on the thought that Charente as opposed to
Cognac was a bad location and that his new competitors' choice of

brandy might be equally injudicious.[37] In 1766 Saule & Co. turned down an offer from Broussards at Pons to buy for them; they may have been conforming to local wisdom in doing so, as there were doubts about the Broussards' capacity. In any event, Saule & Co. engaged the house of Dubourg. Given the fact that Saule still seemed to refrain from entering directly into the market as a buyer, Lallemand congratulated himself on 30 July that 'la façon d'agir de Messrs Saule est réellement noble'. Three days later, however, it turned out that Saule, far from hesitating to integrate shipping and buying, had rented a house in Cognac.[38] That meant ominously that they intended to go behind the buyers to purchase from distillers directly on their own account.

This alarming news also scotched a rumour that he was on the eve of returning to Dublin. The move to Cognac – and perhaps the rumour of the return to Ireland – had occurred in the context of a rift between the Jennings and Saule families. The divide was notorious enough for Lallemand in 1766 to be able to follow its course. At this stage Jennings took ill, and died unexpectedly in late September. Saule himself was also ill, and Lallemand thought that the wish to flee from Charente (like Rochefort, a malaria plague spot) would quicken the execution of the transfer to Cognac. Lallemand also noted Saule's intention to rival Ranson & Delamain.[39] Soaring demand in Dublin (where distillation was temporarily halted by harvest failure) made it possible for both houses, well connected as they were, to take advantage to the full of the new circumstances. The Dublin trade slackened briefly at the beginning of 1766 with traders waiting in hope of one of the taxes on spirits being lifted. The conclusion of MacCarthy in Bordeaux in January, however, was that 'let it end as it may, I am of opinion that Ireland will return ere long to the charge, and import smartly'.[40] There were six ships from Dublin in the Charente in July, five in October, and Lallemand confided to his Charente shippers in November that 'la maison de Jarnac surtout brille plus que jamais, la votre de Charente [*i.e. Saule*] ne manque pas d'ordres non plus'.[41] In January 1767 there were already seven vessels in the river, rising to ten at the beginning of February, a record figure. In March Arbouin, one of the French houses in London, gave preference to Saule's house, and Lallemand was mortified that a newcomer was preferred.[42]

A combination of high prices in Cognac and business failures in Dublin houses was soon to reduce activity in Dublin. By April 1768, Delamain was seeking to place one of his clerks in Bordeaux, finding that 'we have really at present in our counting house more hands than we can well find employment for'.[43] A slowing in the brandy trade was quickly translated into difficulty in turning bills on Paris into cash on the spot. Saule responded to this problem by having 50,000 livres brought in silver from Paris to Saintes. At the current prices of brandy this would purchase 417 hogsheads or 11,259 *veltes*, a quantity as large as the purchases for an entire year by Richard Hennessy.

Saule died on 20 September, two years to a week after Jennings. At the end of 1765, the out-turn already had been below his expectations.[44] Ten months later he was to note that 'this is a dreadful country to do business in'; a revenue receiver had decamped with funds which should have honoured rescriptions in Saule's hands.[45] An inventory on 1 October valued his effects at 32,252 livres, not including his furniture.[46] This figure does not include all his assets. In December Delamain reported to the relatives of Saule in Dublin, Davys & Jennings, a balance of 29,716 livres as the proceeds of a joint speculation by himself and Saule.[47] In addition his London correspondents held a balance of £240 sterling to his credit.[48] However, there had been large losses in the high-priced brandy sent to a falling market in 1767. Of ten vessels in the spring of 1767, when the trade was at its peak, Stritch, Lallemand's correspondent in Dublin, reported in mid-year that 'seven have given so much profit to their owners that they are now out of the trade'.[49] As there was remarkably little brandy in Saule's inventory of 1 October 1768, much of his brandy must have been thrown on the market at low prices. Price cutting on brandies purchased in anticipation of orders was certainly in evidence in the spring of 1768. This seems confirmed in a later admission by Hennessy that in May he had sold brandy at five livres below the price at which he had purchased it, in order to match rivals' prices.[50]

Laurence Saule left a number of dependants relying on the little capital that survived the successive misfortunes of the two businesses: his wife; a nephew and niece, John and Elizabeth, who had been taken into his establishment as early as 1760; Eleanor Jennings, widow of Doctor Jennings, and her two children; and Laurence Saule's own sister Bridget Saule. Although Saule's business in Dublin was in his own name and the premises he sold in 1763 had been held in his name also,[51] Jennings may already have been a partner, perhaps a sleeping partner. The terms of the 1760 will suggest an existing Jennings interest, and in addition a cousin, Theobald Jennings, was Saule's 'shopkeeper'.[52] The will, after providing for a pension of £60 p.a. to his own wife, and £40 to his sister, left the residue, less stated legacies of £310, in trust to Dr Jennings, half for the support of Jennings and his wife, and half for the maintenance of the Jenningses' two children, Saule Jennings and Bridget Jennings.

DISAPPEARANCE AND SUCCESSION: EDWARD JENNINGS, LAURENCE SAULE, AND NEPHEW JOHN SAULE

The Jenningses formed part of a network of successful Co. Galway families in business and in the professions in Dublin and abroad. A Jennings uncle was established in Bath, the retirement haven of the well off, and he was said in 1775 to have inherited £14,000 sterling.[53] Given Edward Jennings' profession of medical doctor he is likely to have been a younger brother and to have had secondary financial standing relative to the other Jenningses in business in Dublin. Laurence Saule bore, in Directory terms, the appellation of 'grocer', not the prestigious one of 'merchant', and even Jennings' support of itself did not transform the resources of the house. Connection by family ties with the much more important Dublin house of Davys & Jennings would, however, raise its repute beyond its own resources. Equally, the terms of the will suggest that the business was a combination of the skill of Saule and of the capital, modest as it was, of a cadet member of a rising family.

The complicated terms of the will of 1760, binding two families together, later proved a source of contention and a quarrel broke out in 1766. If the business returns were disappointing, the residue for the Jenningses could be small or non-existent, and there was already sufficient friction before Jennings' illness and death in 1766 for the two households to separate. Shortly after Saule's death, the widow applied to Delamain for the balance in his hands, which he demurred to make over to her as 'we think we cannot with propriety do it at her request alone, the family is far from being united and ... there are two minors who have the greatest pretensions'.[54]

The Jenningses' son in 1768 was being supported in Vienna, apparently as an army cadet, by a regular remittance through the house of Isidore Lynch in London.[55] In 1771, losing his place in his regiment when, in his absence from Vienna, it was moved to Poland, he came first to Bath and then to London. It would appear that it was at this time that he met his rich uncle, who gave him fifty guineas and promised more assistance if he required it.[56] His return seems to have been at the mother's insistence, and John Saule in 1772 thought his cousin 'was a fool for coming to her, and not to stay in Germany'.[57] Mrs Jennings spoke ill of the Saules to Delamain.[58] She had lost little time in returning to Dublin with a tale of how she had been done out of money in France and had also started legal proceedings against the house of Trenor & Grainger. Winning that case may have eased her circumstances.[59] But she appears not to have enjoyed the whole-hearted support of her family's associates. Davys, the partner in Davys & Jennings, after having been prevailed upon by her to put his name to a letter, dissociated himself from it; and when he refused to forward it, it was dispatched by Mrs Jennings herself despite the fact that 'he positively told her he would not forward it'. John Saule, relying on information from Dublin, asserted that she was hated by everyone and that her son in London was in a poor condition, ashamed to appear in public, not having a decent coat to put on: 'she thinks of ordering home her daughter and to write to Bordeaux [*i.e. about the matters in contention*] ... Judge you how her malice pursues me and for what reason, God knows'.[60]

The following year her son returned to Dublin from London, intending to set up in business. But nothing seems to have come of this as in 1773 an officer friend of Hennessy's asked 'why does not her son join her, the small allowance given him to sustain his dignity in England is very short. I suppose he is accustomed to an idle life, that he will not take to any business.'[61] He seems to have gone to France again: two years later he used Saule's services to realize the proceeds of a small bill, but he cannot have been very successful, for Saule's comment on him was prefaced with the words 'poor Jennings'.[62] He counted on the support of his rich family connections: the hopeful claim that 'my friends in county Galway are desirous of seeing me' is made in one letter.[63]

At the end of the year he cropped up in Sarre Louis in Lorraine, where he had gone to recover a small debt of honour from an officer he had known in Vienna. His situation was as desperate as ever, and, according to Saule, 'he finishes [his letter] in his usual strain desiring to send him cash, to bear his expenses from thence to Ireland by the way of Dunkirk where he'll meet daily opportunity per the Rush wherrys for Dublin'.[64] Jennings' letter itself survives and reveals that his plans had now gone beyond Bath or Dublin, 'to get what I can from my grandfather and other friends in the county Galway and to set off directly for Jamaica to join my uncle established there. This is what I am fully determined upon, and I don't despair of recuperating with interest the time I have already lost.'[65] Saule referred sardonically to Jennings' letter as 'a letter from the baron de Kilmaine'. His late father, the medical doctor, was a younger sibling of the partners in the Dublin house of Davys & Jennings and the Jennings uncle of Bath. His own travails – and travels – reflected the problems of a cadet branch plagued by business losses and death. The letters from this Edward Saule Jennings, *soi-disant* M. de Kilmaine, document the inauspicious origins of the future General de Kilmaine, distinguished military officer of the Revolution. He must have enlisted in the French army some time or other after the mid-1770s.[66]

In 1772 Mrs Jennings was still intent on commencing a law suit against Delamain and Saule. Still more disagreeable news from Dublin was retailed by Saule to Hennessy in 1775: 'I've a letter last post from Kennedy, a long epistle, concerning all our family but therein nothing new, mauvaise conduite and dirt. When I can more agreeably hold my pen, I shall give you some particulars. Jennings has no commission he says.'[67] With offsetting liabilities, the Saule estate had left little for either side of the family, and the matter dragged on into the 1780s. Saule's own sister Betty had to ask Saule to engage Delamain to give him her money from the estate to remit to her.[68] This would have been £100 provided for in the will of 1760, though, whether she received it or not, by January 1773 her position was relieved by finding a place in the house of a person of 'quality'.[69]

The executor of the 1760 will was one of the richest of Dublin's rising Catholics, Valentine Brown, described as a former brewer and gentleman. The list of Saule's Dublin correspondents was impressive, larger at the time of the great expansion in the Dublin trade in 1767 than that of either Lallemand or Delamain.[70] In 1768 he had no fewer than fifty correspondents there. His seventeen Irish correspondents outside Dublin testify to the contacts created by the politics of Saule's former involvement in the Catholic Committee: they included Walter Woulfe of Carrick-on-Suir, Barth Rivers and Dominick Farrel of Waterford, Michael Sutton and Robert Devereux of Wexford and Philip Roche of Limerick. He had three London correspondents: the houses of Arbouin, Wenman & Broughton, and Rice & Belson.

The fact that Davys & Jennings took over Laurence Saule's premises on his departure reflected his public association with them. A Jennings had been his 'shopkeeper' before 1763, and a Davys his bookkeeper. A later letter suggests that the Jennings principals (there were apparently two) in Davys & Jennings were William and John. Whether the house already existed as a force in its own right, or emerged by the employees of the old Saule concern launching out on their own in Saule's old premises, it is hard to say. But the house was prominent in the heady expansion of the 1760s. Like many others it eventually failed. John Saule in 1775 noted its failure in 1773 for upwards of £35,000 with effects to meet 50 per cent of creditors' demands: 'Poor Mrs Saule and William Jennings and John have now got the final blow and are reduced to the lowest. This house has been the cause of many failures in this city and in other places. Thus my poor family are ruined …'.[71] The house had become involved in the 1760s in the affairs of George Colebrooke, London merchant and a future chairman of the East India Company. Colebrooke in the 1760s, in part as a result of his ties with his earlier wartime contracting partners, the Irish house of Nesbitt in London, opened a bank in Dublin in 1764. In April 1773 Saule noted that 'I didn't hear anything of Colebrooke's failure but if it be so, I am not surprised at Davys & Jennings stopping, for they are closely linked'.[72] Saule also implied a link between the Dublin house and French & Hobson in London.[73] Such a link would not be altogether surprising because of a County Galway background shared by the Jenningses with Andrew French, London agent of the rich and rising circle in France of Thomas Sutton, a force to be reckoned with in the stormy politics of the French East India company. Sutton's circle, including the elusive Paris banker Isaac Panchaud, had an interest in Colebrooke's speculations. Colebrooke's speculative ventures were unusual in that they attracted both Protestant and Catholic money. John Saule's mother (Laurence Saule's sister-in-law) was a Protestant, and Saule's letters suggest that her substance was tied up in the Davys & Jennings enterprise.

John Saule's cousin, John Saule Kennedy, was a correspondent to the end of Saule's life: in the 1780s, according to Saule, he was his only Dublin relative. He would appear to be a relative on the paternal side, and hence probably the offspring of a marriage of a sister of Laurence Saule. Though he had a brother, David Kennedy, a merchant in Mary's Lane,[74] and other family connections were sound, his own circumstances were modest at the outset. At the outset of the 1770s he was planning to emigrate to the East Indies,[75] not a wild ambition in itself as the Colebrooke interest would have been of practical assistance. Several years later, however, his circumstances were good enough for him to get a place in the business of Oliver Plunkett, a prominent Dublin merchant, and his sister's eldest son was apprenticed to Keogh, 'one of the first mercers of this city'[76] – in other words to John Keogh, destined to emerge as one of the political leaders of Dublin Catholics in the late 1780s and early 1790s. Plunkett, in whose counting house he had found a place, was a brother-in-law of Michael Cosgrave.[77] Though a Catholic, Kennedy became a member of the Volunteers, joining in mid-1782 a corps in Coolock under the command of Colonel Folliott, some three hundred men 'all the most respectable'.[78] Kennedy was himself a brother-in-law to Christopher Gernon of Bordeaux, a member of one of the two richest Catholics families from Dublin to migrate to Bordeaux. The Gernons were to have an interest in Bordeaux's brandy trade in the 1780s.

THE GALWEYS AND THE BELLEWS

If Saule & Jennings seemed to Lallemand in 1766 and 1767 to pose the greatest challenge, Galwey had not been a negligible force. In retrospect Delamain, a shrewd judge, conceded 'the abilities of the late Mr Anthony Galwey of La Rochelle to serve his friends with cognac brandy'.[79] The house had a formidable background in both Ireland and France. Galwey was a son of John Galwey of Carrick-on-Suir. As late as 1775 John Galway (*sic*), described as Esq., was one of some 130 signatories of an oath of loyalty for Catholics in Carrick-on-Suir, the largest number for any town or city in Ireland.[80] The town had what was for provincial Ireland a uniquely large Catholic business class. In the 1760s Walter Woulfe (Wolfe) of Carrick was a correspondent of Saule's business. John Galway's brother, Edward, was a merchant in Dungarvan, a rising town in west Waterford. In addition to Antoine, another son (who died in 1772) was a merchant in Waterford, as was a third in Malaga.[81] The family were probably taking over some of the business activity that had been managed in the 1750s by the network of the Woulfes of Carrick and Martin Murphy of Waterford, then correspondent of George Fitzgerald of London, at the time the most cosmopolitan Irish businessman abroad and patron of Sutton. In the 1760s the banking circle of Woulfe and Waters was waning rapidly in France, and George Woulfe of Paris made a poor impression even on the neophyte businessman Richard Hennessy in the mid-1760s: Hennessy soon dispensed with their services.[82]

The Galweys of Carrick were accepted by the main Lotta or West Court family in Cork as an associated branch,[83] and Antoine Galwey used the style De Galwey, which signified higher social pretensions. He first made his appearance in French records in 1756, described as 'Sieur Anthonné Gallué jeune irlandais catholique qui demeure depuis un an dans la ville de Saintes, où il est venu résider dans le dessein d'apprendre le français'.[84] Galwey, obviously in the context of his La Rochelle backing and marriage, had chosen to remain in La Rochelle. Buying in Cognac for him proved the mainstay of the business of two houses, the Broussards and the Augiers, in the mid-1760s.

Galwey's widow, though her expectations were reduced by her husband's death,[85] continued the business. However from January 1768 a partner, a young Frenchman, had to be brought into the house, which was now styled Veuve Antoine de Galwey & Guérin. These were difficult years in the brandy trade. Purchasing, for a time halted, was small in 1768 and 1769 when it resumed, and seems to have ended in June 1770. In October 1770 Augier wrote to her father-in-law in Carrick-on-Suir of 'the unlucky situation of Madame Galwey', and visualized her retiring from business.[86] As late as November, a brave face was still being put on events. William Galwey, temporarily in La Rochelle on his way back to Ireland, assured Broussard *fils* that 'ma cousine doit un peu d'argent mais elle est fort en état de payer tout'. According to him, if the widow's father-in-law sent a partner from Ireland, the house could continue without difficulty, and already had a proposal from Dublin for joint purchases. Broussard *père* had been less impressed: according to William Galwey, 'il arrivait [?] toujours à mes portes sans savoir au juste quoique vous et moi le priaient toujours d'attendre'.[87] By February 1771 a debt against the La Rochelle house was prominently inscribed in the Augier invoice book, suggesting that all hope of recovery by the La Rochelle house had evaporated. The family now had to cope with rumours of Guérin being the author of the firm's growing misfortunes. In November 1770 the widow denied them, assuring Broussard *fils* that Guérin had been six months in the counting house with scarcely a moment out of it and that a suspension of payments in the preceding January had occurred while the firm had funds out to respectable houses.[88] The firm's final *bilan* seems to have been submitted in June 1771; crude calculations suggest that the losses were of the order of 100,000 livres. Those losing included the Irish house of Delap in Bordeaux (4000 livres), Petit the *receveur général* or tax collector (18,000 livres, presumably by cash paid in advance for Galwey's drafts on Paris houses) and Mrs Galwey's father (16,000).[89]

At the outset, the assets would have provided for a mere 15 per cent settlement with the creditors. In March 1771, however, the prospect of accommodation seemed good, as John Galwey and Colonel Labadie, father-in-law and father respectively of the widow, waived their claims on the house, which would make possible a 45

per cent offer to the rest of the creditors. However, one creditor, a
Paris banker, due 20,000 livres, proving less accommodating than the
other creditors, sought to have the partners arrested. Guérin was
arrested (though he later escaped from jail and fled to Paris), and the
widow took refuge in a convent.[90] But French law required settlement
where the bulk of creditors were in agreement, and a settlement was
finally agreed in August 1772.[91]

Assured of a fresh capital of 20,000 livres from her father-in-law
in Carrick, the widow was party to negotiations to set up a new
house with a man named Schaaf who had

> the reputation of a very skilled and honest man. We believe he is not
> very rich ... and that you will run no risk to trust him the interests of
> your grown children, also by that mean can repair by the trade the
> loss they suffered by the bad behaviour of Guérin who was a fellow
> of low extraction and bad manners.[92]

Schaaf changed his mind, saying that he was too old,[93] possibly a
reasonable argument – though he was only fifty – for a man who
would carry the burden of a new house in the crisis-ridden La
Rochelle of 1772. In December 1772 the widow was still hoping for
an associate.

Philip Augier had married Anne Marie Broussard, daughter of
Daniel Broussard, merchant, in 1757.[94] Her dowry was 6000 livres,
and Daniel Broussard & Son in Cognac was probably a house set up
with the help of the Augier in-laws to help a son's launch into a successful career. The letters received by the Broussard house suggest that
Galwey was easily their main correspondent, and that they had no
worthwhile business apart from the commissions they received from
La Rochelle. The eagerness to please Galwey is reflected in the com-
plementary sending of a 'choppe farci de truffle'. Galwey replied that
twelve members of the family of his wife and sister-in-law dined on
it, but ominously mention of illness already crops up.[95] The Broussards looked after the son of Edward Galwey of Dungarvan. Augier
regretted in March 1768 that 'we are sorry that our house is not large
enough for to have take him by ourselves. We had done it with pleasure, but you may be positive that we will have for him the same
cares as when you was her yourselves. We have several young English

gentlemen here. We'll recommend the gentleman your son that he do not keep too frequent company with them, that he may learn soon our language.'[96] A year's board had been arranged for 450 livres.[97] Lingering on well beyond the year, he was due to return home only in October 1770, a course which Augier advised 'because our town which is a very small one and where we have no good masters for any sciences, is not fit to improve a young gentleman'.[98] The Augier business with Galwey was very substantial. In 1765, for example, the invoices of Augier and of Pelletreau (who worked on Galwey account, and whose business was probably confined to the Irish trade) were in excess of 2000 barriques. Other business consisted merely of a few foreign invoices for Bruges and for London, where they had two significant customers.

The Galwey house under the widow had provided employment for the young Saule when he was cast adrift by the death of his uncle Laurence Saule in the autumn of 1768. Young William Galwey, whose original agreement with the Broussards was expiring in March 1769, might, because of his family relationship and precarious prospects, have had expectations of preference for a paid position. In response to an approach from Saule, Mrs Galwey had attached a separate sheet to a letter to the Broussard house in March 1769 as a confidential reply setting out her offer, not to be disclosed by Saule, with instructions

> avant de lui donner l'inclus de ne point dire au jeune Galwey ce qu'il gagne et qu'il soit secret à ce sujet et pour tout autre chose avec nos autres commis, qu'il dise si on le questionne qu'il gagne rien, qu'il ne vient que pour quelques mois avec nous, pour nous obliger.[99]

Such was the Saule reputation, however, that the Galwey house, while agreeing to engage him for a year, feared that, having learned all its secrets, he could set up as a successful rival in La Rochelle, Rochefort or Charente:

> Ce jeune homme peut dans un an nous faire une loi dure; ce qui nous ferait bien regretter alors de l'avoir pris. Que pensez-vous Messieurs de nos réflections – nous les croyons fondées … Dieu veuille que nous ayons affaire à un homme délicat et reconnaisssant.[100]

The realities proved different from the widow's fears. Her own business did not outlive 1771, and while Saule left the house at the end of the agreed term of a year,[101] his own fortunes over the following six years were to be ones of narrow horizons.

Luke Bellew and Richard Hennessy at the end of 1765 were the last members of the contingent of the 1760s. Bellew arrived on the banks of the Charente a little ahead – perhaps by only a matter of days – of Richard Hennessy. They met in Paris on their way to the Charente. Both applied to Anthony Galwey for his support. In regard to Bellew the La Rochelle house in response to a letter in November was assured by their agents in Cognac, the Augiers, that 'nous lui procurerons icy tout l'agrément qui dépendra de nous ainsi qu'à Mr Henecy. Ce dernier n'est pas arrivé. Nous doutons que ces messieurs ayent un grand succès dans le commerce qu'ils se proposent ici.'[102] The pessimistic appraisal at a time of great boom in the trade referred to the shortage of suitable premises to rent: the only stores and houses available were in or near the centre of the town. A year later Lallemand made a like observation that any merchant wishing to settle in Cognac would have difficulty procuring a 'logement convenable'.[103] By June 1766 Bellew had temporarily left his affairs in the hands of Richard Hennessy:[104] he travelled, apparently on a business trip, through Ayr, London and Douai between September and November.[105] Like Hennessy he was an army officer; his debts and his restiveness at being passed over for substantive lieutenant rank can be traced fleetingly.[106] While trade, it seems, may have been on his mind as early as 1762, as late as May 1766 he described himself 'as druging here to be a good officer but am resolved to depart as soon as I can have fair promise for my pension', and in February 1767 others had hopes of the army post he had vacated.[107] He was well connected, a son of Michael Bellew of Mount Bellew, near Castle Blakeny, hence a member of a powerful Galway landed family. A brother Patrick was to make a mark as a merchant in Cadiz and Dublin successively.[108]

This background and the entrée it gave him to the County Galway interest in London may also have helped him to find a London partner. By November 1766 he had formed a partnership with Wenman & Broughton. No Cognac house had done this, and no house of the like sort was to follow. Bellew's progress was followed attentively in Cognac: Lallemand seems to have been under the impression that there would be in fact be two houses, that of Bellew and an associated house of Wenman & Broughton.[109] Bellew's London agent was Isidore Lynch & Co., at that time at the pinnacle of their success as one of the London houses that handled exchange business with France and Spain as well as Ireland. When he died his effects were made over to the house of French & Hobson, another Galway house in London.[110] In February 1767 Bellew's return to the Charente was still being anticipated for a future date.[111] But death stole on him before he could return to Cognac, probably in February itself, if not already before that month. The few subsequent references arise from debts incurred by Richard Hennessy on his behalf.

DELAMAIN AND HENNESSY

While Delamain only momentarily exceeded Martell's in the volume of turnover, he was the sole successful member of the new generation of settlers. More than that, he was also at the centre of their social life. When Laurence Saule died in 1768 Delamain was executor of the estate. He helped to set up John Saule, Laurence's nephew in La Rochelle, in 1769 and supported him when he moved to Cognac in 1776. He provided support on several occasions for Hennessy in his disastrous business in Bordeaux between 1776 and 1787. When John Saule's death in 1788 revealed the insolvency of the Cognac house, it was Delamain's introduction of a nephew, Samuel Turner, which put a new Hennessy house on its feet.

Delamain's success attracted members of his own family to join him on the banks of the Charente. His father was in Cognac in 1784, in Liverpool in 1786, but back in Jarnac by 1788.[112] A nephew by a stepbrother, Samuel Turner, had joined him by 1783.[113] A partnership with one of the Broussards was acquired for him. But it can scarcely have been a very attractive position, and when Hennessy's was in difficulties in Bordeaux in 1787 John Saule was able to report that 'Samuel Turner would willingly join you if you could find means of keeping up the house'.[114] In 1790 a relative in the East Indies, no doubt in response to glowing news from Jarnac, wrote with enthusiasm that 'Samuel Turner's success in life gives me much pleasure. I always foresaw it.'[115]

James Delamain was a man of extraordinary personal authority – probably, once Louis-Gabriel Lallemand withdrew from active participation in business in 1775, the most commanding figure among the merchants on the banks of the Charente. Huguenot though he was by religion and marrying into the main trading family of the minor centre of Jarnac, he quickly befriended the newcomers from Dublin to the Charente without exception, rivals and Catholics though they were. As early as 1768 we can trace them being invited to dine, and in that year Delamain was already an executor of the estate of Laurence Saule. His father William's first wife, James's mother, was a Hannah Frances O'Shaughnessy. Three of the witnesses of Delamain's marriage contract were Irish, two of them probably Catholic: Jacques Horish and Patrice French.[116] Delamain did as much, or more, business with Catholic as Protestant houses in Dublin, and the only sign of his Protestant background (but one also of his Irishness) was that his Bordeaux correspondents were the Irish Protestant house of Delap, and the Huguenot house of Baudry, itself allied to the Irish Protestant interest in Bordeaux by marriage. In 1784 Joseph Cooper Walker wrote to William Delamain, James's father, to the effect that Kellett, son of the mayor of Cork 'who resided many years in Bordeaux spoke of Mr James Delamain as one whom he respected and esteemed'.[117]

His social standing is expressed too in his house overlooking the river. Property was acquired in 1774 from the Comte de Jarnac which formerly belonged to the Récollet monastery for an outlay of 20,000 livres, and this acquisition was enlarged in the 1780s into the stylish building which still stands on the river's edge.[118] No other house compared with it in the town apart from the chateau, and no merchant's house in Cognac, the Martells' excepted, came near to rivalling it.

Despite his Huguenot marriage, he did not look to the sources of French Protestantism, as the Martells did. In 1767 Lallemand was arranging for one of his Martell nephews to stay with a French Protestant house in Frankfurt, another was already there, and a third was studying in Neufchâtel.[119] Delamain sent one of his sons to study

in Ireland, and Saule remarked of Delamain's Huguenot wife on that
occasion that 'I am sure she wished Ireland often to the devil'.[120] In
1783 he indicated to a Belfast merchant, in the course of looking for
a place in a business house for his son that he would prefer Belfast
'before many other places as I esteem it to be one of industry and
moderation therefore fit for a young man whose destination is for
trade'.[121] Though his London trade was smaller than Martell Lallemand's, two sons later settled in England, and his daughter of course
married an Englishman.

Delamain had a fondness for potatoes which he shared with Saule
and Hennessy. In thanking a captain in 1768 for the offer of some
potatoes, Delamain asked him to send from Rochefort to Jarnac 'a
small quantity between this and Tuesday, as that day we have Messrs
Saule and Hennessy's families to dine with us. We heartily wish you
could be of the party.'[122] He may have been the first man to plant
potatoes in the south-west of France. In February he had already
asked the master of a vessel: 'pray have you a few potatoes to spare.
We should be much obliged to send them up here. They are to plant
and we shall return you the compliment in some old brandy.'[123]

It is probable too that he shared the views of Richard Hennessy
and Saule on the political changes in Ireland in 1782 which are
echoed in their correspondence: his positive comments on Belfast, a
radical city in its politics, suggests as much. Irish newspapers sometimes came out on the regular sailings from Dublin to Bordeaux and
were forwarded to Delamain. The news, like the potatoes, was no
doubt shared with Hennessy or Saule. Delamain in May 1768 proposed to visit Dublin.[124] If a visit took place it would have been his
last visit to his homeland. A quarter of a century later, now almost an
old man, Delamain referred wistfully to Ireland in a letter to Richard
Hennessy, then proposing to return on a visit, as 'the land of potatoes'.[125]

Delamain's business correspondence sometimes referred to events
in the wider world. In writing of some legal nicety in 1789 (apparently the Regency crisis) he commented to an Irish merchant in
London that 'your parliamentary debates are very extensive on a
question most easy to resolve'. He went on to praise parliament and
its prime minister William Pitt: 'on its steadfastness are founded the

prosperity and liberty of the nation. We conclude the subject with most cordial wish that so upright so judicious a man as Mr Pitt may ever be at the head of affairs.'[126] A *donation entre vifs* by his widow Marie Ranson in 1813 hints at the scale of the library he had left behind him: fifty-eight volumes of the *Encyclopaedia*, six volumes of the Bible, 818 bound volumes and 212 soft-covered volumes (*brochés*).[127]

He also moved in a wider world socially than the other merchants, not excluding the Martells and Lallemands who singlemindedly inhabited the world of commerce. Like Hennessy and Saule, Delamain was a Freemason, but while Saule took a childish pleasure in the rituals of the Masons, it brought Delamain into contact with the milieu of the region's nobility. In December 1778, for instance, unable to attend an assembly at Loudec (or Coudec?), near Ruffec, he asked for his respects to be conveyed to the comte de Broglie.[128] He had some contact with the duc de Rochefoucauld. He obliged him occasionally with bills of exchange on Paris, on one occasion apparently in payment for brandy received. His most regular contact was with Charles-Rosalie de Rohan-Chabot, comte de Jarnac. The first known contact with him is in an intemperate letter from the comte in 1767, which while it speaks well of Delamain makes clear his resentment of an attempt led, the count believed, by Ranson to avoid the feudal obligation of baking bread in the manorial oven.[129] Before her marriage to the count at the beginning of 1777, Elizabeth Smith, daughter of an Irish landowner, resided in Delamain's house,[130] and on occasion in subsequent years Delamain obliged the count in the matter of remitting money from Ireland to France. The count in turn took an interest in the affairs of the brandy trade, and his representations in 1782 and 1784 at the court were instrumental in securing reductions in duties on exports. In April 1784 he informed a Dublin merchant that 'Count Jarnac who has very great influence at court is now here, the writer is constantly employed with him finishing materials and observations to that salutary end and we shall have the first knowledge through this channel'.[131] Delamain's readiness to speak out on behalf of the trade of the region was in evidence again in 1789 when he wrote to Necker supporting representations for a halt in 'the tyranny' of the tax authorities until the States General met.[132]

In 1790, quite in contrast to others, he favoured a wider circulation of notes by the *caisse d'escompte* to compensate for the shortage of specie.[133] When the *assignats* appeared during the Revolution, he welcomed them. He noted the objections to their circulation, but felt that, if circulated without interest payment and thus avoiding repercussions on other commercial paper, they would be useful for trade.[134] Politically, he saw Necker as a minister who understood the interests of commerce, expressing his judgment to Mallet quite categorically without any deference to the banker's exalted status:

> Il est certain que l'entrée de Monsieur Necker au ministère est faite pour opérer une révolution salutaire dans les affaires publiques, nous désirons sincèrement qu'elles prennent la consistence, suite nature d'une bonne administration.[135]

The pace of events in July 1789 took him by surprise. Towards the end of the month he informed an English correspondent that he would not trouble him with a particular account: 'The public papers will have given it you and however strange you may believe them, not exaggerated, in so much that any man who had been absent from the scene of such action since this day month would cry out it is impossible such things could happen.'[136]

Delamain's only sustained English business arose from the trade in flax-seed which gave him a way into a brandy custom in Hull and Newcastle. The association was very close in particular with the house of Berry, later Knowsley. In 1789 Knowsley had in contemplation an even closer association.[137] The company shipped walnuts on its own account in the 1760s to Cork and Dublin, and dealt in flax-seed for the English market. The latter trade was a time-consuming one because as Delamain explained, it was necessary to 'scour the country'.[138] Ranson & Delamain were prepared to ship from as far afield as Bayonne, and for the vessel's outward voyage from England, were prepared to go halves in a cargo of coal. There would be no great profit in the sale of coal in Bayonne, but they were interested if it provided opportunity of business in flax-seed.[139] Outside commodity trade, he seems to have held some shares in the 1770s in La Rochelle vessels in the Newfoundland fishery; and some investment by way of purchase of shares in the slaving voyages of the La Rochelle merchant Weiss from 1787 to 1791 was not unconnected to what were for Delamain's business very untypical orders of brandy for the vessels.[140] Some plantation property in the West Indies inherited in the 1790s was an acquisition with little economic return in wartime.

Delamain led Cognac in the number of his Irish correspondents, apart from Laurence Saule's short-lived expansion. As late as 1783 he was able to observe that 'from our first establishment here we believe we have done more business for Ireland than all the other houses in the country put together'.[141] Martell Lallemand was the only other Cognac house with a significant share of the trade in the 1780s: in some years it did as well as Delamain. Delamain's foreign correspondence in the 1780s was modest enough for an established merchant: he sent out only twenty-four copies of a circular letter in April 1785 and there was little concentration on any single market: eight letters to London, five to Belfast, five to Dublin, one to Derry, two to Bergen, three to Elsinore.[142]

The Paris trade saved Delamain's business in the aftermath of the crisis in the Irish business in 1767. In August 1768, for instance, Delamain sent thirty-six circular letters to Paris.[143] In 1768, at the end of the great Irish boom, Delamain seems to have had more than one English-speaking clerk. By 1782, on the other hand, when Delamain took ill the English correspondence had to be suspended because no one in the house knew English.[144] Even Lallemand conceded in the early 1760s that Delamain's shipped a stronger brandy, and in 1799 Delamain could write to a London house that 'we have the reputation of shipping the best that leaves the country'.[145]

Bellew's absence and unexpected death left Hennessy on his own, among the Irish Catholic houses. His arrival was unobtrusive, and scarcely recorded in the archives of Augier, or more tellingly in the numerous letters received by Broussard *fils*. Even in the sustained commentary by Lallemand in 1766 and 1767, his name recurs little, and the most explicit reference was dismissive: 'la maison Hennessy a toujours peu de chose à charger. C'est ce que nous saurons mieux dans la suite'.[146] He arrived in Cognac apparently in the second half of December, after trying unsuccessfully to acquire premises in Tonnay-Charente. His Cognac premises, on the rue des Cordeliers with an adjoining warehouse on the rue de la Richonne, and without a direct river frontage, were rented at the end of the month, for 400 livres a year.[147] Arriving at a time of crisis the house had few prospects. Hennessy's thoughts turned early to the idea of leaving Cognac and even France, and from 1776 to 1788 he resided in Bordeaux.

5

The Hennessys at home and abroad

Richard Hennessy arrived in Cognac in 1765. Both his father and grandfather had lived at Ballymacmoy on the river Blackwater in the north-east of County Cork. Of the Cork Catholic landed families the only one, apart from the Cotters, to survive relatively intact were the Nagles: they were the dominant family in an enclave on the Blackwater east of Mallow containing in 1720 the sole large concentration of Catholic landed property in the county. After the execution of James Cotter in 1720, the Ballygriffin branch of the Nagle family, by no means intimidated by the hostile environment in which they lived, became the active spokesmen of the Catholic interest. They also made possible the survival of lesser branches and of related families, including the Hennessys. 'Counsellor' Joseph Nagle, younger brother of the head of the Ballygriffin branch of the Nagles, drew up their leases or defended them in the law courts.

The eighteenth-century family recollection was that the Hennessy family claimed descent from a younger brother of Lord Viscount Iveagh in Ulster, who settled in Munster, changing (or anglicizing) the family name from McEnnis (in Irish MacAonghusa) to Hennessy, and finally forfeiting lands in Dunmahon and elsewhere in Cork in the 1641 rebellion. If they restored their fortunes somewhat, it must have been as a result of an advantageous marriage to a Nagle (a great grandmother of Richard) from the then head branch of the family at

Annakissey in or before 1670.[1] In 1786 the Hennessys held their land from David Nagle of Ballygriffin, and the lease of that year appears to be a renewal of an existing stake.[2] Given that the head rent of the Hennessy holder of the Ballymacmoy estate in 1775 in the haven of the Blackwater was a mere £80, the lease must have an old arrangement, probably drawn up either in the 1670s or 1690s (hence before the 1704 act which penalized new Catholic land transactions). The Ballygriffin Nagles' title seems to have been uncomplicated, if we judge by the later evidence for the Hennessy title. But other Nagles, like the Annakissey Nagles, sank in economic position. The precarious state of the Ballyduff Nagles, close to the Hennessy home at Ballymacmoy, is reflected in the fact that they did not hold their demesne directly from a head landlord, whether the Ballygriffin Nagles or the Bowens who also had land in the district, but in the shelter of a subtenancy under the pre-1704 and hence secure title of the Hennessys. The Hennessys, like the other Nagle branches, owed their survival to the circumstances of the Ballygriffin branch of the family and probably to the formidable legal acumen of its younger son, Joseph Nagle.

James Hennessy, father of Richard, had married a Barrett (before 1691 a family of broad acres), probably, given the evidence of the dates of birth of his children, in the 1720s. The Barretts' later reliance on the friendship or support of Edmund Burke suggests that members of the family were in his intimate circle in the early years Burke spent on the banks of the Blackwater. Contrary to what has often been said James Hennessy did not serve in the French army. The prospects of an inheritance were attractive enough to keep him at home. In turn his own sons followed the same pattern. George (1725–1776) succeeded to Ballymacmoy in 1768. Richard, the second son, drifted into the French army in 1748 and out of it in 1752 or 1753 to his cousins' business circle in Ostend. A younger son, James, was a merchant in Cork city, married to Ellen Nagle of the Ballylegan branch of the Nagle family. A brother of James Hennessy of Ballymacmoy, Charles, born around 1700, settled in Ostend probably in its boom of the 1720s when other Cork families like the Sarsfields had a stake in its business. Charles created the Ostend branch of the family, and it was probably the Barrett alliance of his senior brother in Ballymacmoy that made possible in time a Barrett alliance for an Ostend nephew, James, in 1758. Widowed in 1760, this lady in 1765 married Richard. He was on the spot in Ostend, and her modest dowry of £800 was a matrimonial inducement (though one that does not appear to have been paid in full or at all).

The marriages of three of Richard's sisters linked him to the business houses of Shea and Comerford in Cork and to the powerful Roche business family of Cork and Limerick. A young member of the Roche family reminded Richard in 1774 that 'my mother says she was acquainted with you a vast number of years ago, and knows many of your family'.[3] James of Ballymacmoy (i.e. Richard's father) was also connected to the Goolds, another of the rich Catholic merchant houses of Cork, by the marriage of a sister to Henry Goold. In turn the Hennessys were related, apparently on the maternal side, to the Galweys, and both Hennessys and Comerfords were related to the Kearneys of Tipperary, whose Bordeaux and Alicante business interests were very much a feature of mid-century.

Richard Hennessy's future wife (widow of his cousin, James of Ostend), Ellen ('Nelly') Barrett, was a niece of Patrick Nagle of Ballyduff. As one of Patrick Nagle's sisters, married to an attorney named Burke, was mother of Edmund Burke, she was a first cousin of Burke. And of course, as already noted, in the contortions of Irish land title, the Ballyduff Nagles, at least for their seat and demesne, were legally tenants of the Hennessys under their lease from the Ballygriffin Nagles. Hennessy and Burke knew one another as boys. Moreover, a Nugent family into which a daughter of Patrick Nagle had married was to provide the wife of Edmund Burke. When Richard Hennessy in 1765 visited London in fix up a correspondent for the foreign-exchange dealings of his new Cognac venture, he saw Burke, and the meeting is mentioned in one of Burke's letters to Ballyduff together with news of Hennessy's wife's pregnancy.[4] That meeting would have been in September or early October. Having made arrangements with the Irish house of Isidore Lynch to handle his exchange business, Richard then went to Paris where he made similar arrangements with the house of Woulfe. At this time Richard was still keeping in touch with Burke (though unfortunately none of the letters survive), and complaints must have made from Ballyduff to

Edmund Burke that they had not heard from Richard. At the end of the year, Burke assured Patrick Nagle, his Ballyduff uncle, that 'Dick has been for some time past at Paris. It is true he has not wrote; but no man living loves and values you more; not even myself. He will make up for his neglect.'[5] By the time Burke's letter was written, Dick must have already been at least one week in Cognac.

CAREERS, SOCIAL MOBILITY AND POLITICAL AND SOCIAL STATUS

For Irish families of respectability, as for comparable families in England or in France, in addition to landholding, trade and church, the army was a career outlet for sons. In the middle of the century no fewer than six Hennessys can be traced in the French army. Richard, himself a second son, combined in his career both army service and trade. One of the children of Charles of Ostend, Thomas, was captain in the army at the end of the 1750s, but the contemporary military prestige of the family – which was considerable – rested on an earlier Richard. A spurious later history – in which Richard of Ballymacmoy was given a distinguished career, fighting at Fontenoy (and according to some accounts being wounded) and in which military careers have sometimes also been attributed to Richard's father, and even to Richard's son, another James – grew up in the effort to account for the repute. The reality was that Richard had a short and undistinguished peacetime service, and neither father nor son served at all. While the Hennessy genealogy becomes very incomplete beyond the period of Richard's father, James, the earlier Richard, if related to the family, would almost certainly be an uncle of James, possibly fighting in Ireland in 1689–91 but certainly having entered the service in the 1690s. In all probability he would have been a younger son. From the French records, he entered the service in 1695 and reached the rank of lieutenant-colonel in 1724.[6]

Lord Clare's regiment, which Richard Hennessy had entered in 1695, was commanded at the time by Lee because of Lord Clare's death in 1693, and though he transferred later to Bulkely's regiment, representations after his death in 1743 on behalf of his widow were made not only by the colonel-proprietor Bulkely, uncle of Lee, but in 1744 by Lord Clare. When Richard of Ballymacmoy entered the service in 1748 he entered Clare's regiment; he served in the army until 1752 or 1753. His service was later misrepresented when in 1757 the French overran Ostend. His military record would not have qualified him for French citizenship unless he had completed ten years' service. A false certificate to this effect was provided by Lord Clare's son (vicomte de Clare and Lord Thomond), colonel-proprietor of the regiment and a marshal of France. (The document again proved useful to the Hennessy family in 1824, as discussed in chapter 3.) Only the standing of the family could have warranted the issue of an otherwise wholly unjustifiable certificate. Some later accounts even more incorrectly refer to Richard as having served in Dillon's regiment. The statement is incorrect, and probably rests on the fact that Richard in 1781 secured a promise of places in Dillon's regiment for his three sons. Clare's regiment had been disbanded in the aftermath of the Seven Years War, and its officers and men incorporated in the surviving regiments: in that sense Dillon's was successor regiment to Clare's.

In 1730 the earlier Richard Hennessy had been entrusted with an extraordinarily difficult and unique mission of recruiting in Ireland, which had high diplomatic and political significance.[7] The family's military prestige rested on his service in the early decades of the century when the size of the Brigade and within it its rank-and-file Irish membership were at their peak. He had became a lieutenant-colonel in 1724, and his service file hinted at the difficult missions he had undertaken. His two sons were also captains in the 1740s.

A career officer's complaints revolved monotonously around the fewness of promotion prospects and low salaries. Colonel Daniel O'Connell, from County Kerry, a highly successful officer, provides a striking illustration of this litany of lamentations.[8] Similar complaints by another member of the family, Captain Maurice O'Connell, were later recorded by James Roche,[9] and in 1776 and again in the 1780s the members of the Brigade at large were very restive. With rising rents (which enhanced landed incomes and made middle tenures profitable) and with more opportunities in the expanding trade of mid-century, the prestige of army service declined sharply. When Richard, the brandy merchant, in poor circumstances in 1781 envisaged army careers for his sons (and it is revealing that his thoughts turned to army service for his sons only when his own fortune were at a nadir point), he had no difficulty in securing a promise of future places for them.

The Ballymacmoy Hennessys paled besides the Ballygriffin Nagles, or the urban Galweys. They and many of their relatives, Nagle and non-Nagle alike, are among those reckoned by Burke to be cousins within the fourth and fifth degree, 'numerous indeed, not less, to be sure, than forty or fifty – of which, but a small number are in good circumstances'.[10] A family circle of Nagles and Hennessys comes out vividly in a letter from Pat Nagle in 1772, describing visits not only to the Hennessys at Ballymacmoy, but to the Nagles at Ballylegan, a fact which suggests that he is probably a member of the Ballylegan Nagle branch. Nagle was a medical doctor. In directing Hennessy to reply 'to doctor Nagle if you plase', the impression is given that he was newly qualified, on his first visit home after long studies on the Continent. His father seems to have provided in style for his return, giving him the use of two horses and a servant. The good doctor travelled widely among his relatives: 'I am partly in Corke, partly at Ballylegan, partly at Ballymacmoy, Ballyduff, Ballywalter, Ballynamona and many other ballies too tedious to mention'.[11]

While these families were usually able to provide well for the elder son, the careers of young sons were much more problematic. Thus in the case of the marriage, an apparent runaway one, of James, Richard's younger brother, to a Ballylegan Nagle, in or before 1753, there were problems about his dowry.[12] On his death it was reported that 'his little accounts were in such confusion', and the widow and children were said to be 'very limited in their circumstances'.[13] However, family ties and good connections often made it possible to repair the fortune of such families or at least for some of the sons. Thus the eldest son, George, appeared in the secure position of captain of a constant trader on the Bordeaux run in 1788, and another son, Athanasius, became a cadet in the East India Company in 1782, rising eventually to the rank of lieutenant-colonel.[14] In the latter appointment we can detect the hand of Edmund Burke, and in 1788 he was also to find a place for a Ballymacmoy son (a nephew of Richard Hennessy). Most persistently, as we will see elsewhere, the fate of both Edward Barrett and of one of his sons was to crop up both in Hennessy and Burke's letters repeatedly over thirty years.

James Hennessy (Richard's father) at the time of his final illness in 1767 was recalled by Burke as 'as sensible and gentlemanlike a man as any in our part of the country'[15] and his place in a list of twenty 'gentilshommes du comté de Cork' of 1758, certifying the gentility of an Irish colonel in French service, signifies his standing amongst his Catholic peers in the county.[16] The family estate in 1775 was worth £3400 less £514 in liabilities. The net rental was £470 (rents of £550 less head rent of £80).[17] In other words, the net rental corresponds very closely to the estates of £300 or £400 which Burke in 1778 saw the Catholic relief act of that year as likely to create.[18] The Ballymacmoy gross rents from occupiers suggest an estate of not less than 500 acres. The earliest known lease, a three-lives renewable lease of 1786, provided for a rent of £177 Irish for the townlands of Ballymacmoy, Killavullen, Shanballyduffe, Killisane, and Rahatessenigg, the total acreage being 644 acres plantation measure (or approximately 1000 acres statute measure). The unrealistic level of the head rental itself suggests recognition of an existing Hennessy stake in the land, something which is borne out by the low level of fine – £40 – provided for the entry of a new life in the lease. The Hennessy house of the period at Ballymacmoy – which still survives – is a simple two-storey farm house, narrow in the vernacular fashion of the period and with low ceilings. However, there is a tell-tale symbol of status in the long avenue down the hill to the site of the house perched above the Blackwater. The seat is marked in Taylor and Skinner's *Maps of the Roads of Ireland* in 1778, and Hennessy like the occupiers of all the other seats was conventionally given in the book the style of Esquire. Moreover, however modest in both James's and Richard's generations the standing and success of other members of the family, a second 'Hennessy Esq', according to Taylor and Skinner's maps, held a seat at Ballingrane just outside Doneraile: as it was beside a Nagle seat at Ballinamona, it seems likely that it was a Nagle-related Hennessy and hence either a member of the same Hennessy family or more probably a close cousin.

Thus the family were not going down in the world, even if the horizons of individual younger sons were quite limited. With a rising income already evident in George's modest but real substance of 1775, greater pretensions were emerging, and the 1820s house on a new and commanding site overlooking the tiny village of Killavullen was firmly one of gentry scale and status. As late as 1775 the Bally-macmoy Hennessys, in contrast to the inflated style of Esquire given them by Skinner, designated themselves as 'gent', a term which indicated a gentlemanly lifestyle but in a modest fashion compared with the broad acres, advantageous land title, and large rent roll which were once deemed necessary in order to earn the style Esq. The Ballygriffin Nagles securely fitted into the category of Esquire; the other families, Nagles and Hennessys alike, hovered more ambiguously among the 'gentlemen' or 'gents', now only beginning to be described as Esquire.[19]

This small enclave of prosperous Catholics was gathered on the floor of the Blackwater valley at the heart of a region of intense English and Protestant settlement. A few miles west on the Blackwater was Mallow, social centre of rural Protestant life in County Cork with no fewer than fifty seats within a five-mile radius.[20] In 1733–4 and again in 1760 the district had become the centre of menacing allegations against its Catholics of Jacobite conspiracy. Though these charges were directed against the Nagles in particular, the Hennessys were implicated on both occasions. Indeed, on the first occasion, Colonel Richard Hennessy's mission to recruit men in Ireland for French services, though authorized by the London government and by Dublin Castle, was the catalyst of a political crisis in 1733 which sought victims among the Nagle milieu in Cork. The information used to support the charge of plots was provided by a John Hennessy, parish priest of Doneraile, probably a man under hostile local pressure. In another period of political crisis a plot surfaced again. In 1761 information was supplied to Dublin Castle of an alleged meeting in 1760 of which 'the Nagles and Hennessys were chief promoters.'[21] As in 1733 the allegation was fed to the public just before the start of the parliamentary session. Whereas Colonel Richard Hennessy's mission had made the Blackwater a suspect region, Edmund Burke's position in 1761 as private secretary of the chief secretary in a new administration in Dublin Castle made the Blackwater a centre of events with a national focus. If the alleged plot fixed on the little enclave on the Blackwater, long the sole centre of active Catholic opinion in County Cork, it was because the presence of a man related to the Nagles in the Halifax entourage made his County Cork rela-tives the focus of an attack on an administration already rumoured in advance as being soft on Catholics; and the letter of Fant, a County Limerick attorney to Halifax, with details of the plot, dated 18 Octo-ber, four days before the parliamentary session opened, was politi-cally inspired and carefully timed.[22] For Richard Hennessy, these events were remote. He was out of the country from 1748, visiting Ireland only briefly in the early 1750s and again in 1768 for the final illness of his father.

RICHARD HENNESSY'S ARMY CAREER

Born *circa* 1729 (his marriage contract in Ostend in January 1765 gave his age as thirty-six, and less reliably his army record suggested 1724), Richard (or 'Dick') Hennessy entered the French army in 1748. His full record was not discovered in the course of many modern efforts to trace the origins of his army career. Entering the army in peacetime and before a formal cadet system had emerged, he served in the ranks pending the availability of a commission, and his officer career was so short that there was too little of it to give him a fuller record: in the officer records there is only a terse record of his being granted the rank of *souslieutenant* in 1753 and of his replace-ment in 1754. His actual admission is recorded among the *hommes de troupe* in the regimental inspection of Clare's regiment in May 1751. His enlistment date is given as 29 September 1748: 'Natif de Corke en Irlande, agé de 24 ans, taille de 6 pieds, cheveux chatains, les yeux bleus, visage oval et beau, marqué de rousseurs.'[23]

The inspection records for 1751 have details entered at a later date that that he had been 'fait officer le premier février 1753'. A slightly later inspection notes that because of 'délaissement' he was presumed to have terminated his service. His actual service as an officer must have been nil, as he was already in Ostend by then, and his 'délaisse-ment' must have been noted because he had failed over a protracted period to make an appearance: no leave of absence was recorded against his name. The consequence was that, with other young men pressing for promotion, another man was promoted on 22 October 1754 'par délaissement de Richard Henesy'.[24] During his actual service he must have spent most of the time with the regiment, if, as Roche suggested, he learned his Irish there. This is borne out too by the fact that Richard certainly remained friendly with several Irish officers. Moreover, he had made the acquaintance of another officer, Richard Warren, when the Irish Brigade was quartered in Ostend in 1757. Warren was an inveterate letter writer, sociable and socialite alike; in his huge correspondence, Hennessy's letters survive, illustrating Hennessy's easy ties with a very senior Brigade officer. When Warren was one of the commanders of Choiseul's great invasion project of 1759, Richard Hennessy volunteered his services: 'you must not think that if you embark that I will remain here. I assure you I am determined to take my chance for laurels, or a halter.' When the offer was turned down, his regrets and good wishes came out warmly in one of his letters.[25] Hennessy's friendship with a Nagle officer lasted into the 1790s. Whenever one of the Irish regiments did garrison service in Rochefort or Libourne, he made the acquaintance of the officers, and the letters convey an abiding sense of army friendships.

Probably in late 1752 – as we know from his brother's letter in February 1753 that he had already changed his career and was from at least as early as January in Ostend – he disappeared from the regiment, simply failing to return. He made a short visit to Cork before returning again to Ostend. James's letter of November 1755 confirms that he had made his Irish visit by that date.[26] So he never reached the rank of captain often attributed to him, and does not seem to have even had a day's active service in his grade of second lieutenant. Nor can he have served at Fontenoy as is often stated. Some support might at first sight come from one of the essays in Roche's *Critical Essays by an Octogenarian*. Roche, as a merchant in his younger days, knew Hennessy in Bordeaux in the 1780s. Roche never stated explicitly that Hennessy fought at Fontenoy. What he stated was that 'contemporaneously with' the battles of Dettingen and Fontenoy, where a Captain Maurice O'Connell (whose reminiscences he was repeating) fought, Irish was the spoken language of the regiments, a fact confirmed by what Roche heard from 'Mr Richard Hennessy who entered the service at the same time'.[27] The times as given by Roche are approximate, he did not say that Hennessy fought at Fontenoy, and the regimental record more emphatically rules it out. Lord Thomond's later certificate referred to ten years' service, and in modern times his service has been backdated by subtracting ten years from the officer entry in 1754 to suggest that he entered the service in 1744. However, Thomond's certificate in 1757 makes it clear that the ten years embraced his career 'tant en qualité de cadet que d'officier'.[28] Formal cadetship did not exist at this time, and the term simply meant service in the ranks with a promised promotion in turn with other aspirants to vacancies in officer ranks as they occurred: the period of his career is the years from his entry in 1748 to his promotion in 1753.

Hennessy's effective abandoning of service was almost certainly prompted, as in so many other cases, by the absence of promotion in peacetime. A second lieutenancy itself was merely the starting run on a long and uncertain ladder, and it would have come his way automatically in fulfilment of a promise to his family and by way of rota, even if he was for unannounced reasons absent from the regiment at the time. His absence at the outset of 1753 may have been influenced more specifically by a prospect of employment in the Hennessy house in Ostend. He had already been for some time in Ostend, when James, adverting to his change of career, wrote to him there in February 1753: 'let me know immediately what you intend doing on the change of affairs. I am in great hopes Jemmy will give you an interest in the House. I think for his own sake he cannot do better. If anything in my power can urge him to do it, command me freely.'[29]

In 1757 the colonel of his old regiment, Clare's, in certifying his ten years service as a cadet and officer, stated 'nous l'avons vu quitter son employ à cause des lois rigoureuses faites en Angleterre contre les irlandais qui restaient au service de la France'.[30] Such laws had been passed in 1738, 1746 and 1756. As he was already out of the army, it is unlikely that such discrimination against Catholics or fear of its consequences was greatly on his mind, and in any event there is no evidence that he contemplated settling in Ireland. The dating of the certificate, 15 April 1757, is more significant. The real reason for the certificate was the French invasion of Flanders: under the terms of a 1715 royal decree Irishmen who had served ten years were free from the *droit d'aubaine* (seizure by the state of the property of foreigners who did not hold French nationality).[31] This meant that their property was not subject to seizure on their death, and access to the privilege was tantamount to automatic acquisition of French nationality. In the short term it would ward off expulsion as a subject of the English king from French-occupied territory. At the outset of the Seven Years War, the French authorities took a surprisingly severe view of non-nationals remaining in the ports. This was in contrast to practice in earlier wars and reflected French fears, in the first sustained war at sea, of possible links between English invaders and nationals on the ground. The Irish communities in Nantes and Bordeaux encountered many problems, and only those who already had French nationality were free from interference or threat of expulsion. In Bordeaux Irish Protestants, eventually freed from the expulsion order on account of their economic importance, were required to reside in inland districts.[32] The fact that Hennessy had never formally resigned from the army made it easier to issue the certificate he sought. It was a case of a highly-placed Irishman, the colonel of Clare's regiment, vicomte de Clare, now Lord Thomond and a marshal of France, obliging another Irishman. The prestige of a relationship to Colonel Richard Hennessy and the presence of other Hennessys in the army gave Richard's application a standing, and it was all the easier to grant it. It was less than a perfectly honest statement by Thomond, but Irishmen and men of Irish descent in foreign service were wont to look after their mutual interests.

RICHARD HENNESSY IN OSTEND, 1753–1765

In Ostend Hennessy had some dealings with the Hennessy house there. However, as the correspondence points only to the purchase of some luxury items for members of the family, business orders from James in Cork must have been directed to the Ostend house, not to Richard himself. In 1773 he was to describe a brandy order from

Cork 'as the first commission from any one belonging to me though twenty years in business'.[33] No letter before 1758 is addressed to him as merchant. In 1765 he was, despite more than a decade in Ostend, still unconversant with business methods, as a later letter recalled:

> I told you that I would be under the necessity of having a clerk particularly for keeping the books as what I had learned of them at school I had forgot. To this you consented and desired I should apply for one to Mr John Power of Bordeaux who sent me one who had less knowledge of books than myself.[34]

He can only have made a precarious living from some commissions passed to him by the Ostend house, a somewhat humiliating situation for one who had gone to Ostend in the hope of a partnership and had never succeeded in his object. After a short-lived boom in brandy in 1756–7 Ostend became a wretched place as the lucrative business in transit brandy for London and the French trade for Ireland shifted north to neutral Rotterdam. Apart from Thomas Hennessy, who entered the French army (but retained a fourth share in the house), the business had to provide for two sons – James, already in the business, and Pat, still a minor – and a daughter. The daughter married Thomas Blake, an Irishman living in the Lowlands who also had to live out of the resources of the little firm. When the father Charles died on a visit to Cork in February 1758 a fresh agreement was drawn up, but Richard was not brought into the new partnership, nor into a further agreement in December of the same year which yet again revised the details. With the marriage of the eldest son, James, while on a visit to Cork in October, there was even less prospect of serious occupation within the house for Richard.

A feud within the family made the prospect still smaller. Some light is provided on the course of the dispute by Richard Warren, the Irish army office in charge of the Dunkirk–Ostend area from 1757. At the suggestion of Andrew Kavanagh, an Irish merchant in Dunkirk, Warren had found lodging with the Hennessys, and it was through this that he developed his friendship with Richard Hennessy. The death of James in May 1760 was followed after an interval by the dissolution of the partnership. There were tensions as early as 1757 with Thomas Blake, and they had sharpened even further by

1759. The French occupation of Ostend from 1757 had effectively ended the trade that Ostend had begun to develop as a neutral port in 1756. Years later Warren made a sour comment on Blake.[35] Thomas Blake, eventually excluded from the house by the quarrels within the family, had become a partner of the ailing Kavanagh in Dunkirk by 1766, and with Kavanagh's death in that year he took over the house.[36] The Hennessy house continued as a greatly slimmed-down business, finally under the title of Widow & Pat Hennessy; but, not faring well, many years later moved to Brussels.[37]

The dissolution of the partnership freed James's widow's dowry from the communal fund, thus making possible marriage to Richard as well as a separate business venture (the fact that neither the widow nor her future husband, Richard, were included in the new family partnership shows that the family feud had been more than just a quarrel with Blake). The widow (née Ellen Barrett) married Richard in January 1765. Pat Hennessy was later to be British vice-consul in Ostend, but this was less a reflection of the standing of the house than of the absence of any foreign colony in the port. The Blakes did quite well for themselves: they even fitted out at Dunkirk a vessel for the East Indies in 1776. In 1787 a son, Charles Blake, was in the house of the Murdochs of Dunkirk.[38] Pat Hennessy got little business in Ostend; he had no ties with Cognac, and in 1778 when he passed an order to Angoulême, Richard wrote that 'what surprises me is that Pat seems to ignore our house subsisting at Cognac and hopes I have an active striving friend at Charente'.[39]

Richard's marriage and expectation of the dowry provided the basis for his striking out more boldly on his own account for Cognac itself, centre of the booming brandy trade of the early 1760s. However, it is not clear how much of their entitlement came into their possession: ominously the account was closed only as late as 1787.[40] At the time Cognac must have seemed a good move. His first child now expected, he formed a partnership with the house of Connelly & Arthur of Dunkirk for six years from the first of September.[41] Edmond Connelly had been born in Ballgallane near Lismore in 1711, and as he had married a Mary Roche of Youghal,[42] there seem to have been distant ties of kinship. This was a typical example of an arrangement in which the junior partner put up most of the capital and all the labour and the senior partner provided the goodwill and some support. The house was to be known as Hennessy, Connelly & Co. and to set up in Charente. Hennessy was to provide two thirds of the capital of 24,000 livres. This would have come to over £1000 and, if his wife's entitlements had been received, would have absorbed the bulk of her expectations out of the estates of her late father-in-law and of her husband.

Connelly & Arthur passively handled brandy which shippers in Cognac dispatched to Dunkirk on the order of London houses. Cognac may have figured little in Connelly & Arthur's thinking at all. The decisive impetus behind the new business was the interest taken in Cognac by Hennessy's Bordeaux relatives the Galweys. In August 1765 John Galwey had announced to Richard that he was determined to see him fixed in Cognac. The correspondence apparently went back to July or even earlier, premised on a partnership in Cognac proposed between a Dunkirk house and three Galwey relatives, Garrett (a son of John Galwey's in Seville), Edward Barrett (brother-in-law to Hennessy in Cork) and Hennessy himself. But Garrett was reluctant to leave Seville, and expectations of a good match in Cork blunted Barrett's keenness. By November John Galwey was baffled, as only Richard was left of the prospective trio. Galwey observed that Connelly & Arthur 'seemed to value their interest for procuring the house business too much', and that they had no ground for complaint as Galwey had not sought an interest in the venture himself.[43] The loss of the other two prospective partners meant that Hennessy's capital was absorbed by the business, and that he had no resources to help him weather a rainy day (a predicament made worse by the problems in touching his wife's capital).

Letters from the Galweys in both Bordeaux and Cork, often with more family than business news, were numerous in the 1760s and 1770s. While it was a case of a successful family encouraging a less successful relative, it also corresponded to a past involvement by the Galweys in brandy shipments in Bordeaux and an existing long-standing interest, evidenced by the presence of a Daniel Galwey in Cognac in the early 1750s. In the autumn Hennessy took John Galwey's advice to go to London to find business acquaintances there. His first child was born in October in Ostend, and travelling via Paris he had arrived in Cognac by the end of the year. The first letter in his letter book is dated 23 December and the contract for his premises was signed five days later. His wife had not joined him, as in May 1766 he absented himself briefly to go to Bordeaux to accompany her to Cognac. Though his business was now in operation, he was destined to experience years of frustration. After a temporary lull in the Dublin business in the early months of 1766, the demand soared into 1767. He had counted on large orders from his Cork relatives, and quite unlike other merchants whose business was virtually confined to Dublin and London, in his early years he circularized as many Cork as Dublin houses. However, resumption of regular supplies of American rum and the soaring prices of brandy put paid to any prospect of regular business with Cork. The only serious intimation of an early order was from his struggling kinsman, Edward Barrett, in Cork in 1766, and it was not until 1773 that some effective orders eventuated, and then only from his relatives the Goolds, Galweys and the faithful Barrett.[44] Orders from Dublin came his way, but through the good offices of John Power in Bordeaux (Power had a nephew, Thomas Derham, in the brandy trade in Dublin).

The volume of this business was not large, but without it he could not have survived. In April 1767 he lamented that 'we have so little acquaintance in Dublin'.[45] Even as late as 1771 reliance on Derham was heavy: 'our confidence in him is so great'.[46] The two areas in which he had counted on support, London orders procured through Connelly & Arthur and Cork orders through his own relatives, disappointed: in the case of Cork confirmed orders eventuated only in 1773. His invoices were a mere 218 puncheons in 1766, 250 1/2 in 1767, 185 1/2 in 1768, 314 in 1769, and 302 for the two years 1770 and 1771.[47] In September 1767 after twenty months of business he reckoned his profits before charges at 4614 livres, or 1293 livres net. This would amount to £57 Irish or a fraction above £1.2s.0d. per week. French living costs were much lower than Irish, but this was still a mere subsistence income, one so pathetic that Hennessy challenged his partners to visualize what it would be like for them if they had to be 'accustomed for the run of the kitchen as I am or equal my perseverance in the christian doctrine of patience'.[48] So small was his turnover that, after he had dispensed with a clerk in the early stages, he continued without either clerk or cooper.

It is not clear whether it was Hennessy's easygoing ways or the one-man character of the business which accounted for delays in replies to letters. In late 1766 John Power in Bordeaux had advised Connelly & Arthur to urge Hennessy to attend without delay to correspondence.[49] It was only during his absence in Ireland, which lasted from April to October 1768, that his wife hired a young Dutchman, John Duc, for 600 livres plus diet and lodging (i.e. for more than the Hennessys were surviving on), but Duc in fact was due to take up duties only at the end of March 1769.[50] It is hardly surprising that the relationship with Connelly & Arthur began to turn sour. Hennessy claimed that he could execute orders for double the capital of the house, if they were prepared to buy in advance of orders, and at an earlier stage he criticized them for not allowing him to buy brandy speculatively in anticipation of price rises.[51]

The fact that Connelly & Arthur's interest was a minority one seemed, however, to rule out a claim by Hennessy that they had proposed the 'unlucky undertaking'. He had counted too readily on a stream of London orders, whereas just after his arrival the London trade itself went through an upheaval which upset even established houses such as Martell's. Whatever his grounds for complaint, he was so exasperated that he gave notice in May 1771 that he would prepare for terminating the relationship at the end of its legal term and 'ease you of so disagreeable a connection'.[52] In October 1772, he claimed that his partners had 'retired their capital and left me to shift for myself',[53] though this does not quite square with the story in Richard's own letter book, according to which the initiative to end it clearly came from him. As late as 1775 he was still making adverse comments on the treatment he received, and claimed that the partners strove to hurt him with his correspondents in London.[54] Again these statements contrast with an earlier admission that 'I acknowledge that through your means I have acquired acquaintance and friends who I hope may be of use to you'.[55] This refers to London houses, and concedes that he was indebted to Connelly & Arthur for their custom. In June 1773 he wrote to Daniel MacCarthy of Bordeaux that he had been 'almost entirely thrown out of the Dublin business, not being able to sacrifice more than my commission, which has not been found sufficient. The few English friends who favour me with their commands render more justice to my endeavours, and still stick by me.'[56] His business rose somewhat in that year from a nadir of 180 puncheons in 1772 to 532 1/2 puncheons. There was some glimmer of confidence in his outlook as John Galwey observed of his English business that 'although not considerable [it] proves tolerable and we believe equal in proportion to most of your neighbours'.[57] In 1772 he sought the indulgence of Connelly & Arthur in delaying a payment, 'unless I was to make a public sale of my effects and little furniture: otherwise you must expect to see your efforts for my establishment here prove my ruin and disgrace'.[58] The quantities invoiced by Hennessy evened off in 1774, fell to 446 1/2 puncheons in 1775 and were a mere 240 1/2 puncheons in 1776. It is easy to understand why Hennessy at the end of 1776 turned his back on Cognac and left for Bordeaux.

Richard Hennessy's stereotype as a younger son in trade on little resources is matched by the saga of his brother-in-law Edward ('Ned') Barrett. Roger Barrett, a cousin of Richard's, and possibly a brother of Edward's, was already established in trade in Dublin. Ned and Richard would have become partners in Cognac if John Galwey's original design had come to fruition. Only marriage halted Barrett's plans to go abroad. In August 1766 he was already eight months married, and had opened a house under the style of E. & J. Barrett.[59] The resources the marriage had conferred on him were modest, though not trifling, and perhaps even more relevantly in terms of the criteria for success he was considered by his successful connections in Bordeaux to be 'very careless and giddy'.[60] A series of letters survives from Barrett to Hennessy in 1765 and 1766, very warm in their tone, full of hope for Richard, and anticipating business with him. In August 1766 he ordered some brandy, and also had a more ambitious project of sending a vessel with beef to Bordeaux and onwards in ballast to Rochefort to load brandy for Ireland.[61] These plans all came to naught. Barrett was also in touch with his successful relative, Edmund Burke, in England. With Burke's brother holding an official position in Grenada, Burke held out hopes for him there: 'My brother tells me, that poor Barret is likely to do well in Grenada; he is industrious and active; he must indeed struggle with some difficulty and much labour at first; but it is the road and the only road to an establishment.'[62]

Barrett was still pursuing his prospects with the Burkes in 1767.[63] Unfavourable conditions in the brandy trade meant that his order to Richard was never executed. In 1768 he had, however, planned to visit Cognac, a plan abandoned apparently only because of Richard's own long visit to Ireland in that year.[64] A report from Bordeaux four years later presented a discouraging picture of his business: 'Ned does little. What little it is, is in the wine way. I dont think it can support him and I fear he'll not be able to hold it.'[65]

In March 1766 Burke's appearance in the English House of Commons had been commented on in a disinterested fashion, Ned noting with pleasure that he had 'speached with uncommon applause'.[66] In difficulties in 1772, Barrett no longer concealed from Hennessy his hope that Burke could look after him, and with Burke deeply involved in one of the political circles which meddled in the East India Company's affairs, his hopes turned to the east. He was in correspondence with Burke, and we can follow progress from one of his letters to Hennessy:

> My affairs remained till now in so low a way that I was quite dispirited. I had hoped for a favourable change, which I would and do eagerly impart to you and for the particulars of it, I refer you to the enclosed copy of a letter which I this day received from our worthy friend Mr Burke, to whom I write this day, that I thankfully and cheerfully will embrace such a place or situation as he may get for me, which shall be communicated to you and Nelly as soon as I'll know it.[67]

In October John Galwey noted Ned's plans of going to England and perhaps India with prospects of a fortune: 'Ned is a little slow and dilatory, but the change of air and desire of returning soon may rouse him and cheer him up. He does not want ability and cleverness.'[68] In November Ned was sanguine about his 'good friend's intention of promoting me'. The tenor of a letter at that time suggests too that the prospects of a post in India had been broached for Hennessy, also at a low point of his affairs, as well as for Barrett. That approach apparently had been made in a letter from Nelly, Barrett's wife, a niece to the Ballyduff Nagle family, and hence first cousin to Burke. Hennessy was warned not to write to Burke until he heard further from Barrett:

> The last letter I received from him was wrote about a month ago. As I'll transmit you a copy of it, I'll only observe that nothing was then accomplished. When there will, I wont lose a moment in advising you of it. I cant express how happy it would make me if an establishment could be procured for you in India, though I am fearful of writing Mr Burke about it. I'll exert myself through Dick [*i.e. Burke's brother Richard*] when on that spot – I say in London – to effect it. I'll be impatient to know what answer he'll have made to Nelly, God sent it may be as we wish. He is the best man I ever knew, but I am afraid he may think me too troublesome.[69]

In May 1773 the expectation still lingered that if Burke could do anything for Barrett it would be done.[70] But in fact a revolution had taken place in the politics of the company, and the Burke Whiggish interest, though more vocal than ever in regard to the company, no longer had leverage in the vital area within the administration which controlled jobs. Barrett was destined to wait until 1782 for the expected favour from Burke, and when Burke became paymaster-general, it was in the West Indies, not in India.

THE END OF A DREAM: THE STORY OF OTHER IRISHMEN IN THE CHARENTE IN THE LATE 1760S AND 1770S

As long as the brandy trade boomed, Cognac attracted young men either in search of apprenticeship or of secure employment in a house. Only over several years did the realization sink in that the contraction in exports was lasting and that the Charente offered few prospects of either apprenticeship or investment. Several young Irishmen flitted through the pages of the late 1760s and early 1770s, in addition to William Galwey of Dungarvan, apprenticed in 1768 to the Broussard house.[71] Joseph Connelly, a son of one of the principals of Connelly & Arthur, made an appearance in Cognac at least as early as September 1767. He spent most of his time in Bordeaux – there is a glimpse of him 'busy looking after trade accounts' – but by June 1768 he had created a bad impression as John Power wrote that he was 'sorry to find Mr Connelly the only young man that found the people of this town disagreeable to him'.[72] Another visitor, a brother-in-law of Barrett's, James White, merited from Galwey the description of 'this very idle young man'.[73] A nephew of Hennessy's, John Comerford, gave an impression of being 'wild' in 1771.[74] The last person to seriously consider setting up in the region was Thomas Egan junior. His father, who had set up another son as an importer, had first sent him abroad to the house of Laurence Saule in the mid-1760s, and apparently envisaged setting him up abroad.[75] He can be traced as having returned to the region in 1772, this time intending to turn the ambition into reality. Though he spent a long time in 1772–3, in Pons more than in Cognac, and had some hand in brandy orders from the Dublin house, the trade at large was at a nadir and the prospects for Thomas junior seemed gloomy in 1773:

> I observe poor Tom's proposal to you, poor fellow. I'm afraid that if his father cannot give him a greater capital, he runs a great risk of never getting an establishment, as he should desire … that if his father thinks proper to give him this money and to do business with it in your place, that you would manage the same for him, in executing the commissions his father might procure for him, in which he should have a half or three quarters.[76]

The Egan family was not enjoying much fortune at the time. The other son, setting out in 1772 for London, attempted to discount to his own advantage £1400 in bills which had been entrusted to him.[77] The last Irishman to settle in the region in the 1770s, in the twilight of the great Irish interest in Cognac, was Stephen Geoghegan, a brother-in-law of Val Tallon, a brandy importer in Dublin.[78] As Geoghegan was very much a bachelor in 1775, it seems clear that a sister of his was married to Tallon. Whatever the family reason for settlement, he was in evidence socially in the Irish circle; his name crops up frequently in Saule's letters in 1775. He also seems to have found his feet in business terms from the outset. He settled in Pons, which was developing vigorously at this time, and Saule, who had himself been hoping to make a connection in Pons, wrote to Hennessy that 'if he was an honest fellow he would gain over Lallemand to my side, since there's no more question of the Pons gentleman'.[79] The Geoghegan link in Pons with Lallemand turned into partnership in Bordeaux with Théodore Martell in September.[80] The shift of the focus of Geoghegan's activity from Pons to Bordeaux reflects a new-found role of that city in brandy business. The Irish distiller Andoe in 1774 settled in Bordeaux, and Hennessy, whose thoughts had turned several times in its direction, finally moved there in 1776.

6

A *decade of crises: the 1770s*

The later story of the little Irish colony revolves around three individuals: John Saule, Richard Hennessy and James Delamain. Most remarkable of the friendships was that between Hennessy and Saule. Saule's letters to Hennessy survive from 1769, as do his letters to Saule for the period from 1776 when Hennessy was in Bordeaux. As early as 1770 Saule came back from La Rochelle to spend ten days with the Hennessys, and the visit cemented the already burgeoning friendship.

The close friendship belied the wide gap in age; in 1769 Hennessy was forty, Saule eighteen. Saule was the more literate of the two. He read widely; in 1769 one of the first letters from La Rochelle to Broussard's Irish clerk in Cognac was in relation to books.[1] He was also more confident in the detail of business, in 1771 offering to come over from La Rochelle to Cognac to settle bookkeeping problems, in the midst of Hennessy's difficulties with his Connelly partner. In 1772 he interpreted the nuances in a letter from Hennessy's Paris banker. If Saule's letters are the more fluent, Hennessy made it up in his warmth. Saule in 1770 described him as 'a novelist particularly when there's anything about any of our countrymen'.

The correspondence began from the time Saule had become a clerk for a term of one year in the Galwey house in La Rochelle. His early departure was not occasioned by problems in the Galwey business, as he was immediately succeeded by another Irishman, MacNamara; it may have had something to do with his own urge to better himself, especially as he enjoyed the backing of James Delamain, executor with Richard Hennessy of the estate of Laurence Saule. John Saule was, from later evidence, disappointed of a place in the prestigious Delap house in Bordeaux. Delamain, known to the Delaps, must have been the intermediary in negotiations which broke down because, according to Saule, someone in La Rochelle had blackened his character. At any rate, Saule left the Galweys towards the middle of 1769 for a position in a house run in La Rochelle by Roullet of Jarnac. Delamain's hand is more definite in this step, and the attraction of the position was that Roullet had other interests and therefore needed someone constantly on the spot. Saule was left on his own a good deal, and a share in a partnership was promised either for the outset or for shortly afterwards. The atmosphere of his new employment under an uncongenial man comes across in a letter written in the bantering style adopted by Saule in letters and real life alike:

> Dont be angry with me for not writing you long letters. I could wish I had time, having a vast deal to write you – but imagine to yourself looking at me writing on a desk in the office a letter to you, my man being gone out, in a hurry to finish before he came in to surprise me. I hear his tiger's voice or his foot coming in. Imagine to yourself my fright, away goes my letter to you under the desk, into the desk, into a book, into a bundle of other letters which I am perhaps writing for him etc. Judge how I sweat for fear he should discover it, his suspicious mind always suggesting him something bad … This letter has fell under the desk and in my pocket twenty times since I have began it.[2]

The prospective partnership was put on the long finger by Roullet. By July 1771 Delamain had already provided some of the capital for this partnership. On one occasion Delamain had sent 1200 livres; on another he gave Roullet another 1800 livres, but whenever Saule sought by letter for the cash to be accounted for, Roullet avoided the issue by reference to the haste with which he had to reply. The balance of the capital was to be in the form of a guarantee by Delamain of a credit with a Paris house, but Roullet dragged out the execution of the credit. In June 1771 Saule was optimistic about a favourable outcome, by September 'miserably cast down, living in the most terrible state of incertitude'.[3] In July he had set out to Hennessy at some length the problems of the preceding eighteen months:

> He has behaved comically with me. 1. You know he has abused me these 18 months, that I have been doing nothing, so shall not enlarge on that article. 2. You may remember the difficulty he arose about the signature [*i.e. a partnership*]. When that was over, there was nothing more to do but come off here and conclude a society for five years. No sooner was I here but he desired a guarantee, and liberty of withdrawing his funds at the end of the year. When we consented to that, I went to Jarnac, this last turn. Then he left me entire master to terminate but that he could not furnish me the cash, but would give me a letter of credit for your friends in Paris but begged of me above all things not to speak a word of that to Mr Delamain.[4]

Saule was tempted to break with Roullet,[5] but did not do so for fear the blame for a rupture would attach to him: 'a man adrowning grasps at any thing which seems to give him any hopes of life'.[6]

As long as the arrangement with Roullet stood, Saule seemed to have the use of a large house. In June 1771, when prospects still seemed good, he was able to extend an invitation to Hennessy's family to visit him for sea bathing. While with Roullet, Saule became acquainted with two young merchants, Hébert and a Swede, Hoogman. Hoogman's sister-in-law was to marry a friend of Delamain's in 1773.[7] It is possible that here again it was through the Delamain connection that he made Hoogman's acquaintance. All hope of the Roullet partnership seems to have been finally abandoned in the autumn of 1771, and Saule henceforth resided in Hoogman's house. He was now without employment, a mere *toiseur de pavé* as he put it himself.[8] Saule, who had had hopes of Bordeaux in 1769, now entertained them again of the same circle, although this prospect soon collapsed.

Hennessy's business prospects had been deteriorating at the same time, and as early as 29 September 1771 Saule had written to him that 'I should be extremely sorry for your sake that we both were in equal situation'. Within a few months Hennessy's plight was to seem the worse of the two. As Saule put it, 'I must own that you are worse than myself when in the dumps, you were formerly preaching courage to me, must I now do as much to you?'[9] Hennessy toyed with his prospects first in the East Indies, then in Bordeaux. Saule observed to him that 'you must have a great opinion of your ill luck to think that because you thought of Bordeaux the vines had suffered there'.[10] At one stage in the spring the two men seem to have had plans for some partnership together. However, prospects of an association between Hennessy and his relatives the Bordeaux Galweys ruled out such a partnership, and Saule reminded Hennessy that he had a young family and that he should put their interests before Saule's. He advised Hennessy to go: 'he would do ill to stay and loose his time. You'll spend in two years waiting more than you'll gain in a good year'.[11]

Saule advised Hennessy as to whether it was best for him to visit his relatives in Bordeaux or to wait for them to visit Cognac. In May Saule commented that 'Mr John Galwey is not a polite nor a friendly cousin it seems, since he gives you no invitation, he has no bottom – his bragadoccios of the great fortunes of his brothers does not augment yours. Should he say that he can give or help you by a part of it, it would be another matter.'[12] The Galweys finally visited Cognac in July. Nothing came out of the visit, and Saule observed that 'I believe them both to be chaps who think only for themselves … Certainly its cruel for a generous heart to stoop to demand a favour from such persons.' Of course 1772 was a phenomenally difficult year in the southwest. The bad vintage of 1771 had left its mark on export business in both wine and brandy. In a letter of 17 May 1772 Saule painted a graphic picture of the lack of business confidence in La Rochelle and of the numerous failures. The bad harvest too ensured that misery spread down the social scale, and Saule, a generous observer of the troubles of others, commented that 'were you to see some of the poor peasants here, crying out misery it would make your heart ache'.[13]

SAULE'S PURSUIT OF A MARRIAGE PARTNER: VICTOIRE BERNARD

At the end of April 1772 Saule observed that 'I can assure you (between us) that was it not for matrimony I would be also acquainting you with others moving their bob to some place'.[14] With an antic-

ipated dowry in mind he wrote that 'I am not desponding entirely as
you may imagine … Things may turn out better than expected. Who
knows the luck of a scabby colt?'[15] At this stage Victoire Bernard,
who was to absorb so much of his thoughts and to consume so much
ink from his pen, enters the story. Her father André Bernard held
posts as Entrepreneur des Travaux du Roi and Conseilleur et Pro-
cureur du Roi at the Hotel de Ville in Cognac, venal posts which
bespoke status and the income which made their purchase possible.
Victoire is first referred to on 6 June 1771: 'last night I had the
advantage of conducting along with Dardillouze Miss Victoire and
her sister to the play, and I am to receive to-morrow night'. In 1775,
when the family had become much less enthusiastic about Saule's
attentions as a suitor, he denied her brother's accusation that he had
long been forbidden to speak to her:

> This is visibly false; I had her every day at the play, she went no place
> without me; I went with her to Rochefort, staid with her four days,
> went to Charente with her, to the father's knowledge and presence.
> Then again, whilst I staid in Cognac in 1772, I was daily with them,
> this also well-received. I'm the only one who ever played a card in
> their house perhaps.

After Victoire's long stay in La Rochelle, which lasted to the
summer of 1771, he often visited her in Cognac. The father who frequently met Saule in La Rochelle was in September 1771 a prospective companion for Saule on a visit to Cognac, and within the same
year Saule seems to have begun to arrange visits to Cognac to coin-
cide with the father's sojourns in La Rochelle. In January 1772 Saule
observed to Hennessy:

> The papa is to be here in 8 or 10 days. I'll let him stay here for some
> time 'ere I make my tour, as it would look to the rest as too suspicious
> if I was to part directly. It might be said we were playing at blind-
> man's buff – for it was already remarked to me that as soon as he
> appeared at Cognac, I hopp'd off, though it is not he who I have any
> dread about.

A few months at most after first meeting her, he had drafted a letter
about his feelings to her uncle, a priest, apparently at Victoire's sug-

gestion, as she feared a direct approach would meet her father's opposition. He added that his feelings were reciprocated. It is not known whether this letter – dated 22 July 1771 – was ever sent. It was written at a time when he was sanguine about the outcome of his negotiations with Roullet: in the course of it, he claimed that 'j'ai aujourdhui dieu merci un établissement en cette ville assez honnete, notre maison fait un commerce considérable'. Although he declared to a member of the family that a dowry was not on his mind, the subject was very much so, and he was also aware how painfully poor a suitor his own predicament made him. These circumstances added urgency to his quest for an establishment, and to negotiations with the Hébert & Hoogman partnership in the middle months of 1772. Under a draft agreement Delamain, by 'un principe d'affection', guaranteed a credit of 10,000 livres for the young Saule at the Paris house of Mallet & Le Royer for five years. This draft would seem to have been the basis of a final agreement which came into effect on 1 September and Saule's name was to be introduced into the style of the partnership from 1 January 1773. The latter condition did not enter into effect, apparently because some minor episode occurred as a result of which Saule did not want to have his name associated with Hébert's.

The partnership, though one of three young men, was an active one with a small but significant trade. While his relationship with Hébert was at one time strained, his relationship remained equitable with Hoogman, whom he regarded highly and whom he described as 'vastly clever at everything by which a man can make a penny'. He had already been living in Hoogman's house since 1771, and continued to reside there. The two senior partners held country properties, and moved around a good deal in the hinterland and in the Île de Ré. They also had business interests outside brandy: a vessel in the Newfoundland fishery, and trade with both Amsterdam and Scandinavia. They had more orders from Amsterdam for colonial goods in August 1773 than they could supply from La Rochelle. In addition at that date they had an order from Berne for cotton. Had they been able to execute all the commissions in hand, they could have earned, in Saule's reckoning, in all some 3000 livres or 200 guineas. Thus it was quite a creditable business with a stake mainly in traffics which held up well in the 1770s; the house escaped the depression evident in La Rochelle's Canada trade and in its foreign brandy trade.

In a small city like La Rochelle, every trivial matter became a subject of comment. On several occasions in correspondence with Hennessy the question of giving money, or of reluctance to refuse it, to associates came up. Although Saule deflected a first approach from a young man for a loan in 1773, a second followed. The young man, while recovering 'from a malady which I have reason to suspect the fair sex caused him', had his allowance cut off by his indignant father. All three partners had the right to draw 500 livres per annum from the partnership's cash for their own subsistence. At the time of the second approach, Saule was temporarily in charge of the partnership's cash, and advanced the suppliant 402 livres, 'the more so as we had money useless in our caisse'. The failure of the borrower to repay the money soon left Saule in dire straits. He even had to draw 300 livres from Delamain to cover the cost of clothes. The irregular use of the firm's cash, and for the benefit of a young man with venereal disease, already cut off by his father, seems to have been one of the happenings which the Bernard family were later to hold against him.

How well founded were the Bernards' grounds – apart from his obvious lack of fortune – for turning against him? Saule was a young man who grew up rapidly in the interval between the simple letters which survive for 1769 and the increasingly fluent ones of the early and mid-1770s. He was a prodigious reader, and the literary allusions in his letters are unselfconscious and natural. In December 1772 we find that he had been reading the *History of the Siege of La Rochelle* late at night, and resumed reading at day break. When his friend left the house, he continued with the book, which had been left

> on a chair by my bed-side and after my friend's departure I began to read it until 10 1/2 o'clock in the morning. However, finding it late I got up, went downstairs, found my other partner in our office writing. I went to breakfast. At 11 or 11 1/2 he took his horse and parted for his country house. I returned to the house, wrote a letter, went to mass at 12, returned at 1. I dined, went again to the office, wrote another letter, left the two for the clerk to copy. I went out and staid at a friend's playing of whist till 5.

The reference to whist merits noting, because gambling was also later held against him by the Bernards.

While Hennessy's letters were directed to the immediate ends of friendship, Saule's letters often observed the events of the day with deft revelations of his somewhat ironic view of personalities and political events. One of the things held against him almost from the outset was, according to Saule himself, his 'malicious laugh'. He was aware of bigger events and interested in them, and Madame Bernard's view of him as a *philosophe* – another of the vices attributed to him – had a point. He played a lively role in the Freemason politics of La Rochelle. Saule's personality turned him into a fervent Mason, using Masonic references in his letters, and taking advantage of the unrestrained or freethinking atmosphere of Masonic lodges to become a debater of the momentous issues astir in the France of the 1770s. He was more critical than others, lacking the facile optimism for the political fashions of the hour which many affected. While Turgot's reforming regime was welcome among the merchants in La Rochelle in 1774, Saule shrewdly and sardonically thought that his endeavours would have no practical outcome. Such views were probably behind his differences with fellow Masons, which seem to hint at a move to another and more radical lodge:

> I have retired from the old freemason lodge here which has caused great fright among some of the brethren as they were vastly desirous of keeping me, but thing were not upon proper footing. *Il vaut mieux etre seul qu'en mauvaise compagnie.* Have you tinkers, surgeons, hatters, goldsmiths, watchmakers etc among you.[16]

This would seem to have been the outcome of what Saule had described on 29 September in a letter to Hennessy six weeks previously as 'vast masoning here this month. I hope to participate in your august misteries when I shall see be with you'. He followed Irish and English politics as well. Commenting in 1779 on Edmund Burke's not making a motion in the Commons for the arrest of the English ministers, his observations on the intended invasion fleet for Ireland reveal something of his cynical realism and a practical concern for the people of his homeland in a situation when success could by no means be taken for granted: 'I hope that notwithstanding all the reason they have to complaint [*sic*] of cruel England, they will remain quiet for should they join the enemy and that peace ensures, these who may have joined will be marked out as victims, to the common security hereafter.'[17]

Saule's self-confidence made him dismissive of the timidity of others. When the mayor of Cognac billeted troops on the English-speaking residents in 1774 – arguably a violation of the 1713 commercial treaty – they were reluctant to challenge the action publicly. Saule went to see the *subdélégué* (the administrator in charge of the Cognac region in the La Rochelle *intendance*), drafted a letter for Hennessy who had been complaining about the billeting (and continued to make heavy weather of it), and observed that 'whilse I have a tongue and hands to write, no rascally mayor or any other officer shall deprive me of those [rights] I am entitled to'.[18] When he encountered insolence from an official who boarded one of the partnership's vessels, he replied in terms which could have boded ill for him, and later in January 1779 a letter to Victoire assuring her that his last thoughts were with her, suggests that he was about to fight a duel.[19]

Saule had a bantering manner which made him a success with ladies. His relationship with Mrs Hennessy was friendly, and in his letters to her in Hennessy's absences on business he went beyond business into long and lighthearted commentary. He charmed the ladies, married and unmarried, whom he met in Gothenburg on a business visit there at the end of 1773. Mrs Erskine after his return wrote that she was 'extremely glad to find by it [*i.e. Saule's letter*] that you are well and happy. Indeed one of your tenor ought never to be otherwise.' She added – and it is perhaps a revealing index of the impression that Saule created – that 'I allow you to be one of the best souls ever breathed, yet there wants in the composition a very essential ingredient which is absolutely necessary to render the marriage state eligible'.[20] Mrs Erskine's unmarried sister, Elizabeth Gordon, who declined to send a copy of her own journal because it was too personal a document to trust to the post, wrote: 'I join with Mrs Erskine in begging you for the sake of your future, not to think of marriage for at least some years, vous etes encore à ce que j'ai vu trop inconstant.' The reference to a journal by Elizabeth Gordon was prompted in part by the fact that Saule kept one of his journey and had promised to send it to them. A copy in his hand exists in the Hennessy archive, and they also received their copy. The issue of matrimony seems to have been prompted by Saule's speaking freely of his love for Victoire. His journal at the outset, describing his departure from France, states that he could not lose sight of land 'without the greatest grief, my heart was full of a charmer who remained behind …'.

In his journal he observed that 'le commerce des femmes adoucit toujours les moeurs de l'autre sexe', and the gulf between men and women in Scandinavia surprised him. Much later he observed that the best way of learning French was though the country's womenfolk. While this interest was part of his sociability, a positive preference for female company, especially if allied to a gay and flippant manner, could be taken for a less innocent interest. It is fair to add, however, that Saule made a strong impression too on men, such as John Mehigan, an Irish officer of marines known to Hennessy as well as to Saule, and also a man of masonic leanings.[21] Saule's letters to Hennessy are full of mention of his male friends, almost invariably kindly and sympathetic to their misfortunes.

A rich imagination could belie the seriousness that underlay his personality. John Mehigan, paraphrasing for Hennessy the contents of a letter from Saule, including a fantasy account of his journey overseas, conveys something of its quality:

> He had private audience from his Danish Majesty, made both a defensive and offensive league with him; at the Hague he was introduced to the Prince of Orange, and established an uninterrupted commerce with him. When in Paris he went to Versailles and partook of a feast the King gave to the Count and Countess of Artois, where he danced with that princess, who was delighted with his performance as was all that noble assembly.

He also related to Mehigan 'a great curiosity' of a rabbit coupling with a hen with the consequence that the offspring were chickens, all feathers on one side and fur on the other. This fantasy had already been the subject of good-natured banter from the Gordon ladies, and was to catch the fancy of quite a number of individuals in the southwest of France as well.[22]

The trip to Gothenburg, in which he was charged with the partnership's interests, shows that he enjoyed the confidence of his partners. He had set off for Scandinavia at short notice, taking advantage of the departure of one of their vessels on 28 August 1773. He wrote to Hennessy with a message for Victoire, communicated to Hennessy from Sweden, and again from Paris on 28 December 1773 on his way back. In Sweden he was – or, exercising his fancy, said he was – frequently at court, 'and a right dull one it is'. On his way back, he passed through Hamburg, Hanover, Holland and the Austrian Lowlands. In Holland he got a brandy order for 'the quality to be of the most superior sort to be found', and passed it on to Hennessy. Holland had impressed him more than any other country: 'Never did I see so dear a country for living as in Holland. I was obliged to count upon a ducat per day for living for my expenses but I have not seen a neater or handsomer country for buildings, particularly the country houses.' However, his thoughts turned to Victoire:

> I'm still foolish enough to be over head and heels in love – though almost ashamed to pronounce this last word – but the sweet little creature's merits excuse my weakness. I hope I have got no formidable lover since my absence. Has she always someone or other always hanging after her?

Prior to his departure, if his business circumstances were modest, he was still at least *persona grata* to the family. In March 1773 the father still behaved 'most kindly' to Saule.[23] In April a visit from the priest uncle of Victoire 'had nothing but what was flattering for me in it, his conversation and manners were most amicable'. Saule was even informed that the father would give each of his daughters ready money on the day of her wedding, having resolved not to follow the 'unjust' custom of Saintonge of making the daughters renounce in favour of the son, and assured Saule that when he was in Cognac the family would 'always be glad to see him'. When asked whether he intended to marry, 'I replied that I was too young and had not yet laid in hay enough, upon which I received a compliment.' The conversation left Saule sanguine, though he still saw his lack of fortune – or 'hay' – as an obstacle, and he speculated whether Victoire would be prepared to wait the four or five years it might take him to make his fortune.[24] In July he looked forward to seeing the father and the priest in La Rochelle again.[25]

Yet when he came back, it was to changed circumstances and to opposition from the family. Why was this? Whatever his concern about making money for his marriage, he kept up an excessive style of life. He was inordinately fond of the theatre: even when his vessel for Scandinavia put in to Lorient, he went to the play house to see *Adelaide du Guesclin* by Voltaire, observing that 'had Monsieur de Voltaire ever imagined his Adelaide should fall into such hearty hands I don't think that he would have ever published it'. When in Paris on the way back he allegedly purchased a coach (though this statement can only have been an expression of his self-mocking fantasy). Certainly from what we know of his income he cannot have saved anything, and more seriously did not show signs of attempting to do so. His sanguineness about a fortune in the future may have given the impression of a lack of serious purpose. Delamain gently remonstrated with him on one occasion.

Moreover, with some justification, the Bernard family also turned his fondness for the company of women into a serious charge. Saule later complained that the father read 'more particular connections' into Saule's associations.[26] But his conduct was reckless to say the least, and his attempt at more prudent behaviour later in the same year was an effective admission of indiscretion. Even then, it persisted, and possibly the major episode occurred in 1776:

> I observe the papa's exclaiming against my connection with the lady in question; I'm the most unlucky fellow perhaps in the universe on such occasions; my neighbours and fellow citizens if they see me in any way assiduous with any woman immediately imagine a closer intimacy: the one mentioned is a woman of note here; *petite maitresse, fine* woman, young and giddy, enjoying 20,000 livres per annum; in her house I frequently pass my leisure hours. She keeps a great house, open table, etc. I accompany her everywhere and from

> this attention, surmises are drawn of more particular acquaintance.
> It's natural I behave with attention towards a woman, who shows me
> and my friends on every occasion the utmost marks of friendship and
> surely she and I can act without having any *crim. con.*? [27]

A clear statement of the gravamen of family charges against Saule
occurred in a long letter written in 1777 by the priest uncle, the Père
Sillion in Nantes, to Victoire. It painted a picture of a debauchee sink-
ing from 'la cour aux femmes accréditées ... descendant d'étages en
étages ... aux grisettes et filles communes', gaming with the firm's
money and catching venereal disease.[28] While Delamain's backing of
Saule's establishment (which could be construed as making up for
Saule's own want of substance) was conceded by the priest, Delamain's interest in Saule's welfare was interpreted as mere self-interest
to recover the 10,000 livres already advanced for the share in the
Hoogman and Hébert partnership. Even the fact that Saule on his
return did not succeed in seeing Victoire is turned into further accusation against him.

In a letter of 27 September 1774 Mary Saule, Saule's mother, who
opposed the match, wrote that 'upon what I am informed she has
several brothers of whom fame does not give so agreeable a report
and it has been assured me that you have yourself been very ill treated
by them'. By November 1774, untypically, Saule was very down-
cast.[29] In late November reports of Victoire's engagement to someone
else reached him, and he declared he was giving up hope. In fact,
whatever the views expressed in the letter, Saule's hopes were by no
means at an end. On 19 March 1775 he declared that he was 'as hot
in love as ever I was'.

He had, however, been suspicious about the authenticity of the
wedding plans. When meeting the father in the spring and compli-
menting him on the news, the father's response that the occasion was
still somewhat distant only added to his suspicions. At this stage he
attempted to communicate with Victoire, but one of several letters,
none of which resulted in a response, certainly came into the hands
of the father. Saule, considering the possibility, slight though it seemed
to him, that she had actually handed the letter to the father, resolved
that 'I shall never write nor see her whilst I live, at least till I'm certain that she has not been in the fault'.[30] The family front was by no

means a united one, and Saule even thought – wrongly as events were to prove – that there were hopes of winning over the mother. In April 1775 he commented, 'it's very high that I should have all the devotees of the place at work for me, moy surtout – il ne manquerait plus que de la y joindre quoiqu'elle n'a point de voix au chapitre. She would be an advantageous acquisition, mais je passe pour philosophe avec elle. Voilà mon grand tort, sans compter celui d'en avoir point 80,000 livres.'[31]

In Saule's case, given his winning ways with women, it would seem to be a case of encountering male opposition more than female. A sister was on Saule's side, and in coming months a cousin, Mademoiselle Lafargue, became the channel of communication. The sister's position represented a conversion from former opposition; Saule contrasted her view with exhortations 'to return to her duty and obedience to her family' in letters from the sister to Victoire when she had been temporarily sent to Ruelle.[32] Hennessy had already assured Saule of Victoire's faithfulness, and while Mademoiselle Lafargue became the subject of family suspicion as a channel of communication, Victoire was able to deflect the priest's enquiries on the point. Letters were conveyed mainly by Hennessy into the hands of Mademoiselle Lafargue, who lived across the road from the Bernard household. That meant that letters could be delivered by stealth. Saule's instructions to Hennessy were quite detailed:

> Be so kind to send it to her as late as you can at night. *At seven and a half in the evening* will be a good hour – Pierre can go with it. For heaven's sake don't let it be found out. If he chuses to go to the back door which opens on the old *hall*, its the second, but I believe the street door would be the surest. Its just facing Bernard the attorney's windows.[33]

At times Hennessy resorted to other channels, including his own children, on Saule's behalf.

By late May, referring to the family opposition, Saule wrote that 'I hope my ladies are now a little more easy. I have a queer card to play with them, I must own, for they [*i.e. the father and his supporters*] are a comical sett, and, what's more, vexatious. They ever discovered of themselves, for if anybody tells them they know a thing, instantly they own to it, which perhaps was only suspected.'[34] In one of the rare direct contacts in La Rochelle at this stage, Bernard apparently advised Saule to give up any thoughts of Victoire. Any semblance of friendship with Saule had now gone. Saule in April had a letter from Mlle Lafargue 'by which [I] observe all the disturbances in the family, but the brother's resolution of coming to me is admirable ... I however don't think he will put it in execution. If he does I shall revenge myself by an abundance of politeness.'[35] The meeting that the brother had proposed does not seem to have taken place,[36] though he did communicate with Saule by letter apparently in November. Some months earlier Mlle Lafargue advised Saule that the frequent appearance of Hennessy's boys in her quarters gave grounds for suspicion. She suggested that the next letter should be delivered by Hennessy himself and that 'she would concert proper measures to convey said letters in future'.[37] No fewer than three ladies seem to have been the recipients of the letters destined for Victoire. Many letters were left unsealed for Hennessy or even Mlle Lafargue to read, and on one occasion Saule left Hennessy with the discretion of deciding whether it should be delivered. By this time the family were becoming more desperate in their effort to break the contact, and a threat of putting Victoire in a convent had been issued: in October 1775 she expressed fright at the prospect.[38]

A week later Saule was in a quandary, because while a message came back to him from Mlle Lafargue for a message to be sent through her, Victoire's last written communication had desired him not to write until she gave him leave.[39] Worse was to follow. On 4 November Victoire indicated by letter that she withdrew all promises made to him. The letter's formal tone led Saule to conclude that it had been written under pressure, and he replied to it, as he told Hennessy, 'in conformity to Miss Lafargue's advice I tell her I'm sure it was not her heart dictated her, but a passive obedience to her parent'.[40] Difficult though the position was, at least Victoire's own views were not in doubt, and Saule was free from the gnawing uncertainty he experienced in 1774 and early 1775. In January he sent his picture – 'ma triste figure' (an allusion to Don Quijote) – hidden in a box with a double bottom for delivery through the usual good offices of Mlle Lafargue.

The income in a commission business, even if it held its own, was modest, once spread over three partners. Plans were however beginning to take shape between Saule and Hennessy, who was now thinking again of Bordeaux: Saule would retain his interest in the house in La Rochelle, but would move to Cognac as a partner in a new firm of Hennessy & Co. to handle the brandy business after Hennessy's departure.[41] It was the prospect of winning Victoire's hand that motivated Saule: 'Thanks to God our business here goes on well, but we are three and as I am working for Victory, it is necessary to do the best to augment my little avoir for to maintain a wife. As my heart is afired on her, so it is on doing my endeavours to entitle me to obtain her and to render her happy.' Arrangements for the joint moves – Saule to Cognac, Hennessy to Bordeaux – gradually progressed.

Not all went smoothly. Much was made by the Bernards of Saule's associating with a particular woman in La Rochelle. On 19 March 1776 Saule wrote to Victoire 'a long letter hereon, it has taken up all my day'. Hennessy's support as an indulgent friend was also counted on, 'for you can surely pardon a young fool's falling in with a pritty woman when there's nothing dishonorable on one side or other'.[42] Victoire had already been placed at one stage with an aunt at Ruelle: the longstanding threat to send her into a convent was put into effect in May or June 1776.[43] At the end of 1776 Saule finally returned to Cognac. We know less of the affair at this stage, because Hennessy was no longer an intermediary in the contacts with Victoire. But if the move was intended to help Saule, it disappointed in its outcome as the brandy trade was disastrously bad in 1777 and 1778. In the two years from 30 September 1776 to 14 December 1778, Saule shipped a mere 121 1/2 puncheons of brandy, a figure which, converted to an annual rate, would have been a mere third of what Hennessy shipped in his worst years between 1766 and 1776.

Opposition did not end with the father's death in late 1776, and Victoire and Saule, finally giving up hope of winning consent to their plans, decided by early 1778 to fly in the face of opposition. One of the problems about a runaway marriage was that in French law both males and females attained majority only at twenty-five

years, and marriage formalities required for both parties an indica-
tion of parental agreement. From the convent in Cognac, Victoire
wrote to her mother on 2 March 1778 of her intentions. In the same
month Marie Saule in Dublin gave powers of attorney to convey her
assent to the marriage of Saule and Victoire.[44] On 29 September Victoire addressed the Lieutenant-General of Angoumois asking him to
enjoin two named notaries to act. The request must have been
granted, as on the following day Victoire gave her powers of attorney to two named notaries and a witness to go to the address of her
mother. Later the same day a summons was made to the mother at
the grill of the 'grand parloir' of the Benedictine convent to which
she had retired several months earlier. According to the signed
recital of the events the mother 's'opposait formellement autant qu'il
était dans son pouvoir'. The procedure was repeated on 3 October,
and on 7 October. There were nineteen witnesses to this document,
including both the *curé* of Cognac and Delamain. More significantly
still, the witnesses included a large number of members of the
family, thus signifying the fact that the family itself was split on the
issue. On the day the third requisition was both delivered and registered or controlled at the Greffe (a step necessary to give it legal
effect), a declaration was signed by both Saule and Victoire supported by a recital of the documents and events of the preceding
eight days, and the marriage contract was signed. It was a day of
feverish writing for the notary and of high drama for all the other
participants.[45]

If business prospects were bad, at least the lovers were now
together. Moreover, the volume of business recovered modestly and
finally in 1782 at 595 1/2 puncheons it had reached a new peak for
the house. Saule's better fortune had really set in in the spring of
1781: 120 puncheons were shipped off in a vessel in April 1781 and
he was looking for a vessel to ship off another 100 puncheons.[46] The
long and bitter family opposition seemed to melt, and in March 1779
Saule told Hennessy that 'the Bernards' family reconciliation was
received by me with pleasure'.[47] The settlement of the father-in-law's
estate now came on, in which Saule as Victoire's husband had a stake.
At the outset of May, he was 'in pretty good favour with my mother-
in-law, brother-in-law and the elder uncle, who came to pay me a visit

and to assure me how desirous he would be to be in the way of being serviceable to me – but it is now too late – I have now not seen the younger *cordelier* Sillion, nor will I see him'.[48] By this time too Victoire was making the acquaintance of Saule's circle. At his own suggestion Delamain had dined simply with them, bringing with him Roullet and L'Epine 'who gives us a feast on Thursday à la vénérie – my wife for her first acquaintance was highly satisfied with our friend as he seemed to be with her'. Delamain was also to send his carriage for Victoire and Saule to go and spend a few days with him in Jarnac.[49] Even before the end of 1778, no more than a month after the wedding, they had visited Bordeaux to stay with the Hennessys, and on her return Victoire added her own note to Saule's letter to Hennessy, repeating an invitation for the Hennessys to come and stay with them in the following spring.[50]

Saule's mother, Mary Saule, came out from Dublin in 1781 to visit her son. She had opposed the idea of marriage in 1774, but, as a letter on her return from Cognac to Bordeaux to take shipping for Dublin suggests, the visit had been a success, and it ended with an expression of 'my love and blessing to my valuable daughter [*i.e. daughter-in-law*]'.[51] The visit was a short one in the middle of 1781, and she was already back in Dublin by the outset of September. Richard Hennessy had taken pains to send her back, because of the perils of wartime sailing, under the care of a trusted master in the Irish trade, Captain Darcy. Hennessy had assured her with his characteristic and kindly humour that the captain 'is a brisk widower, much about her own age, and that I suppose he will be making love to her all the voyage'.[52] Captain Darcy seems to have looked after her well on what was a tense voyage in which the vessel was halted twice by hostile privateers, and on arrival he took her to his own house.[53] At this stage, our knowledge of Saule's family life and of Victoire fades. There are fewer letters on family life in the 1780s. The main reason is that Saule was now writing from Cognac and not to Cognac. A busy Saule, preoccupied with the growth of his own business and with his friend's problems, touched little on his own life: his romantic life in any event had now become secure and Victoire was a member of the little Irish circle.

A NEW BUSINESS IN 1776: SAULE IN COGNAC,
HENNESSY IN BORDEAUX

During the 1770s, Saule's love affair with Victoire took precedence over all other matters in the correspondence. As far back as August 1775 Hennessy had an interview with John Galwey, and by the end of November his intention of quitting Cognac was sufficiently well-defined for Saule to refer to the proposal of his taking Hennessy's place in Cognac.[54] In the wake of the poor 1775 vintage, Hennessy's turnover was halved. So desperate was he that he envisaged the possibility of setting up with Galwey's help in Cork or Le Havre. Bordeaux itself of course remained a possibility, and Saule advised Hennessy that it

> would seem to me to suit you much better than any proposed plan as yet, should you be determined to quit Cognac. There your friends in Ireland could be of use to you, and Mr Galwey himself render you most essential service. There again you might reap still some advantage of your settlement in Cognac. You would only change places, the trade would continue the same, and he that gave satisfaction on the shipping cognac brandies may surely do as much in the Bordeaux brandy, beside other branches which may fall in your way.[55]

Hennessy's abandoning any idea of trying his luck in Cork or Le Havre was due to an upturn, in contrast to Cognac's fickle fortunes, in Bordeaux's brandy trade. Some Bordeaux brandy had even made an appearance on the London or Dunkirk markets, and some brandy in the Entre-deux-mers region was being distilled up to spirit strength.[56] Bordeaux also expanded its markets in Russia, and in the Guinea and colonial trades. The distiller Hilary Andoe from Dublin had already settled there in 1774. Hennessy brought a distiller with him from Cognac. In theory at least, his experience as a *négociant* combined with the professional skills from Cognac should have equipped him to do well in the boom that the Irish circle optimistically read into the fickle demands of the 1770s. The loyal Saule, in a letter to the master of an Irish vessel, described his departure with a flourish: 'he is settled under his own name and has got surprising encouragement from all our worthy countrymen there which in same manner ensures his success in his undertaking which principally consists in brandy distilling'.[57]

As in the past, however, the Galwey support did not prove as helpful as Hennessy had hoped. In part, as in the mid-1760s, bright prospects were undone by unanticipated external and climatic variations. The year 1776 itself had been exceptional in its demands, and Bordeaux distillers were not to experience a comparable upsurge until the early 1780s. Even in the practical matters of getting premises and custom, the Galweys may not have been very helpful. It was another Irish house, Coppinger, admittedly one of Bordeaux's major houses, who made the enquiries on his behalf.[58] If any one of the Galweys was at fault, it must have been John Galwey, over-optimistic in giving advice, and not personally offering any practical assistance when Hennessy acted on his advice first in 1765 and now again in 1776. However, loans from two other members of the family in Bordeaux were vital to Hennessy's survival in the early years.

Hennessy's problems were twofold. The first – and more long-term one – was the erratic nature of Bordeaux distilling. The second, and more immediately serious problem, was Hennessy's want of capital. Before going to Bordeaux he was seeking a partner, and even had in mind Roullet, the man with whom at an earlier date Saule had had a disastrous partnership. Saule sought to dissuade him from this step, advising him, given the needs of his family, not to seek a partner at all.[59] His shortage of capital explains why he took a partner, George Boyd, despite Saule's advice to the contrary, shortly after he had set up. Even with that he needed the support of Delamain who guaranteed Hennessy's credit in Paris, and even provided 9000 livres for Hennessy's establishment.[60]

When the partnership was concluded, the style of the firm remained Hennessy & Co. Boyd's entry was a typical case of a younger merchant making his debut with a more experienced man. His attraction for Hennessy was the capital resources provided by his family background. Skinner was a forceful and successful figure in the business life of Bordeaux. Deeply involved in trade with Britain and Scandinavia, his interest in the distilling trade was no doubt similar to that of the Galweys: he provided both brandy and spirit for his foreign customers, and had rectifying commissions to give out. In later years Skinner in association with Fenwick sent in 200 *pièces* for making into spirit: it was a specialized order from England, probably for the East Indies.[61]

The partnership was already in effect at the outset of 1777 when William Coppinger observed to Saule that Hennessy's 'association with Boyd proves essential and good. They will do a great deal in the burning way.'[62] But Hennessy was already living on the firm's capital: at the beginning of 1778 'my heavy expenses, furniture, clothing etc has left on the balancing our books the other day a large disproportion in the capital'. The deficit over sixteen months amounted to a total of 6000 livres. When the deficit came to Skinner's attention he insisted on Hennessy making good the deficiency, and he was obliged to borrow the amount from Richard Galwey on a nine-month promissory note.[63] George Boyd was a strong and, as later events were to show, an unpleasant personality. Hennessy's debts were personal ones, not debts of the partnership. Some inkling of the future was evident by 1781: the partnership itself, though strapped for cash, had advanced near 6000 livres to Boyd's father on a promissory note which proved impossible to negotiate in 1781. In other words the partnership, though in theory Hennessy was the senior partner, was hitched more to the Boyd interest rather than to Hennessy's.

HENNESSY'S BUSINESS AND DOMESTIC PROBLEMS IN BORDEAUX

In 1776 distilling was a prosperous business. In early 1777, with a sudden credit crisis in Dublin, its fortunes collapsed. In April Hennessy retailed the business failures in Dublin which helped to make 'brandy a very bad article there. God preserve our friends.'[64] So bad were conditions that Hennessy's stills were to remain unlit for two months.[65] Things then recovered a little but in February 1779 he lamented that 'I am again idle'. In some respects the situation was even more serious, because while the Dublin credit crisis (a by-product of financial stringency in London) had lifted, war produced a deepening one in Bordeaux. On 18 May eighteen failures were reported in a single day, and many married people had taken refuge in the countryside to avoid their importunate creditors.[66]

Even Boyd could raise no money on the strength of his connection with the Skinner interest. Things seem to have picked up towards the middle of 1779, at least in the Irish trade. By means of masked vessels the general commodity trade with Ireland remained quite buoyant during the war; any upturn in demand for spirits would be quickly felt in Bordeaux, the more so as in wartime neutral vessels were scarce in the Charente in contrast to Bordeaux. By the end of the year, however, things were again desperate, perhaps even more so than at any previous juncture. Hennessy seems to have borrowed 10,000 livres at this stage from Henry Galwey. [67]

Illustrating the volatile nature of the distilling business, the bad conditions of 1779 had turned into 'a terrible hurry' in the following April, with six ships loading at one time for Ireland. From 18 February to 23 March 1780 Hennessy's twelve stills never stopped, and the partnership had purchased 400 *pièces* for rectification.[68] As late as August six to ten stills were still working, and even in September, despite the cash shortage in Bordeaux, Hennessy reported that 'we will have a good deal to do for three Irish ships'.[69] New wine duties that had come into effect in Ireland accounted for the upturn in the spring: some 3000 tons of wine had been shipped for Ireland in a short space of time.[70] The presence of vessels loading wine always generated some demand for brandy, and hence commissions to redistil brandy to the right strength. However, news of the seizure of some of the masked vessels in July threw doubts over this method of conducting trade. Though the doubts were later resolved, the crisis halted the boom in the trade for Dublin, and when it could resume wider problems had emerged.

The activity of more numerous and more daring privateers under French or American colours (often with Irish crews) reached a peak in 1781, greatly adding to the risk of wartime trade.[71] Enormous pains had to be taken to ensure that the true ownership of vessels was concealed, and the crew, disguised as passengers, were supplemented by genuine Danish or Scandinavian sailors. The tension under which trade was conducted is shown in the experience of Mary Saule on her voyage to Dublin in the autumn of 1781. The master, Captain Darcy, was disguised as a passenger, and Mary Saule was to pass for his sister. The vessel was twice boarded by privateers; the second instance of this took place off Waterford, where the vessel was 'a hellish one full of guns and Irishmen'.[72] Mary Saule's account survives in a letter to Saule: 'I kept to my instructions. I was going to Norway with my brother. The[y] still douptd [*i.e. doubted*] me. The[y] broke open my truck, took what they liked. I concealed my drafft in my stays.'[73]

By December 1780 a number of the Irish houses had halted payments. Significantly, the houses that did so were all deep into the Dublin wine trade: J.A. Byrne, Gernon, one of the Barton partnerships, and Gledstanes.[74] Hennessy commented, 'you can judge how those faileurs have hurt the credit of the factory particularly the young and striving part ...'.[75] In March 1781 he wrote, 'the credit of the factory is now at the lowest ebb, there are not people wanting to say every house of them will stop'.[76] In December 1780 he had noted that some had proposed supporting him, but had dropped the idea because of the badness of the times.[77] In July 1781 Henry Galwey refused to extend the 10,000 livres loan, and compelled Hennessy to repay 6000 livres of it;[78] Hennessy was reduced to asking Saule for help. Hennessy's brandy business was at a dead stand at this time.[79] In October he was still hoping for support from Galwey, adding, 'indeed he keeps me in boiling water, as I have unfortunately no other recourse and that he is so dilitary and fickl'd a man'.[80]

There was a limited pick-up in business subsequently which helped to save Hennessy from utter disaster. But with brandy more freely available, the Dublin market by February 1782 was said to be glutted.[81] Hennessy experienced successively in September and October 1781 the greatest personal tragedies of his life. On 4 September he recounted the death of his wife Nelly to Saule. She had been ill, called for a confessor, but lost her senses before the sacrament was brought. Hennessy was stricken: 'thus I lost my poor dear Nelly, when I wanted her most as did her poor children ... I attempted twice last post to give you the melancholy account but could not succeed.' Mrs Hennessy's health was never very good: there were frequent references to it in Saule's letters in the first half of the 1770s. Saule's mother, who had seen her as recently as a month or two before her death, wrote a year later that she had not many hopes for Mrs Hennessy, adding that 'she had too early notions of womanhood'. As if this loss was not bad enough, two other tragedies followed. In October his two younger boys took ill with scarlet fever, which was raging in Bordeaux. J.A. Byrne's four daughters had it as well, and the youngest died. In writing to Saule on 27 October, Hennessy added a postscript that the boys had passed a very indifferent night and that he had not quitted them till 3 o'clock when the fever abated a little. Six days later the two boys died within three hours of each other despite the attentions of three doctors and a surgeon.[82] For a warm-hearted and affectionate man like Hennessy the burden was enormous. In response to advice from Saule, he could only say that 'conjugal and paternal ties and affections get the better of my resolution, and often obliges me to give way to the losses and griefs which heaven has pleased to dispense to me'.[83]

Nelly's death added to his economic problems. He was defrauded by an old woman whom he employed, on his wife's death, to look after him and his children. He had then decided to put himself into boarding, and also to board the two younger boys (Biddy was already in a convent, and James in the Douai College), and he hoped he could make an arrangement with a Mrs Good for them and rent the house.[84] Though the Boyds turned down the house at the time, in the aftermath of further family misfortunes of their own George Boyd moved into it in the spring following. Hennessy was now truly at the nadir of his fortunes and, as in 1772 and 1775, the question of abandoning France altogether came up. On this occasion, improving prospects for his brother-in-law Ned Barrett (brother of Nelly), who had virtually disappeared from the correspondence in the mid-1770s, were the basis of fresh hopes. Barrett was a singularly unfortunate individual: when he reappears in 1782, his circumstances had been impaired by a lawsuit which he had lost. However, the appointment of Edmund Burke as paymaster general to a new British cabinet opened an avenue for him. Burke had already made promises to him in the 1770s which had, to Burke's regret, come to nothing, and Barrett's welfare was still preoccupying him in 1781.[85] Now he secured for Barrett the posts of deputy paymaster of troops in the West Indies, and controller of the island of Barbados. The emoluments were reckoned to be worth £2000 per annum. Though Barrett

was appointed only on 1 May, employment had already been offered
by Barrett to Hennessy, presumably some form of deputyship to execute office work, 'though my name would not appear'.[86] It is not
clear whether this offer came only from Barrett (a loyal and generous man) or whether the prospect of looking after Hennessy was
part of the design conceived between Barrett and Burke. The Galweys advised caution: they pointed both to the climate (a killer) and
to Barrett's age (in all probability he was the same age as Hennessy,
hence no longer a young man, and employment would die with Barrett). In fact, the prospects which Barrett had held before Hennessy's
eyes disappeared abruptly. Burke resigned from the government: this
meant that Barrett lost his position as paymaster, though he retained
the post of controller, which however was worth only £400 to £500
a year.

Barrett now suggested that Hennessy should go out with him, and
settle in Barbados or one of the neighbouring islands. This time he
was not proposing employment, though the implication was that in
his official position he could be useful to Hennessy. What Barrett proposed was that Hennessy's brother-in-law Shea, a merchant in Cork,
or other friends there would give him the consignment of a cargo or
two, and that this would help to put him on his feet.[87] He was
already in receipt of pessimistic appraisals of business prospects in
Bordeaux. According to Henry Galwey, 'you rate your profit too high
and make no allowance of rent and very heavy charges and expenses
… the work decreasing yearly'.[88] Hennessy took the new proposal
very seriously. He wrote to the Sheas, and Henry Galwey also wrote
to Barrett. 'I scarcely think of anything else,' was Hennessy's summary of his thinking in a letter to Saule. He could not count on assistance from his relatives in Bordeaux ('I had but little reason to hope
for friendship from my relations in that city'), and could not count on
help from Barrett ('himself £300 to £400 in debt, a wife and four
children, three of them daughters, and a spirit equal to the highest
employment he can arrive at'). However, he expected that the sale of
his interest in the Bordeaux business would cover his own debts.
Moreover his expectations were modest: 'if there was a possibility of
obtaining the management of a plantation in his or any of the neighbouring islands, I would think myself equal to it'.[89]

A post of overseer required no capital, and it was usually an outlet for a younger man of limited prospects. That this was the hope of a man of fifty-three years shows how desperate he was. Over the months of summer the plans seem to have changed, as Hennessy in the end did not sail with Barrett as the latter had proposed. After Barrett's arrival in the West Indies, Hennessy's eldest son was to go out the following year. But even the altered plan came to naught, as misfortune again struck the hapless Barrett. 'This poor victim to ill luck', as Hennessy described him, sailed for America in November under neutral colours in a vessel belonging to Henry Shea. It sprang a leak seven miles out from Waterford, passengers and sailors had to take to the boats, and Barrett lost his commission of appointment and his outfit on which his outlay had been £400.[90] By January 1783 Barrett himself was dead.[91] Mishap and death brought the design for Hennessy's son to an end. Hennessy had not pursued further the plan of himself going to the West Indies. One reason for having already changed it in 1782 into a simpler plan of carving out a modest career for his son, was that with prospects of peace in 1782 and a bad harvest in Ireland the fickle distilling business in Bordeaux staged an upturn.

During this time Hennessy's economic problems were enlarged by the responsibility of looking after his family and providing for their future. In fact, at the time Nelly died, the only daughter, Biddy, was already lodged in a convent at Pons, and Saule and Victoire cared for her in the period of mourning after her mother's death. Biddy's placement in a convent must have occurred at the time of Nelly's final illness, and the fact that her only complaint was said to be about the breakfasts implies reporting on a new experience.[92] The eldest boy, James, had been at Douai since 1777. Richard does not, however, seem to have envisaged a military career for him, though he did for the other two boys. But in the economic difficulties he was experiencing he altered his plans for James as well, and at the outset of 1781 he obtained places for all three boys in the Irish Brigade. The places were obtained through Count Dillon, who informed Hennessy that a recommendation in favour of his sons would be dispensed with, 'knowing my family had served in the Brigade with distinction and credit'.[93] In February Richard informed James in Douai that he

Richard Hennessy (1729–1800) as an officer of the National Guard. Hennessy was a lieutenant from 1789. (Hennessy collection)

Interior of distillery, with two stills, from engraving in the Encyclopedie, *1750s. Few if any distilling premises had fewer than two stills, and some had many more. The letters* **C** *and* **D** *indicate the boiler encased in brickwork;* **A** *and* **B** *indicate the small wood-burning furnaces, and* **F** *the flue.* **K** *and* **M** *indicate the woodwork encasing the condenser through which ran the coiled pipe – the* serpentine *or* worm *– and which held cold water introduced by the pipe above the woodwork (the pipe at the base evacuating the flow of water is at the rear and hence not visible). The cold water condensed the vapours from the still into liquid, which was directed by an outlet pipe into the basins* **L** *and* **N** *at the foot of the still. The figure on the right has a prover or* éprouvette *in his hands; it contains brandy taken from the flow into the basin. If, after the prover was shaken, the liquid in it seemed of the right consistency, the basin containing the inferior early flow was replaced, and the new basin received a liquid deemed to be of good quality. The prover was supplemented in the 1760s by measuring instruments which, dipped into liquid, indicated if it had reached the required alcoholic strength.*

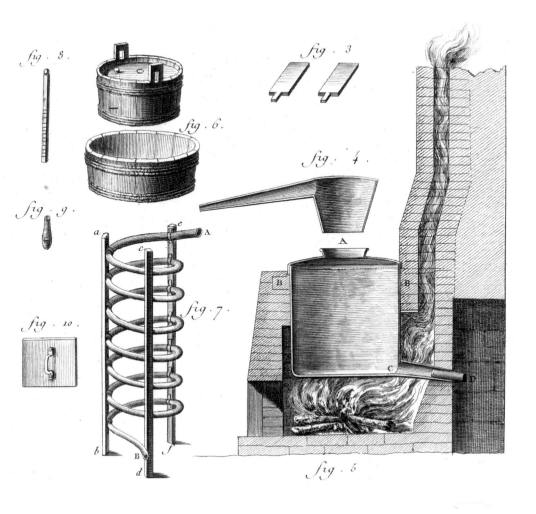

fig . 8 .

fig . 6 .

fig . 3 .

fig . 4 .

fig . 9 .

fig . 7 .

fig . 10 .

fig . 5 .

Cross-section of a still (fig. 5) and of the head or chapeau, *which conducted the vapours into the condenser. Fig. 7 shows the* serpentine.

Left: *James Hennessy (1765–1842), son of Richard Hennessy. The portrait is likely to have been made in 1816 or 1817, when he served as commandant of the National Guard of the* arrondissement *of Cognac. (Hennessy collection)*

Below: *La Billarderie, painting of c. 1830. The house was purchased by the Hennessys in the 1790s, and was Richard Hennessy's residence during his final years. It was greatly remodelled in the 1860s. (Hennessy collection)*

Right: *James Delamain, 1738–1800 (Madame Noël Sauzey, with kind permission)*

Above left: *Delftware plate made by Henry Delamain in Dublin for the wedding of his nephew James Delamain to Marie Ranson in 1762. The shield carries the Delamain and Ranson arms impaled. (Monsieur Alain Braastad collection)*

Above right: *Marie Ranson, daughter of Isaac Ranson, wife of James Delamain (Madame Noël Sauzey, with kind permission)*

Above left: *Thomas Hine (1775–1822), husband of Françoise-Elizabeth Delamain, manager of the Ranson & Delamain house from 1800 until 1817, and co-partner and manager of Thomas Hine & Co. until his own death. (Hine collection)* Above right: *Jean-Jacques Caminade de Chatenet, second husband of John Saule's widow, Victoire Bernard (Musée municipal, Cognac)*

Above left: *Charles-Rosalie de Rohan-Chabot, comte de Jarnac, probably at the time of his marriage to Elizabeth Smith in 1776.* Above right: *Elizabeth Smith. Their son, a future comte, married Lucy Fitzgerald, a daughter of Lord Edward Fitzgerald. (Portraits reproduced in R. Delamain,* Jarnac a travers les ages)

Gabarre under sail on the Charente at Saintes: detail from a lithograph by L. Le Breton, c. 1850, based on a sketch by E. Thiberge, 1801 (M. Christian Vernou, with kind permission)

Bordeaux in 1776, the year in which Hennessy arrived there to start his distilling business. The business would have been located in the Chartrons district (in the background of the engraving), the main business area of the port. (Engraving by Le Gouaz after Ozanne)

Rochefort looking downstream, by Joseph Vernet, 1762. Rochefort was the major arsenal of the French navy for south-west France. Irish vessels usually loaded their cognac in Rochefort, probably at a point slightly upstream from this scene. Hence masters sailing from Rochefort or from Tonnay-Charente farther upstream passed the arsenal and, sailing to neutral Hamburg in wartime, were a source of information on the forwardness of French preparations for invading Ireland in 1798. (Musée de la Marine, Paris / photo by P. Dantec)

Detail from a sepia sketch by Nicolas Petit showing a loaded gabarre at the quayside at Jarnac, outside the Delamain residence and warehouses. The barges struck their masts to enable them to pass under the bridges. (Dr Jean-Louis Plisson, with kind permission)

had obtained a commission for him in Dillon's regiment 'with permission to continue your studies at Douai'. He set out the reasons for the change in his plans for James:

> I did not destine you for a military life yet I could not refuse so advantageous an offer for you. I was the readier to accept it as the hopes I had of forming an establishment for you here daily diminishes, owing partly to the war and other unfavourable circumstances. In the little time I am here I have several examples of the little dependence we can have on a mercantile establishment. Houses of long standing, with large capitals, great repute, good business and irreproachable conduct, are now fallen to nothing.[94]

Richard regarded a military career itself as a *pis aller* for an eldest son. He made it clear to James that he was still free to reject a military life. By mid-year it was established that James disliked the prospect, and Hennessy had written to his Lowlands relatives now in Brussels and to the Blakes in Ostend. As a result, James found a precarious niche in the Ostend house.[95] By late 1782 the more desperate expedient of sending James to the West Indies was in the air. That came to nothing not only because of Barrett's misfortunes but because the outlook in the brandy trade had passed its nadir. That made it possible to find a place for him in Saule's counting house in Cognac (where the upturn in brandy was quicker than in Bordeaux), and James began his apprenticeship with his father's closest friend.

SAULE & CO: JOHN SAULE'S INDEPENDENT BUSINESS

This brings us back to Jack Saule and to his progress in Cognac from 1776. We gradually begin to lose sight of Saule's daily life and thoughts after his marriage in 1778. When Hennessy's plight in 1787–8 necessitated detailed personal letters, the old fantasy and whimsy were entirely absent. We can best tell the progress of Saule's business from the impersonal record of quantities invoiced and shipped. The figures reveal a virtual collapse of brandy shipped in 1777 and 1778. By January 1778 Hennessy noted that the house's credit with the Paris banking firm of Mallet was greatly overdrawn and that the banker whom he met in Paris seemed uneasy.[96] Recovery in turnover was slight in 1779 and 1780, and in 1781 at 416 1/2 puncheons it was still below the level of the mid-1770s, itself hardly satisfactory. When Hennessy went to Bordeaux in 1776, he retained an interest in the house which now traded under the style of Hennessy & Saule. That arrangement ended in 1779, and from September of that year Saule traded independently under the style of his uncle who had arrived in 1763, Saule & Co. The partnership had effectively ended a year earlier in September 1778 when Hennessy agreed to leave his name associated with the partnership for the purpose of helping the house with its London orders.[97]

The original joint interest in the Cognac house was probably less for the purpose of securing a profit to Hennessy than to retain an established name for the house in the first stages of a new merchant setting out on his own. In 1776 Saule was still unknown in business, not featuring even in the style of the La Rochelle house in which he was partner. In January 1779, after the partnership had ended, Saule experienced difficulty in getting an account in his own name with a Paris banker. Saule attributed this to the jealousy of Lallemand. In 1779 he still had to make his mark. However, whatever the circumstances behind his problems, the fact is that the business had staged an upturn, however modest, in 1779. In June 1779, writing to the house of Connelly, to whom he could speak frankly, he admitted that 'we are young beginners and are uneasy and constantly in dread of losing our customers'.[98]

The letter book reveals a keen interest in developing the London market at this time, and it was in the course of this year that Saule proposed to Hennessy that they should both make a trip overseas. (Nothing came of this.)[99] By January 1780 a more sanguine Saule reported to Connelly & Co. in Flushing that 'we are gott in in a degree to the London trade'.[100] From the Hennessy business he had inherited the custom of the London house of Steele. Steele, of course, as most big houses did, divided its custom between several firms, Martell and Augier as well as Saule.[101] But regular commissions from such a house conferred a standing on Saule's. Saule's business made little advance in 1780 and 1781.[102] In both years the two friends were in dire circumstances, neither really able to help the other. Saule's situation improved somewhat in 1782, but Hennessy's, which we can only measure more impressionistically from personal letters to Saule, remained bad. Late 1782, however, bore fortune to him as well. The long dark business night of 1776–82 had ended, and both friends experienced a welcome relief from the almost unremitting cares of seven years.

7

Bordeaux and Cognac: brandy business in two centres in the 1780s

THE BORDEAUX BRANDY MARKET

The two friends, Hennessy and Saule, were still to experience years of trial and years of success. Hennessy benefited from an upturn in the Irish market in late 1782 which continued at least into 1785. The reasons for the upturn were a combination of bad harvests in Ireland, a temporary clamp on distilling, and the introduction, independently but coincidentally with the harvest crises, of rigid administrative regulation of distilling.

Hennessy was by no means the only distiller serving this market. While Hennessy seems to have served the Catholic circle of Galwey and French, Andoe supplied the Protestant partnership of Barton, Johnston & Barry. But Hennessy sometimes got their business also: in November 1784 he was very pleased to report that they had done well in getting the custom of the major Barton house.[1] Weak or inferior brandies, drawn from Bordeaux's hinterland, mainly from the north side of the Gironde reaching from Mortagne to Royan and even beyond, were redistilled on the coastline or, more frequently, sent to Bordeaux.

This brandy was in demand especially, though not solely, from smugglers. Smugglers often arrived in the river Garonne without notice, demanding not only brandy but frequently spirit rectified to three-fifths strength or higher, strengths executed only in response to a direct order. This caused sharp swings between idleness and bouts of frenetic activity. Thus, according to Hennessy in January 1784, 'since dispatching the above vessels, we have not had a still going, tomorrow we shall set 16 of them to work'. This was in response to the arrival of three vessels from Ireland, for which between 600 and 700 *pièces* of brandy for rectification were purchased in a single day.[2] By April, with four cutters loading the ankers beloved of smugglers, and 'traders' also loading for Dublin and Cork, the sixteen stills were at work 'with an appearance of their continuing so some time if we can get brandy'.[3] A capacity of sixteen stills was impressive for the period, and it reflected the rather special circumstances of the Bordeaux business. At 30 to 40 *veltes* per still, this could amount to a total distilling capacity of 480 to 640 *veltes* (or 960 to 1280 gallons), which would have approximated the size of a large Irish distillery of the 1770s (though not of the 1780s). In intensive use, this could amount to an output of 15 to 20 barriques of spirit a day.

Inevitably, interest emerged in a larger still than the traditional size. Not only did Boyd, Hennessy's partner in the Chartrons business, open premises at Royan further downstream than Mortagne, but it was he who there contrived the first large still in the region. The activity there was in the hands of Boyd, while Hennessy remained in charge of distilling in the Chartrons and of the loading of the vessels for Ireland. In December 1784 Hennessy advised Saule 'to wait the trial of the great still we are making which we hope to have up in the course of this month. The make of it I think must be better than the common ones.'[4] A month later he reported that 'we have got home this afternoon our new still, it has now 300 veltes water in it, and it will work …'.[5] The prospect of continued success encouraged Boyd to erect yet a further large still: in September 1785 he was busy fixing up the still at Royan, 'which is to be the Non such. It forms an oblong square with two worms.'[6]

From a peak in 1784–5 business proved only fitfully good in later years. In October 1787 Boyd was without an order for three months. Business revolved mainly around orders from three Galwey partnerships and from the house of French, with regular orders also from Barton, Johnston & Barry and from Forsters, more intermittently from Coppingers and Morgan.[7] When demand was weak in late

1786, 'deux grands fraudeurs anglais' – Irish vessels – and vessels for the Île de France prompted such buying as there was, and even a month later 'on compte toujours ici sur les besoins pour l'Irlande et pour l'Inde, ce qui soutient le courage de nos propriétaires'.[8] Business was all the more erratic because London did not import spirit (as opposed to brandy): in fact it had been made illegal in the 1780s to do so.

A large and uncontrolled cash flow continued between Royan, a business conducted by Boyd in a partnership with a man named Guiliory, and Bordeaux, location of the joint venture by Boyd and Hennessy. While the Royan venture supplied badly needed spirit for sale in boom times in Bordeaux, the arrangement was indefensible because, while it used the capital of the Bordeaux partnership, any profits went exclusively to Boyd. The problems were made infinitely worse by Boyd's insouciance and irresponsibility. Despite having a partner in Bordeaux who could handle business on the spot, Boyd also spent much of his time in the city. At Royan the books had long been neglected, and required balancing. In the books which survive because of Boyd's later bankruptcy, and which show signs of hasty updating in 1787 and later, curious inconsistencies are immediately evident, as in the case of the invoice book which was written up either later or intermittently from loose papers. A frantic Guiliory wrote repeatedly to Bordeaux about problems in October 1787. He broached the bookkeeping and the larger questions of overcapacity. His questions went unanswered, and despite Guiliory's urgent pressing of him to go to Royan, he seems to have been slow to return.

The two businesses – Boyd's in Royan and the joint one in Bordeaux – were on parallel courses to disaster. Hennessy, unable to make good losses in the Bordeaux company, had to vacate the premises in Bordeaux to Boyd as the price of a rather good composition with the creditors financed in effect by Boyd and his family. The business in Royan was wound down under pressure from Guiliory and closed in March 1788. Hennessy had vacated the premises in Bordeaux in the autumn of 1787 in the internal arrangement with Boyd, and the Boyd business was transferred to it.[9]

HENNESSY'S LIFESTYLE AND BUSINESS PROBLEMS IN BORDEAUX

In the heady days of 1785 a touch of extravagance entered the lifestyle of Hennessy for the first time. Hennessy, though a man of fifty-six years, moved in a circle of much younger men. He related to Saule that he was 'these three months father of a society of young men such as I heard you say you had at Rochell'. He went on to relate:

> We are fifteen who joined in taking a little house and pleasant garden, about half a league from town, where we dine and amuse ourselves every Sunday and holiday, very much to satisfaction. It is called Liberty Hall, already pritty well-known and envied by many, gambling not admitted, nor more than a bottle of decent wine for each, when we have no strangers, and even then we take but little more. One of us [is] every month, charged with providing and keeping the accounts. We have laid in a stock of wine; an excellent cook who buys and dresses our dinner. We live very well, drink good wines, coffee, liquers, teas, lemonade etc and costs from 4 to 6 livres each day, our rent 540 livres per annum and 200 livres do. for our gardiner and house maid … The expenses settled everyday, wine, cook and wood etc and divided on as many diners, he who brings a friend pays for him as for himself.

Apart from two or three Frenchmen, the participants were 'countrymen' (i.e. Irish or English, and in the case of Carey, from Guernsey): Andoe, Thomson, Barry, Johnston, Bradshaw, West, Lawton, Seally, John and Henry Martin, Carey and 'papa Hennessy'.[10] There was something sad in all this, as Hennessy's life at this stage should have revolved around a circle of older men. Moreover, in spending time and money on such a circle, he was ignoring the fact that the larger distilling capacity of Hennessy & Boyd and their consequent higher overheads left them vulnerable to undercutting by smaller distillers determined to carry off an order.[11] In the 1783–5 period, when demand was at a peak, they made a handsome profit.[12] However, as capacity grew and demand failed to increase in proportion, in trying to keep to their old rates of charge for distilling, they found that they were undercut by other distillers.

The bookkeeping in Bordeaux – characteristically enough given Hennessy's easygoing ways – was left to the younger associate Boyd, who of course was maintaining (or neglecting) the books of another concern as well. The first and apparently last balance, before nemesis overtook the house in 1787, was struck in 1783. In 1783 Hennessy's capital in the books was in excess of 32,000 livres. In subsequent years bookkeeping deteriorated further, and even the posting of entries into the books was several months in arrears. Given Hennessy's lack of taste, or more accurately incapacity, for bookkeeping, he had little inkling of how serious things were, though he registered some ineffective protest: 'there has been ever since a constant intercourse of cash and notes between the two houses. I always thought and complained that our capital was laid out there.'[13]

The most noteworthy aspect of Hennessy's lifestyle in the mid-1780s was that he pursued it despite the fact that his engagement in distilling depended entirely on borrowed money. It was not in itself a particularly happy relationship for any man, and for an older man a potentially humiliating one. In 1787 Saule reminded Richard that he had gone to Bordeaux to dissuade him from entering into the partnership.[14] Later he amplified his comments:

> I see you now begin to know the people you are concerned with, but unluckily its too late ... they never deceived me from the first hour your connection with them was proposed and I have only the satisfaction to say that I always strove to guard you against them, but your friend Delamain prompted you on, and the only man he guarded you against is the one who has not yet hurt you.[15]

Of course Delamain's support for Hennessy's partnership was at the time understandable. Hennessy had no cash behind him, and while his relative John Galwey put orders for brandy in Hennessy's way and two other members of the family lent him money when he was in difficulty, none of them was prepared to invest capital in the enterprise. Alliance with another merchant was in those circumstances inevitable, even if the normal convention of the older man providing the capital and the name, and the younger man the work, was reversed. Delamain provided him with a loan of 30,000 livres, and in

1781 he borrowed 10,000 from the banker Gastinel in Paris on Saule's security.

When the difficulties came to light in 1787, the first thought of both Saule and Delamain was that Boyd had run away with the substance of the Bordeaux house and that Hennessy had a real choice of either forcing Boyd to settle his debt to the partnership or compelling Boyd to join him in a common bankruptcy.[16] Saule advised Hennessy to avoid ceding his interest to Boyd and allowing him to settle the debts of the house. In the worst circumstance there should be a bankruptcy either of Hennessy & Co. or of Boyd's separate venture – Boyd & Co. – in Royan. As far as Hennessy & Co. was concerned, he should remain on the same footing as his partner in settling the debts of the house, and resist any attempt by Boyd to set him adrift. In this way Hennessy would not only retain an interest in any composition with creditors, but as a consequence of having done so, with the support of his friends, he might be in a position to buy back from the creditors the stills and stock and set up in business again.[17] Delamain took up much the same position as Saule. Writing to Hennessy in August, he assured him that he would go to Bordeaux shortly and exhorted him:

> I hope you and your partner will settle so as justice may be done with-out any hostile measures. If he has, as there appears no doubt, taken the funds of the house to employ elsewhere, they must be found, and let him depend on what I assure you that he will be far behind his reck-oning if his intention is not to settle in an amicable legitimate manner.[18]

A fortnight later, apologizing for further delay in leaving for Bordeaux, he added that 'I am in great hopes our affairs will be settled amicably'.[19]

Delamain eventually visited Bordeaux. A settlement with Boyd followed broadly on the basis Boyd had proposed. Given Hennessy's situation, there was no alternative to Hennessy's ceding in October his interest in the partnership to Boyd, who was therefore left in control of the liquidation of its affairs with the creditors (which dragged on into early 1788). As soon as he heard of the arrangement, Saule was furious, still believing that Boyd more than Hennessy was at fault, and he was critical of Delamain's role:

> I must frankly tell you that its my opinion that your conduct from the
> beginning to the end was all of a piece and Delamain in letting the
> blackguards give him 80 per cent and leaving you upon your arse was
> as bad. The rascal frightened you by talking of failing. Boyd's reputa-
> tion was already up by his father's, and I dare say he dreaded such an
> *éclat* more than you could.

In fact the settlement was not precisely on the basis Boyd had proposed. The payments to creditors were reduced by 20 per cent, not by
the 25 per cent originally proposed by Boyd, and debts to Delamain
and to Gastinel were not left unhonoured as Boyd had proposed. In
other words, the actual costs of settlement to Boyd were high, though
the main principle of what he had proposed had to be conceded.

 Hennessy's grasp of the situation was shaky. His debts he reckoned in 1787 as 60,000 livres, in effect the amount of the sums he
had borrowed from Delamain, Gastinel, the Galweys and some
others. This was simply crude arithmetic of what he had borrowed
over the years, and he had no idea in a bookkeeping sense of what
was the precise situation of the house.[20] The timing of the crisis had
been determined in 1787 by Boyd's employing an accountant to draw
up a statement of affairs. Both Hennessy and Boyd had counted originally on a distilling commission of 20 livres per puncheon, whereas
it had fallen to 9 livres. He proposed the cession of Hennessy's interest to him in return for 30,000 livres from Boyd towards settling
Hennessy's debts, and Boyd's then paying off the creditors of the partnership at a 25 per cent reduction in their entitlements. He proposed
that Delamain would wait for the payment of his 30,000 livres, and
that Saule would answer for the 10,000 livres due to Gastinel.[21]

Not only was the statement of the situation drawn up entirely
from Boyd's side, but Hennessy, with no clear idea of what was
amiss, was totally unable to rebut Boyd's case. He stuck to the idea
that the bookkeeping (which Boyd had neglected) was the root of the
problem, and that there were funds enough in the house to pay all. In
his view the situation was precipitated by the Boyd group's interest in
driving him out: 'Skinner wanted to drive me out of the business.'[22]
But the fact emerged that, without taking his share of the general
debts of the house into account, Hennessy's resources would meet
only a quarter of the sums borrowed from Delamain, Galwey and

Gastinel.[23] In other words, Hennessy's situation was quite desperate. The situation was brought home to Hennessy and his friends only after Delamain visited Bordeaux, and what he established then explains why he no longer advised Hennessy to hold out for more advantageous accommodation with Boyd. While Saule had been critical of Delamain when the outline of the news first reached him, his opinion was later reversed:

> Since I wrote you my last I had a conversation with Mr Delamain about you – he says that it was impossible to secure you the establishment as there was a balance of cash against you of 140,000 livres whereof no account could be given and for which he says worthy Mr Skinner would have got you arrested. If such was your negligence, its unpardonable on your side, having a partner, and by this you lay at their mercy. Still Delamain looks upon them equally as a pack of rogues.[24]

Arrogance and a hazy bookkeeping sense alike are evident in Boyd's attempt to get from Saule the balance which he alleged was due to the Bordeaux partnership, whose interest had been ceded to him. Saule, in bookkeeping terms, however, was a tougher nut to crack. Boyd had lost little time in November in writing to Saule, claiming a balance due from him, on the basis of the cession of Hennessy's interest. Saule went back over the transactions between the two houses as far as 1778, and reminded Boyd that 'had you gentlemen been so kind as to have furnished your account in November 1784 when we begged you would and since been constantly calling for, you should have saved yourselves and us a vast deal of trouble overhauling old accounts of near 11 years standing'. Saule found that articles to the credit of his house of 9430 livres had been omitted from Boyd's account, and articles to his debit also in a total of 2137 livres. The result was that far from there being a credit due to Boyd's house, they were in debt to Saule & Co.[25]

No reply was received to this letter until February 1788, although Boyd later claimed that a letter, entrusted to a negligent cooper, miscarried. He acceded to the substance of the adjustments proposed by Saule. However he claimed that not only should this sum be scaled down by 20 per cent, but that reimbursement of the guarantee on

Gastinel's 10,000 livres should be treated in like fashion. To this proposal Saule replied with spirit that 'you surely do not expect that we should take upon ourselves 20 per cent loss on this article whilst we had no other interest in that affair than by striving to oblige you in introducing you to our friend and procure you a facility you wished for and stood in need of'.[26] Eventually through his insistence, Saule was given promissory notes for the payment of his outstanding balance in nine months (less 20 per cent); Gastinel was given notes maturing in 12, 18 and 24 months for payment in full.[27] If the affair had been disastrous for Hennessy, it was not advantageous for Boyd either, which rebuts Hennessy's charge that Boyd's family circle simply wanted to get rid of him. Boyd's unscrupulous dealing is hinted at too in the fact that Delamain, who had employed Boyd to handle corn purchased on the orders of the *intendant* of Guienne, found that it had been sold by Boyd and the proceeds converted into brandy.[28]

Hennessy defended himself from the comments of his friends by alleging that other distillers were in the same plight, and were reduced to leaving their stills idle.[29] While conceding that their Chartrons business was ruinous in its want of profit, he attributed their problems to the partnership's high rent of 4000 livres. His defence of the rent was simply that 'you'll say a less would serve but its very difficult to find a proper one for the business as many will not admit of a distillery in their houses'.[30]

Leaving aside personal expenditure by Hennessy or a siphoning off of resources by Boyd, the fact is that Hennessy's capital seems to have fallen from above 32,000 livres in 1783 to effectively 15,000 livres in 1787 (25 per cent of his outstanding debt of 60,000 livres). In other words, for whatever reason, the business had used up 17,000 livres of capital. He was totally unable to account for the change: 'what should become of our friends' substance is what I cannot account for'.[31] Hennessy's ineffective role in the later stage of the house's existence left a residual bitterness even in Saule's recollection of the episode. In April 1788, in the wake of his own final settlement with Boyd, he observed: 'I can never conceive how you my friend quitted the house without seeing justice done to all your correspondents'.[32]

The settlement of the affair, according to Boyd, took up both his private fortune or patrimony (upwards of 23,000 livres), and the sums which his brother-in-law David Skinner had invested in the house.[33] Delamain, the largest single creditor of the house, received his reimbursement not in Boyd's notes but in Skinner's.[34] Whatever the nature of the transactions between the Chartrons and Royan houses, and the degree to which one partner or other made free with the resources of the partnership, the public outcome was that, for a firm in difficulties, a rather handsome settlement had been made with the creditors. In the short term the loser was Hennessy, who lost his interest in the distillery and who was now both without resources and was revealed more clearly and more publicly than ever as the ineffective businessman that he was.

Boyd in the autumn of 1787 gained possession of the distillery in the Chartrons, either the largest in Bordeaux or second largest after Andoe's, ahead of composition with the creditors in the following spring. The long-term outcome was more problematic. The settlement had not been a cheap one for him, and he was now short of capital. Guiliory, already Boyd's partner in the old Royan venture, was partner in the new venture.[35] Guiliory's association with the two Boyd ventures was the typical case of a man of standing and resources lending his name and only some capital. In the new venture Boyd's capital was 30,336 livres and Guiliory's 17,633. Guiliory himself was an honest and competent man, described by Saule as 'un homme plus qu'aisé'.[36] It was his examination of affairs in October 1787 and the long letters that he wrote to Boyd at the time that were the first stage in realism being forced on Boyd, and the Royan enterprise being wound down. With his losses, Boyd was short of capital from the start even in the reduced venture of 1788 in Bordeaux, and he relied heavily on the support of Skinner, who in January 1789 guaranteed a large credit with the Paris house of Mallet for the business.

In ceding the business Hennessy also vacated his living accommodation on the premises. On 24 October 1787 he had already, for the second time in his Bordeaux career, retired to lodgings. Biddy, his daughter, already in the country for several months with the Caseys, was to go for a second time into a convent. Hennessy had the run of the kitchen at John Galwey's. His son James, visiting Bordeaux almost a year later, found his father unclear about his plans, and wrote in exasperation to Saule: 'I find my father as I expected in a cruel situation, but what surprised me more is that he does nothing nor has he any establishment in view. How can he afford to pay the necessaries of life for himself and poor Biddy I cannot imagine.'[37] At fifty-nine Hennessy was becoming a old man, and his never great grasp of business may have been further impaired. Saule described him to Gastinel as 'ce brave homme mais faible et actuellement sur le déclin de l'age'.[38]

Rectification, the most speculative branch of the brandy business, declined in the second half of 1787. The fact that the crisis in the affairs of Hennessy and Boyd began before the fall-off in smuggling demand suggests that the problems lay within the business itself. Of course, though the brandy business at large recovered, reaching a great peak in 1789, the highest since 1720, the Bordeaux spirit business moved more fitfully. It promised very well in 1788, and then tapered off, with, on the evidence of the *congés*, only six of the year's twenty-nine suspected smuggling voyages occurring in the last four months of the year. Difficulties were still more acute in 1789 when London and Paris buyers paid over the odds for brandy. Boyd's new business had maintained some momentum, profiting also from the custom of Hennessy's old customers and brisk business for much of 1788. The sudden moves in demand and the swings in output in Bordeaux spirit business even provided scope for Hennessy acting as a brandy jobber and picking up lots in late 1787. He shared the commission with distillers, 'which I hope will be sufficient to defray Biddy's and my expenses until something better may offer'.[39] Hopes of getting back into distilling lingered on. A connection with Andoe was a mirage of late 1787, and later some hope of Samuel Turner, a nephew of Delamain's, joining him in Bordeaux was afloat. Throughout 1788 Hennessy hoped that his jobbing and brokerage might, if some capital could be put together, lay the basis for a renewed interest in distilling. His friend Knight even proposed that if Hennessy went into distilling again and Turner agreed to join, he would come in for a quarter share. The intermittent upward swings in brandy sustained persistent hopes of better times.

Boyd's bold new venture went under in the autumn of 1789 as a result of the soaring price of brandy in mid-1789 as much as the credit crisis. His turnover to September 1789 was only 626 *pièces*, well down on his turnover in the preceding year. Moreover, brandy or spirit supplied in ankers came to a mere 85 *pièces*, suggesting that the downturn in smuggling demand in late 1788 had proved permanent. By July 1789 his wild promises of orders to Cognac reflected his desperation. His partnership with Guiliory was dissolved in the same month.[40] Bankruptcy was then the only recourse. James Hennessy, advised of the Boyd bankruptcy by his father, told Samuel Turner: 'Marquez donc ce qu'on dit à la fin. On traite le voleur comme il mérite.'[41] In a letter to his father, the family resentment against Boyd burst out in all its force:

> The news you give me of the bankruptcy of the rascal who was formerly your partner does not surprize me. I only wish he may be used as he deserves. What does the great Skinner say to it? I have a mind to write him a letter of congratulations on the occasion.[42]

According to Hennessy's Bordeaux friend Thomas Knight, 'the entire of this affair is looked upon by all people as the most dirty affair that has passed here and the general remark is – how its easy to be seen how poor old Hennessy was plundered'.[43] Hennessy was owed 3000 livres on foot of recent transactions with Boyd, which prompted Jemmy to lament: 'Is it possible that again we must be the victim of that scoundrel.' In 1790 Richard, while in Bordeaux, attempted to pursue his interest in the creditors' settlement in the affair. The existing bad relationship with the Boyd circle may have complicated it. Richard reported that: 'I yesterday complained to Mr Fenwick [*i.e. Skinner's partner*] that I should not be treated as well as other creditors which he seemed surprised at, and advised me to apply to Skinner. I told him we were not on speaking terms.'[44]

Though author of his own misfortune, Hennessy was perhaps somewhat vindicated by the fact that not only was Boyd declared bankrupt, but a criminal prosecution was also to be launched against him,[45] and Guiliory, Boyd's partner, who paid many of the calls on Boyd, spoke of his 'follies and irregularity'.[46] On this occasion there was no escaping, and he seems to have forfeited the support of Skinner. James Hennessy asked: 'Where is he now? If the great Skinner said he was guilty of every villainy, I suppose he must fly the country

for without that man's protection there is no living in Bordeaux.'
Boyd did indeed disappear from Bordeaux: he last crops up in 1792,
about to take ship for the Île de France.[47]

HENNESSY'S RETURN TO COGNAC: THE NEW HOUSE OF HENNESSY & TURNER

One possible solution to Hennessy's problems was, as already mentioned, the prospect of an association with a nephew of Delamain.
This did not eventuate in Bordeaux as Hennessy had hoped, but it
came up again unexpectedly after October 1788 when Saule died. Out
of the resulting partnership the modern house of Hennessy grew.

As Delamain had several sons of his own, there was no hope of a
place for Samuel Turner in his uncle's house. In August 1787 Turner
seems to have communicated to James Hennessy, at the time a clerk
in Saule's house in Cognac, a proposal that he should join Hennessy
in the distilling business in Bordeaux.[48] Nothing came of it, probably
because investigation revealed Hennessy's affairs to be desperate. The
Hennessy problem in Bordeaux was that they had no capital, and
Jack Saule in the following January advised Hennessy's son James or
'Jemmy' to marry if a proper match could be found.[49] Given the
London trade's reluctance to buy in early and mid-1788, Jemmy was
able to spend much of mid-1788 in Bordeaux, perhaps looking for an
heiress. Such a need was all the more critical because Turner had now
formed a partnership with Broussard of Pons, a house with both past
and recent Irish associations.[50] The idea of a partnership was kept
alive less by the London market, which was at a stand in 1788, than
by the siren song of Bordeaux distilling: Pons supplied some brandy
for Bordeaux's rectifying stills, and some of the benefits of this had
come the way of the Broussards.

Saule's unexpected death opened up an unforeseen avenue. Delamain refrained from seeking an interest in the house, leaving it to the
widow and to James, if they so chose, to conduct the business in partnership.[51] The widow finally decided, given the poor prospects, against
continuing in business. The goodwill of the business was ceded to
Jemmy, but that itself did not make a start any easier. Jemmy wrote

almost immediately to the father that, unless he could get a partner with capital, he too would be unable to continue in business.[52] The question of partnership with Turner, though this time in a novel context, came up again, even as early as 20 October, and James had apparently commented sanguinely on the prospect.[53] Perhaps it was with this prospect in mind that Richard finally decided to abandon Bordeaux and that the house of Hennessy & *fils* emerged in December.[54]

The execution of the partnership with Turner was deferred by the fact that he was still partner in a business in Pons, but it was agreed in principle by May: one of the Hennessys' main Bordeaux correspondents was informed that month that 'Mr Turner will have the pleasure of seeing you and of telling you his intention of associating with us on his return here.'[55] Only in August was the contract signed. While the Hennessys seem to have had the major share of the capital of the new house, Turner's share made him the largest single partner. Turner was not brought in because of any demonstrable lack of experience or confidence about Jemmy. The key problem was one of capital. As soon as Turner entered as partner in August, James lost no time in visiting London to cultivate importers. Murdoch had already advised this course months earlier, and James's departure took place within the month of signature of the contract. Waiting to sail from Charente and with bitter memories of what had happened to his father in Bordeaux, he wrote to him on 30 August, imploring him to make a proper inventory of their effects so as to know where they stood, and also to pay attention to the business: 'pray, my dear father, to get well-acquainted with all that regards us in the business line. Above all things [see] that the books are kept regularly.' There was little need to fear. Turner was a man of quite different mettle to Richard, and Jemmy too proved from the start a man of determination and single-mindedness.

JOHN SAULE IN COGNAC: THE EARLIER
FOUNDATIONS FOR THE NEW HOUSE OF 1789

The house rested on the foundations laid by Saule. Victoire's dowry and a loan from Delamain may help to account for the change in the fortunes of the house. He shipped 596 puncheons in 1782, the highest figure attained by the house since its inception in 1765. The figure rose further to 945 puncheons in 1783, but it fell back in 1784 to 581 puncheons. The importance of his London trade prompted him to visit London in 1784, the first true business visit abroad by the house. He left Cognac on 12 June. We have a fleeting glimpse of his week or so in Paris, its news a combination of up-to-date fact and fantasy: 'I go this evening to Versailles to a ball at court where I shall meet my old acquaintance Gustavus, incognito Comte de la Haga. To-morrow I shall be at St. Cloud at the departure of a famous ballon.' Hennessy seems to have left Bordeaux to look after Saule's affairs in Cognac during his absence,[56] which illustrates all too well Hennessy's readiness to neglect his own affairs. There was admittedly a quid pro quo, though the thought of a good turn requiring a payment in kind would never have entered the mind of either friend. Saule was to take James Hennessy to London with him.

After leaving school in Douai, James had been employed in the Blake house in Dunkirk transcribing letters as every apprentice did. Too many young Blakes meant that James had no future in the house. The main purpose of taking James to London was the hope of securing a place for him in the house of Herries, with a base in the Austrian Lowlands and an interest in the Mediterranean brandy trade. This came to nothing. Saule and James seem to have spent seven weeks in London. We know little of what Saule did in London, apart from a reference to 'sundry expenses at Windsor': the parallel with the visit to Versailles is evident. His total expenditure on the round trip came to 5207 livres. Of this, 478 livres were spent on various commissions executed for Delamain and other friends, and 763 livres was James's share of the outlay. Purchases for himself and his wife at 1508 livres seem rather high.

There were important consequences of the trip. The first was that, failing of a place in London, James entered into Saule's house as a clerk. The second was that the long visit provided the basis of an expansion in Saule's business. On his way he had been given letters of introduction by his Paris banker to the Arbouins of London.[57] This introduction did not lead to great things, though Arbouin did order some brandy from Saule in subsequent years. More important was the acquaintance struck up with the house of Yeats & Brown, and especially with one member of the house, Tim Brown (nephew of the original proprietor of the business, Yeats). Even after his departure warm memories of Saule's visit lingered on. The magical quality of his presence, seen when he had been in Sweden a decade earlier, glowed again.

Several years later Saule contrasted his fortunes during six years 'like a slave' with the 'unexpected success' which followed his London visit:

> Was it not for the accidental acquaintance I made with one house in London, to whom I had the good luck to become afterwards useful, I know not how my establishment here would have proved. That acquaintance alone has almost ensured me all the business I have.

In 1787 he had seventeen London customers, and his volume of business with one, John & Walker Gray, was slightly larger than with Yeats & Brown. However, the two houses were his only large customers, and some major importers were totally absent from his invoices: what he seems to be saying is that the goodwill of Yeats & Brown helped to enlarge his business. There were over sixty importers in London, usually dividing their custom between several Cognac shippers. Hence Saule's acquisition of a large house like Yeats & Brown was a stroke of fortune or genius. We may see in it a consequence of Saule's charm, and of an association between a young Cognac man and a new generation in an established London house. Yeats (with Joseph Brown as a partner) was the founder of the house; a new generation was taking over in the mid-1780s, Tim Brown in London and a brother Isaac in Dunkirk. The phrase 'us beginners, peddlers in the trade' occurs in a letter from Yeats & Brown to Martell in 1785.[58] The same letter in fact refers vaguely to the problem which Saule helped to solve, and which cemented the new friendship, and goes on quite frankly to refer to business they were passing into Saule's hands: 'Mr Saule's very great attention and politeness to us in the affair of the *Zee paard* merits everything but we have told him that his rival [*i.e. Martell Lallemand*] as our oldest acquaintance must not be quite deserted. We wish we could sell as many as you both would trust us with.' While the first contact between the two houses was a favour by Saule relating to a ship, it rapidly ripened into close friendship. On both sides, letters were full of warm expressions of friendship, and gifts, sometimes expensive ones, were exchanged. Tim Brown in July 1788, writing about his daughter who was going to stay with the Saules, gave mock-serious instructions: Saule was to keep all books written in loose language out of the way, also all priests.[59] While Saule's letters to Hennessy were now very sober, the tone of Brown's reply suggests that it may have been prompted by something of Saule's old bantering spirit in his letter.

LOSSES IN DEALINGS WITH THE IRISH SMUGGLERS

Saule's business seemed to promise well. The one dark cloud before 1788 was his disastrous liaison with the Irish smuggling interest. In itself at the time it held promise of a more sustained link with the smuggling interest than that held by any of the other houses: he provided brandy for four voyages by a small Irish smuggling confederacy which promised to become regular customers.[60]

Troubles within the confederacy itself began to emerge with the fourth voyage, and Saule later had an unpleasant initiation into the problems of dealings with his new contacts. In the wake of the success, as far as he was concerned, of four cargoes, he was less than wise in future dealings with Robert White, front man of the former group, who, when the confederacy collapsed, proposed to deal on a large scale on account of a new business interest. He came out in 1786 in a large vessel said to be 100 to 150 tons, unheard of in the smuggling trade. Moreover, though Saule did not appreciate the significance of it, his links were not with the established business interests in the tiny smuggling port of Rush, fairly regular customers in 1783–4 with whom Hennessy in Bordeaux had close and satisfactory business dealings, but with a motley confederacy which was not part of the established shipping interest in Rush. The true story began to unfold only after bills for White's new and enlarged venture, which Saule foolishly took, bounced.

Though even the last of the original four voyages had a safe outcome, despite near disaster for the smugglers both in France and Ireland, it did not have a happy effect on the smuggling concern itself. The chief organizer of the venture, Tallon, a brandy and general merchant whose ties with the Charente went back as far as 1772 when he visited it as a youth of fourteen, was simply an outside investor in a motley confederacy of small business interests, which fell out over the irregularities in the management of the fourth voyage. The association had originated in 1784, and Tallon had been put in contact with the other investors in the project through an attorney named Browne, married to a cousin-german of Tallon's. According to Tallon, 'Mr Browne ... proposed to me to take a concern in a cargo of brandy and pointed out to me the plan and place of landing in such a manner as seemed to have no doubt of success.' Tallon's contacts were in the town of Drogheda: 'many particular friends of mine in Drogheda declared to me they had never more satisfaction in dealing with any man than they had with Mr White. On this the *Hamilton* was [*word missing*] and a security lodged with me for three quarters of the supposed cost of the cargo'. The first three cargoes were all landed safely, and successfully sold, even if in typical manner accounts were slow to be settled and no general settlement among the partners had taken place. In Tallon's words, the first cargo had been 'shipped and every cask safely landed and sold. I was given to understand the cargo would net £800 but it was so dispersed and charges not brought in that no settlement was made. A second cargo was safely landed ... Great part of these cargoes was sold in the country, the amount of which it seemed was not coming in, and on pointing out this to Mr White he agree with me Dublin market was the best and every single cask of the third cargo, 200 small casks, was safely sent to Dublin and sold.'[61]

Tallon's interest in the operation was a mere fourth. The balance of the venture was financed by Browne, his attorney relative and two more disreputable parties, Robert White from Rush, a failed businessman, now attempting to re-establish himself by an active role in organizing smuggling ventures, and Thomas Collins, a Dublin merchant in linen and printed cottons, who like White had failed, and who was not only ready to invest in such ventures but also saw in them some outlet for his textiles. For such figures, smuggling, rather like drugs today, seemed to offer an apparently easy method back to riches and success. Collins had failed, owing £16,000 to £18,000, and the creditors had been paid very little.[62] He was to achieve later notoriety. Though making a start in business again, he failed once more, and in need of money became an informer for the government, reporting regularly on the activities of the first society of United Irishmen. His letters to Dublin Castle from 1792 to 1794 were the prime source of information for government on the first Society of United Irishmen.[63] They illustrate an intelligent man, somewhat disabused of people's motives, in financial straits, and surprisingly, given his previous activities and associates, both God-fearing and anti-Catholic.

Smuggling operations inevitably involved a coming together of urban interests – in this instance Tallon, Browne and Collins – and a rural or coastal interest which held the prime responsibility for executing the actual operations. White was the key figure in Rush. He was not part of the established group of Rush operators, and he and those around him represented new interests pushing into the business in its boom in the early 1780s alongside more seasoned operators. The mistake Tallon and his Dublin associates made was to be too easily taken in by White. Hennessy, reporting to Saule from his enquiries about White and Boyle among the established smugglers plying to Bordeaux, had to report that 'the old captains in the Dublin trade now here can give me no account of them'.[64] According to John Saule Kennedy's reports too, there was no more 'infamous villain than said White, he failed here some years ago and made it up with his creditors for almost £25,000 and before the first payment became due he was detected in making off to America with all the effects …'. A statute of bankruptcy was secured against him in consequence, and he paid only four shillings in the pound.[65] White was married to a Miss Rice whose father was a distiller in Monaghan. Thus he fitted into a diffuse network of small interests reaching in the case of the distiller as far afield as Monaghan. Small distillers, in the habit of defrauding the revenue of some of the taxes on their own distillation, were familiar with the market for illicit spirit. Moreover, in the wake of new revenue restrictions, they found it easier, at any rate in the relatively law-abiding province of Leinster, to import spirits rather than to run risks in evading the new regulations on production. White's doubtful business activities extended even into Dublin port, as at one stage he had a project afoot in partnership to secure the repayment of the duty on 35 to 40 hogsheads of tobacco by fraudulently declaring it for export and relanding it the next day. Such activities ensured that he was known to and useful to 'respectable parties' like Tallon and Browne. According to Saule's cousin John Saule Kennedy at a later date, 'White's intimates were Browne an attorney, Collins and Tallon; they were seldom asunder'. However, the real appeal of White rested on his contacts and relatives in the countryside, necessary for the dispersal of cargoes, such as Moncks the distiller, or Boyle, 'a poor rucker in Fingall not worth £50 and married to a sister of White's',[66] the latter only emerging in the story when White drew doubtful bills on him in part payment of a later cargo.

The enterprise, which had so far prospered on the growing popular market for spirits, was soon marked by conflicts in the motley confederacy itself. Tallon's account hints at their early appearance, as White had marketed the first two cargoes in a rural and slow-paying milieu in which he had his own contacts and relatives. Tallon's insistence, however, directed the third cargo to the more solvent urban market. The problems became still more acute with the fourth cargo. One of the problems of these loose confederacies was that of controlling the subordinate members. In this instance, on the homeward voyage, a large quantity of tea, some five hundred chests of nankeen, was taken aboard. The tea was not part of the original plan, as far as Tallon, the more conventional figure, was concerned, and as leaks sprung on the homeward fourth voyage, the prolongation of the voyage by calling at Lorient for the tea added to the wear and tear, and put the vessel at risk from the sea. The venture had already run the risk of seizure in France by bringing out cloth, which was contraband in France, and which, after it could not be landed in Charente, was still aboard when they reached Lorient; as Collins had a business in printed cottons and linens, we may suspect that this was a private venture of his. No sane businessman would have put a commercial venture at risk for the sake of what was in commercial terms a very small speculation like Collins' cloth. Such risks, combined with the unscheduled visit to Lorient, sowed the seeds of dissension. The tea, moreover, was in Irish revenue law automatically contraband if found on a vessel from the continent. A consequence also of the investment in the tea which enlarged the outlay was that it was harder for members to discharge their obligations among themselves. Tallon was left unpaid some £300 (later said to be £400) by White, and was unable to recover it. According to Tallon's later apologia to Saule, 'this the first thing that made me an unfavourable idea of his principles: I was determined to have no more connections.' The whole operation fell apart at this stage.

White's ambitions, on the other hand, were whetted by his operations so far, his methods even catching the attention of the sober Martell house itself. In intimating that the *Hamilton* would be back soon on a fifth voyage, White envisaged moving to a larger scale of operations: 'I expect to be out here directly in a large vessel, finding a large field for business'.[67] The fifth voyage of the *Hamilton* never happened, and the reason is clear: the confederacy broke up in quarrels over the fourth voyage. By early 1786 White took a concern in a large vessel reportedly of 150 tons and went off for Charente in February.[68] The vessel's name was the *Good Intent*, master Richard Hore: the Hores were a major business interest in Rush, Richard Hore's stake in the vessel outlived the confederacy, and the standing of the Hores gave the venture a cloak of credibility. The partnership was, according to John Saule Kennedy in a letter of 26 October 1786, one of four men: White, John Moncks (in County Monaghan, where through Rice's wife he had ties), Thomas Kelly and William Keough. Her departure on her return voyage from the port, burthen one hundred tons, is duly recorded in the Charente *congés* on 10 March 1786.

Tallon, the more orthodox businessman, and Browne, a lawyer however shifty, had by now fallen out with their associates; and the rump of the confederacy continued on their own, supported by some new recruits. Saule, who knew nothing of this, was warned on 14 February by Knight of advice from an unnamed friend who 'cautions how you deal with Mr White, when he arrives with you, to do nothing with him without such bills as you very well know'. Knight added that this friend's advice was disinterested, and he would stand to be paid £400 which White owed him if the success of the venture were to put White in funds. Unfortunately, through anxiety not to reveal to Saule the full extent of Tallon's own past relations with a doubtful party, his name was not divulged. As the Tallons had dealings with either Hennessy or Saule as far as 1772, had it been attached to the warning, it might have given it the weight it warranted.

Unfortunately Knight's advice was not heeded by Saule. Saule had formed a high regard for White. He retailed the news of what he regarded as his good fortune in his letters to Hennessy. Hennessy routinely replied that 'you have a stout order from Mr White who I hope has given you good credits', and later, no doubt in response to further news, commented that 'White's plan is a very good one the vessel and casks being of such gauge diminishes by much your risk'.[69] The point in Hennessy's letter was that on technical grounds a large vessel and large casks in place of a smaller vessel and small casks lessened the risk of a revenue seizure (at law vessels with brandy had to be of a minimum tonnage and brandy casks of a minimum size).

Hennessy, experienced in dealing with smugglers, had adverted to the need for caution with regard to bills of exchange. Saule on the other hand was influenced by knowledge of White from four preceding voyages, none of which had presented problems as far as payment to him was concerned. White's order was a large one for 200 hogsheads (100 puncheons), and Saule's sanguine state of mind as his business expanded has to be taken into account. He now made the cardinal sin, in disregard of accepted trade practice, of accepting unorthodox bills. Smugglers either secured through their Dublin associates credits at recognized London houses which their French contacts then drew on, or they brought out cash with them. Out of the total of over £900 in White's purchase, only £80 was in a recognized trade bill. The balance was paid in quite unorthodox paper drawn by White himself on North Dublin associates, one of them his brother-in-law, Boyle, and the other a partner in the enterprise itself. The bills were two on Keough for a total of £335, and one on Boyle for £550, all later protested by Saule.[70]

The full picture was gradually pieced together by John Saule Kennedy, who had already observed as early as 15 April 1786 that 'you could not possibly form a worse connection than you have done'. One of the bills, for a total of £310, was on one of White's partners, William Keough. Kennedy eventually tracked down one of White's other partners, John Moncks, in Donabate, who stated that there had been four interests, each for a quarter, in the ownership of the *Good Intent*: Moncks himself, White, Keough and a fourth or joint interest of 'Kelly and some other in Rush'.[71] As always in smuggling ventures, there were further interests. Collins, whose venture in textiles had nearly brought the fourth voyage of the *Hamilton* to grief, had another small consignment of cottons and printed linens on board, the proceeds of which were to be invested in brandy on the joint account of White and Collins.[72] Moncks admitted his management and sale of the 200 hogsheads of brandy. Hennessy, inquiring from the masters of Rush vessels in Bordeaux on behalf of Saule, had been able to inform him that the cargo had been safely disposed of. One of the masters reported seeing 'of a morning 46 carts loaded with White's cargo of brandy come into Thomas Street accompanied by four custom house officers and that all was delivered safe', a success even if he also reported that he had heard that some days later ten hogsheads had been seized.[73]

White himself was the only member of this rogues' gallery with whom Saule had dealings. The bill on Keough was protested, and White assured Saule that he would honour the bills himself, though tellingly all that came in the wake of protest was assurances, not new bills. In attempting to recover money, there was a problem in 'gripping', i.e. in delivering court summons, as White 'resides mostly in Fingall at a place that I am told no bailiff dare be bold enough to venture'.[74] Saule Kennedy eventually confronted Moncks and in person served a subpoena on him drawn up by Browne. Moncks had the effrontery to tell Saule Kennedy that in serving a subpoena on him a wrong method had been taken 'to get Mr Saule his money as he could get people enough to swear he had not one single hogshead on board'.[75] Tallon – whose doubtful frequentations gave him some knowledge of unorthodox business methods – thought it a mistake to send a bailiff after White, as bribe-seeking bailiffs often intimated in advance to their quarry news of the impending visit. Tallon advocated accompanying the bailiff or 'gripper' to White's residence.[76] In this case, the subpoena was eventually served, by setting a thief to catch a thief. The bitterness of the quarrel among the parties to the fourth voyage of the original partnership meant not only that Tallon introduced Saule Kennedy to Browne but that Browne himself eventually served the subpoena on White.[77] Saule, accustomed to the more orderly style of business of France and fearful that Browne was in both camps, observed that 'its evident that he was much in White's confidence'.[78] However, whatever Saule's misgivings in leaving matters in such hands, Hennessy approved of it on the principle that 'a rogue is the fastest man to deal with thieves such as you have been unlucky to deal with'.[79]

Saule had been scandalized by the fact that all reports made it clear that White had been very much in evidence in Rush. A smuggling master told Hennessy in September that White was to be seen every day in Rush, and that he might have an interest in the prospective cargo from France in a further voyage by the *Good Intent* which was being got ready to go to sea again.[80] Tallon reported that the vessel lay quite openly in the port of Rush 'where she went through a great repaire and I am told £500 or £600 laid out on her'.[81] She eventually sailed for Bordeaux, appearing there in November 1786 under the same master, Richard Hore, 'a tall lively clean man who commanded her when a cutter at Charente'. The master told Hennessy that when she had been at Charente White had had a half interest in the vessel (Moncks' information, probably more accurate, suggested a quarter).[82] News of a past interest implies that he no longer had an interest in the vessel, and other information suggested that his original interest had been purchased with bills which later were not honoured.[83]

Saule was quite scandalized at the openness of the contempt for legal niceties:

> Ireland is perhaps the only part of Europe where a man cannot obtain justice of such a villain ... incredible that such a fellow should arrive and stay in the capital and 12 miles round it and that he cannot be laid hold of ... having given you the slip and got off with his vessel and property. Has he no effects to seize? ... If so a man might as well trade with savages.[84]

News had come from several sources, including Captain Hore, master of the vessel on her Charente visit, that Keough had funds in hand to pay the bill drawn on him by White. The problem was, as one correspondent observed, 'to prove this and force him to refund this. I must leave to your good care, as also to obtain proofs who the dormant partners were and render them responsible for their shares in the cargo'. Tallon had suggested that Saule should have the vessel arrested in Bordeaux, but without a judgment in advance in Ireland in support of the claim, he could leave himself open to counter action in France for heavy costs and damages. Thus without a warrant from Ireland Saule, or Hennessy in Bordeaux on his behalf, was powerless to proceed against Forsters, who loaded the *Good Intent* and who might have funds of White's in their hands, or against the vessel itself, should it reappear in Bordeaux.[85] Nor did Tallon, who in any event had probably cast his own involvement in a somewhat more passive light than was the case, continue to be of much assistance. In the autumn he had played a useful role in getting Browne's services in tracking down his erstwhile associates. His falling out with White had alienated him from his former Rush brandy milieu; the failure of Clem Cosgrave of Dungarvan, a grain trader with whom he had a partnership, gave rise to a decree of bankruptcy against Tallon as well.[86] He made arrangements with his creditors at the end of the year, and left for Dungarvan.

Nothing good came of White's bills apart from the small one on a London house. Deducting from the total due to Saule the value of some of the cottons and linen brought on the vessel – which had been successfully landed and some of which had been sold to the firm of Dumoustier & Jarnac in La Rochelle – the net indebtedness to him amounted to £812 Irish or 18,509 livres.[87] The failure of the La Rochelle house in the interval added to Saule's losses, as it was likely to pay no more than 40 or 50 per cent.[88] The proceeds of the textiles came to £119. If this sum, now in doubt, is added to the rest of the debt, the total was almost £1000.

White himself was not on the *Good Intent* when it finally appeared in Bordeaux in the autumn of 1786, and he does not seem to have had an interest in this voyage. He left Ireland by October; Saule Kennedy heard that he had gone to Liverpool under the assumed name of Rice. Kiernan, an attorney with whom White had lodged in Dublin, said he had powers of attorney to offer 15 per cent settlement of his debts. Reports were abroad that he had sailed for Norfolk.[89] However, he was still in Portsmouth in February 1787 and had the effrontery to write to Saule, promising to make good Saule's loss in the end, but asking for the proceeds of the linen and cotton to be remitted in the mean time to him.[90] Eventually from Norfolk he wrote in April professing that it was Saule's pursuit of him that had compelled him to sail to America: 'your friend pursued me so close, [I] could not stir out to look after any matters without endangering my person, nor could I ever find who that person was, that I might lay my situation before him'. He professed that he would return shortly with powers of attorney to take possession of £500 in Bordeaux which would reduce his liability by half. If he could settle his affairs in Dublin, he would remit the balance. This seems to have been an alleged legacy to be paid into the hands of the house of Barton in Bordeaux from a relation of his wife (her brother resided in America). The matter was still alive in June 1788, when Saule entertained the hope of receiving the funds.[91]

Nothing further came of these promises, and silence tells its own story. It is conceivable White himself was wronged by some of his associates; in April 1787 he referred to them as villains, which, while it could represent White's infinite capacity to put himself in the best light, could also be true. Knight, who through his Tallon connection had information from this milieu, thought that White had received but a small part of the proceeds of the last cargo.[92] He was a plausible man and made a good impression. Edward Connelly of Barcelona referred to his vanity.[93]

His long letters in the spring of 1787 putting the best gloss on things are certainly consistent with this appraisal. Saule, taken in in the past by White, was once more greatly impressed by the letter of April, and in June wrote to Saule Kennedy suggesting that, if White returned, he should not be arrested in case that might exasperate him and damage the prospect of settlement.[94] In March 1787, he had threatened White rather helplessly with 'the extensive connections I can tell you that I have in every part of the globe'.[95] In the wake of White's letter he wrote a conciliatory letter, stating that he knew of White's interest in going to America as his wife's relatives were there. Referring to White's letters he said that 'they and my wife (who is a great advocate in your favour) have changed my resentment against you to pity'.[96] But even a year later there was no further news from White, and in the autumn of 1788 Saule himself was dead.

SAULE'S SPECULATIVE BUSINESS EXPANSION IN 1787–8

Saule's loss, about one tenth of his turnover, must have wiped out profits for the year. Its impact was all the more serious as Saule was carrying a large stock of brandy and in late 1787 an acute credit crisis set in. At the outset of 1787 he had it in mind to go to London to further his business, and did so later in the year. His invoices in 1787 at 1470 puncheons were above the previous year's level, and in 1788 (up to 1 September) rose further to 1562 puncheons. This understates the expansion of business in 1788 because, as a result of laying in large stocks in 1787, he was left with substantial amounts of brandy in his warehouse unsold in September 1788. The invoices to September plus stock he had on hand in his warehouses at the time (450 puncheons) would amount to 2000 puncheons.

This figure would roughly match Martell Lallemand's turnover. The 1780s were a decade of growth in the brandy trade, something that does not emerge in the interested representations in the early 1780s from the region seeking to make a case for tax concessions. They painted a picture of gloom and doom, seizing on the secular decline and eventual disappearance of the Dutch and Hamburg trades. In reality the Paris trade reached new peaks and the English trade was larger than at any time since the heady days of the Guernsey stake in 1720. The significance of Saule's expansion was its almost total dependence on London. The tensions with Martell's arose from the fact that they likewise, a few Irish orders apart, had an exclusively English and largely London custom.

Over the decade Saule had a string of successes. Even as early as 1780, the London house of Steele divided their orders between Martell, Augier and Saule.[97] In the mid-1780s Yeats & Brown switched their business from the Martell house to Saule, and in the short-lived upsurge in smuggling business Saule's five cargoes for White seemed to presage that there too he might outshine Martell Lallemand in a field which was novel and specialized. In late 1787 he outbid Martell Lallemand for brandy, in the most concentrated buying spree by a merchant since 1720. The pace in London visits too was set by Saule with journeys in 1784 and 1787.

Martell's, ever since the time of Lallemand's problems in containing opposition in the 1760s, had shown resentment of the Irish challenge, and no social contact existed before the 1790s between the Irish houses and Martell Lallemand. Saule regarded them as hostile to him, and retrospectively attributed to them his failure as far back as 1769 to get a place in Delaps. The bitterness was already established in 1779 when Saule, referring to Lallemand, wrote:

> ... my lot is to find him everywhere. It was he who prevented my going to Mr Delap in 1769, it was he was the first informer against my wife and me, and now I dare say he has thrown me out of the way to obtain this small credit. I am sure the Augiers are incapable of doing me any prejudice, and I know full well that Lallemand is very sorry to see me doing anything this year, therefore if Messrs T. & B. wrote that house I am sure that they could not get from thence a satisfactory answer.[98]

In 1787 he told Richard Hennessy that he lost business through 'my envious neighbours, rich competitors who thought to crush me 'ere I could have wings to fly! They seem to love Hennessy now because he is not dangerous, but were he so, they would soon run him down.' [99]

On Saule's second visit he took his wife with him. They left at the end of June, and they did not get back till 1 November. Saule obviously had a good deal of confidence in Jemmy, whom he left in charge. Enquiries about the prospective trends in the new season needed sensitive handling as brandy importers maintained lines of communication with several *négociant* houses. Incompetence would be quickly detected and would prove damaging to the reputation of the house. Saule on his return wrote to Richard: 'I hope and pray that my long absence four months must have done a great deal of good to your son, who was obliged to work on his own bottom. I have not had time to look over his operations as yet, but think they must be satisfactory.'

We can suspect, knowing Saule, that the London visit was extended for social reasons, though once he left London in October, with a new buying season about to begin, he lost little time in getting back to Cognac. He spent eight days in Dunkirk, itself an important centre of the brandy trade, but only three in Paris. Isaac Brown of Dunkirk had been in London in the course of Saule's visit, and both men returned to Calais together, sharing expenses. Purchases made in London during Saule's stay amounted to £66.11s.6d., including a ring for Victoire for £4.14s.6d., a coffee urn, 1000 needles, eight knitting needles and a service of flint ware. Some other purchases were business ones, humdrum domestic ones or little commissions or presents for friends in Cognac. The Brown influence was reflected in the friends made in London. Returning with Saule and Jemmy to Cognac was Peter Cherry, son of George Cherry, head of the admiralty victualling office in Somerset House. They arranged for his accommodation in Angoulême. A number of warm letters from the father followed in 1788, suggesting that a very close relationship had been established in London. Letters from the Browns remained numerous and affectionate. Tim Brown sent out a peacock and hen for Victoire, a cask of porter of his own brewing, and a Gloucester cheese. To this dispatch Mr Cherry added a cheese also and stuff for a gown for Victoire. Other items came from London at other times, including, in February 1788, a dumb waiter from the brandy importer Thomas Bevan. In the aftermath of the visit too they looked after the son of Timson, a major brandy importer in London.

The first real expansion in Saule's business had come in the wake of his 1784 visit to London. By 1785 his turnover had increased threefold, and from 1785 to 1788 it was never to fall below 1398 puncheons. This was all the more creditable as conditions which had been brisk in 1785 were somewhat less so in late 1786. In early 1787 prices were not rising.[100] However, the calm in early 1787 was largely artificial as there was a hitch in the application of the new Franco-British treaty reducing tariffs: 'at present our trade is almost at a stand, until the treaty of commerce takes place'.[101] Hence the British trade was very much on Saule's mind. With the prospects of a larger trade in the wake of reduction in the duties, less brandy was likely to be sent to Dunkirk and in future brandy merchants would ship directly, taking brandy from Dunkirk only in the winter months.[102] He had hopes of becoming British consul, and Delamain entertained a like hope. It is not known whether either man knew of the other's interest in the post. But Saule's business had made a new man of him, a phenomenon which Hennessy had detected in 1785, when Saule saw even Delamain as a rival. Hennessy chided Saule for being 'a hundred times more jealous about your business than you were two years ago when you had not half so much of it'. By January 1788 Saule observed to Hennessy that 'Had I not profited a little of the instruction given me in my youth and in time had the good fortune to marry, to see into the dangers of my many years of dissipation ... I might now be a beggar'.[103]

Coming back in late November to the Charente, armed with what he thought was sound intelligence of impending war with France over the political crisis in Holland and of consequent rising prices, Saule was in something of a frenzy to buy before others set to as well. In the three weeks to 19 December 'I have not stirred out of the house but on Saturdays markets and Sunday nights'. He had, he said, 'large orders'.[104] His purchases in this concentrated period exceeded the total in his invoices for the first nine months of the entire year 1788. London purchasers, unimpressed by the high prices in January 1788, held off buying (and were at first all the more content to do so because London credit was tight); on the other hand with the first direct vessels coming and more expected, *négociants* in the Charente laid in stocks in advance of orders. In May he had stocks of 900 puncheons, and more particularly as he said to Hennessy in May, 'We must say that we have thus almost in our hands all the old brandies which remain in the province.'[105]

Worse still for Saule, with his credit overextended, he had to admit that 'we have only a prospect of a round loss, and unluckily I have distressed myself by having on hands 1500 hogshead of brandy, which run up a large sum, and the best hopes I have is to lose what I earned this last year'.[106] While Charente *négociants* had laid in stock in anticipation of a lively demand (Saule in November and December, the other *négociants* with a time lag and at more favourable prices), the London importers, little enamoured of speculative buying by local *négociants* ahead of orders, were aware of the unreal expectations in Charente. An undeclared war of nerves developed between the two sides, in which in a concerted fashion the

London importers held back, confident that the market would eventually break.

Surprisingly, Saule and the other *négociants* did not realize that the importers' need to combine to charter vessels created what was in effect a ring of buyers among the influential brandy houses in London. This ring was already in the making in 1787: at that time the important London house of Bevan, referring to new houses in the trade, told Martell's that they would confine space in their vessel to the 'old' importers.[107] Even into August and September brandy stocks were not clearing.[108] Many London importers were holding back in unison in the hope of a killing when the market collapsed. At the end of August some two- or three-year-old brandy had sold for 106 livres, and Yeats & Brown intimated to Saule that they had been advised to expect the market to fall to 65 and 70.[109] Bevan observed in August that 'it proves we were not much out in our opinion near 12 months ago'.[110] From what Martell Lallemand had retailed to Saule, even their house was resigned to a large loss on their business in 1788. Martell Lallemand, the house with the largest business and the closest contacts in London, suffered least. Quite apart from special circumstances in 1789, their huge and unprecedented volume of business in 1789 was a consequence both of London awareness of their 1788 caution and judgment, and of the havoc the gamble in 1788 had caused among their local rivals.

Given that the London market was holding off, the Paris trade was inevitably the most active market in 1788, and houses there, quick to realize that the 1788 vintage would not be a good one, enlarged their cognac buying by the onset of autumn. These rising orders for Paris alone prevented a disastrous fall in prices at the end of the summer, and even Saule, who had little business with inland houses, in September sold 100 puncheons of brandy and 25 puncheons of spirit to Pierre Nouel of Angoulême: 'by this means I shall clear my stores of 100 puncheons brandy which you may judge I shall pick out of my hardest flavoured ... This is a losing sale, but I am glad of it as I may buy new brandy in time much cheaper'. Some brandy he had held in Dunkirk Saule was able to sell at a profit, but the loss on the deal with Nouel cancelled out that gain.[111] The downward slide in prices expected by London did not materialize. That inevitably meant the collapse of the London ring.

Saule took ill in September. Jemmy had gone to Bordeaux but he was advised by Saule not to hurry back as there was no business to execute. In his financial difficulties, Saule, so fond of show, had cut back even on clothes:

> My clothes are grown threadbare. Still I regret buying a coat being much in want of funds and having made such a bad year. However if you can get me a fine *white* cloth very white, buy me enough to make a coat only. I believe that an ell and a half will do. I will want a hand-some button for my corbeaux coloured coat but am afraid buttons *à la mode* will cost too much. If I could get 18 for 18 livres you may bring them. A trifle more or less will be of no consequence.[112]

Saule's correspondence had been free of mention of ill health so far. In retrospect what he said three years previously gains significance as the first portent of serious illness:

> I was taken very ill the night of good Friday. I thought I was going off on the Saturday morning. Since that time I have been recovering slowly. I unluckily caught cold about three week ago and since that time I have not been able to get rid of it. It seems to have fallen upon my breast, and I am just as if I was an asmatick. I walk with pain, and hardly can get up our street. The worst is that it prevents my sleeping.

He attributed the illness at this time to 'a too great application to business during four or five months of this winter. Our correspon-dence is a laborious part and I have been constantly tied down to the desk.' He promised that if the vintage turned out well he would get an English or Irish clerk to help out 'as I am grown tired and dis-gusted with slavery'.[113] In the aftermath of this illness James Hen-nessy, no longer assured of the continuance of the place in the counting house of his Ostend relatives, found employment under Saule.

Sadly the end was not long in coming. Illness in September 1788, only the second one of consequence in his correspondence of many years, quickly turned into progressive decline. He first felt unwell at the beginning of the month. In reply to James, who meantime had returned to Cognac and reported on Saule's condition, Richard Hen-nessy expressed unease on 23 September. What proved Saule's final illness began the preceding day, and he died on 5 October. Hennessy junior wrote the following day to Tim Brown that Jack Saule

> fell sick the twenty-second of last month with fever that turned out bilious and putrid. Since the thirtieth, he remained almost in constant delirium and yesterday morning at half past seven he expired after a long agony. I remarked as did his servant man that was with me that the last name he mentioned was yours.[114]

For the widow, the death was a tragic blow. According to Hennessy, she was 'almost motionless and quite inconsolable'. Delamain told Yeats & Brown that 'his poor widow is in a most miserable situation, and it must be a work of much time to alleviate her grief'. Economic problems can only have added to her worry. At first it seems to have been her belief that she and James Hennessy could continue the business together. Writing on the day of Saule's death, James, while conceding there would have to be a forced sale of brandy which would reduce the value of the assets, assured Mallet that 'les affaires … se trouvent bonnes'. Delamain speculated whether Victoire would continue the business on her own 'or perhaps she may in conjunction with a very worthy young man Mr Hennessy'.[115]

Within days inspection of the books revealed a parlous state of affairs, and she decided to make over the interest of the house to James Hennessy, who would bring in a partner.[116] The problem had been broached with Delamain even before Saule died: 'Young Hennessy is a most honest worthy lad. He two days before Saule's death called on our J. Delamain who as far as was decent looked into matters.'[117] Delamain suggested that the house could cover only 30 to 35 per cent of its liabilities. A fuller appraisal by Delamain and Augier was completed in days after his death, and on 14 October they reported in somewhat more optimistic vein than the house could cover 50 per cent of its engagements.[118]

The matter was complicated by the fact that some brandies had been purchased on the account of two London houses who had put Saule in funds for the purchases.[119] Delamain thought that the claims of both houses to these brandies would not pose problems, as the creditors of the house would be interested in a quick settlement.[120] Substantial losses would be occasioned by brandy purchased up to

January at prices as high as 148 livres whereas the market price on 2 October, three days before Saule died, was 120.[121] Delamain noted that 'Poor Saule's situation has particularly been occasioned by too great desire to do extensive business, buying large parcels at high rates from the country people who go about to the farmers' houses exceeding the market price and thus being obliged to reduce afterwards in order to preserve his commissions. As the writer was his friend he often remonstrated with him on the inconsistency of this conduct.'[122] The estimated losses of at least 70,000 livres were made up of 24,000 livres incurred by the cargo provided to White, 10,000 livres in miscellaneous losses 'hereabouts', and the expected loss on the sale of brandy purchased at a higher price.[123] No doubt, if death had not intervened, Saule could probably have warded off disaster. As young Hennessy put it, 'had he lived by the many resources he had, and the plans he had adopted, I am convinced he would have retrieved his losses'.[124] Delamain's more authoritative view was not discordant: 'the deficiency is easily accounted for. Had he lived (as he had much cleverness) he would probably have got above water but never arrived to easy circumstances, being too fond of parade in every particular.'[125] Even Martell (probably Frédéric-Gabriel), whose comments on Saule's demise were cold (reflecting their strained relations), observed that 'il aurait encore pu continuer longtemps, peut-etre réparer ses imprudences de cette année'.[126] The straightforward nature of the failure is reflected in the fact that a 50 per cent payment was made to creditors by the end of the year.[127]

With an inventory drawn up at Augier and Delamain's directions, a general meeting of creditors was scheduled with little delay for 8 November. At the meeting Augier and Delamain were appointed syndics on behalf of the creditors and empowered to proceed to sell the brandies and also to determine to what extent the two London houses were entitled to claim the brandy, already branded in their name and paid for in Saule's warehouses.[128] Fortuitously the sale of Saule's brandy coincided with a rise in the market – London buyers who had held back earlier were now coming into the market strongly – and 10,000 livres more were realized for the creditors than had been anticipated.[129] Saule's brandy, purchased in haste at the end of 1787 and apparently embracing all the older brandy available, proved 'of very indifferent quality'.[130] Martell Lallemand took 160 of the 450 puncheons of Saule's stock to meet orders in hand.[131] Good news though this turn of events was, the plague on Saule's affairs persisted. If the brandy had been held off the market for another few months, it would have realized much higher prices. As early as the end of December the Martell house were regretting that they had not made a larger purchase of Saule's brandy. By the end of January prices of brandy taken at the still had reached 120 livres, and the market price had climbed to 135 and 140 by late March. Allowing for some further premium for old brandy, sales at those prices would have eliminated entirely or greatly reduced the losses on the various parcels which made up Saule's stock.

The decision of the creditors was registered only on 22 January. The fact that its registration was held over for almost three months and that there were no other meetings suggests that, while the affairs of the estate were cut and dried as far as the creditors were concerned, some form of dispute took place with the officials of the *contrôle des actes* who valued the estate more minutely to ensure full payment of the registration tax.[132] This seems to correspond to the fact that the inventory in the notary's files is not complete on the value of the estate. Untypically the *contrôle* affords not simply a gross valuation of effects amounting to 218,790 livres but a division into two components, 152,218 'pour les effets valués par le notaire' and 66,572 livres 'pour ceux qui non l'ont pas été et qui auraient du l'etre'.

Saule's furniture was substantial, and was minutely described in the inventory whose preparation proceeded intermittently from 8 October to 3 December. To be deducted from the gross total were also a number of small debts (twenty-four in all), of which only two were of any size, one for 3377 livres to Richard Hennessy in Bordeaux, the other for 740 livres, characteristically to a bookseller. As the gross estate of 218,790 livres was inflated by brandy in stock, deduction of its market value at about 180,000 livres would, before taking other debts into account, suggest in very crude fashion a personal estate of 38,790 livres. This figure, if approximately correct, would correspond to the status of a moderately successful commission merchant. Indeed, it is probably also some measure of his dowry.

The only tangible personal assets into which his resources were turned were his furniture and books. There were no buildings, and Victoire on his death was in danger of being turned out of their rented house.[133]

The irony of the situation was that precisely because the liquidation was straightforward and the winding up had occurred with little delay, the losses were much greater than they would have been in a more protracted settlement. The sale wiped out Victoire's interest in the business, and much of her fortune, which was the guarantee of the Gastinel loan, must have been lost as well. The creditors' meeting had a further unfortunate and unexpected result for her. The convention on these occasions was that the expert valuation of furniture and other personal effects was accepted by the creditors, and the widow was free to buy them back at that price. On this occasion the value of the furniture was pushed one third above its valuation by one of the creditors. According to an unsigned letter in the Saule archives, 'la raison de cette injustice vient de ce qu'un créancier qui connaissait tout le faible de Mr Saule pour son mobilier a eu la barbarie d'offrir une summe supérieure a l'évaluation convenue, bien persuadé qu'elle ferait un dernier effort pour se le conserver. Elle l'a fait et elle a été dupe. La bibliothèque fait partie de cette acquisition qui est de 12,000 livres.'

Saule's great romance had ended as all things must. There were no children of the marriage. Victoire at least had a comfortable family to fall back on. In the way of the times, that meant not only material support but a possibility of remarrying. She remarried on 20 June 1791.[134] Her new spouse was Jean Jacques Caminade de Chatenet, an *avocat*, a widower with two younger sons. There were no children of her second marriage. She thus was absorbed back into the family circle which had been reluctant to give her to Saule in the first case, and who probably both chose her new husband for her and from their own milieu. She disappears from the correspondence; a fleeting reference from Thomas Shoolbred, a second son of a London merchant friend of Richard Hennessy, after he had left Cognac in 1795, asked his regards to be sent to 'that worthy woman, whom I shall never forget, Madame Saule'.[135]

JAMES HENNESSY'S ENTRY INTO BUSINESS

Continuity in the house was provided by James Hennessy ('Jemmy'). After his studies in Douai he had spent some time copying letters in the Blake house. With too many young Blakes on the spot, this occupation held out no future. His entry into Saule's business can be dated to some point between April and June 1785: in the latter month, Hennessy, referring to projected absence by Saule, already had occasion to observe, 'I am sorry to think your elleve may not be clever enough to supply your place'.[136] As late as November reports from Cognac must have been still discouraging as Hennessy, in response, wrote on 4 November that 'he must be very dull and cearless, not to have profited more from copying so long years Mr Blake's letters'. Richard complained too of his accent,

> which is shockingly vulgar, and renders him a laughing stock in every company ... he never could acquire so great a brogue but by affecting it. I wish you could break him of it. I must own to you that my greatest dislike to it is that with all strangers it denotes a mean and low education.[137]

However Jemmy proved to have more aptitude than first reports had suggested, and also soon began to display more social ambition that Richard may have anticipated. By 1787 Saule left the affairs of the house in Jemmy's hands when he went to London, and was happy with them on his return. Back from London, Saule was to write: 'I am sorry to tell you that he is far from being clever, but this is between ourselves.' However, in the next breath he conceded that 'he is well-disposed. Time, experience, assiduity and inclination will bring him on to what I wish he would be.' As Saule observed to Richard, who was once again in the depths of business difficulties in Bordeaux, 'I am keeping your son at work and striving to put him in a way of earning his bread. I had foreseen your misfortune long ago and prepared him for it, frequently represented to him what little dependence he could lay on your success and to conform his conduct to the circumstances.'[138] James proved to be quite a hard-headed young man, and he adverted quickly to matrimony as one way out of his shortage of capital. Saule's words to his father repeat some of the story: 'I did observe by your last letter to your son that he must have talked seriously matrimony to you. How he may go through with that plan I cannot say. Its true I frequently mentioned it to him formerly and I wish he could put it still in practice for your and his own sake, but then the question is to find the proper match.'[139]

Young James Hennessy's shrewdness showed up in seeking the advice of Delamain even before Saule died. It is revealed too in his cultivation of Delamain's nephew, whom he, not Richard, turned into the needed partner for the business. Delamain's comments on James were uniformly favourable. In little over two years in business, the gauche Hennessy of 1785 seems to have turned into the shrewd and respected figure of 1788, capable the following year of forming a partnership with another young man, equally if not more astute and ambitious, and enjoying resources and backing from his uncle James Delamain.

In default of matrimony, a partnership was the best hope for the Hennessys. Letters from Hennessy to Madame Saule when she accompanied her husband to London already reveal an ease of manner and a self-confidence, even if it was not the more showy one that would impress Saule. The year 1787 was not an easy one in any business and in the case of Saule's business it was particularly difficult: Richard Hennessy's problems in Bordeaux, combined with his son's presence in the Cognac house, led to suspicion of a hidden association between the two houses and a reluctance to accept paper from Hennessy junior. In a postscript to a letter of 4 August James referred to the problem in a casual and confident manner: 'you will easily conceive how disagreeable this is. Babin is continually about me for to know if Mr Pineau is paid. I want about 26,000 livres and as yet I can not get above 6000 to 8000. Patience.'

As soon as the new partnership agreement was concluded in August 1789, James lost no time in visiting London, in the fashion of Saule, to improve their business there. Through friendship with Tuffon (whose goodwill was another of the fruits of Saule's London sojourns), they acquired some custom from Timsons, who had hitherto dealt with Martell Lallemand. Tuffon assured Hennessy that while the firm would continue to do business with the Martell house, they would like to give some of their orders to Hennessy's. James apprised his father how the orders should be executed, advising him to consult Saule's invoices to see how things were done for the London market. He described brandy from their house as 'foul and much too pale', and observed that rivals' brandy was in better condition.[140] The transition to a new house had posed problems in keeping up standards, and one London house at least complained of the brandy being inferior to what they had been accustomed to receive in Saule's time.

The first half of 1789 was difficult for the Hennessys, both because of Saule's failure and the Hennessys' own problems, arising from the Bordeaux debacle. As early as November 1788 Hennessy was discussing the question of raising money with Daniel MacCarthy and Forsters, but with financial stringency growing, this was a very bad time to attempt to raise money.[141] Even so, the new partnership in August 1789 was quick in getting on its feet. The ledger suggests that discounting 170 puncheons on hand at the outset, 1036 puncheons and 11 1/2 barrels were purchased in the period from 13 August 1789 to 30 September 1790. This is quite a good figure, given the fact that buying started in the high noon of Martell Lallemand's ascendancy and in a buying season that became progressively more difficult. The rivalry bordering on hostility between Saule's house and Martell's, which we might easily think to have existed only in Saule's head, was a real thing to James. In London he was shown a letter in which 'Mr Frederick – for I suppose he dictated it – throws some of his venom at us, but I hope the sting won't poison us'.[142] The house was also cementing its existing relationship with Shoolbred, and James actually lodged with them. The friendship, while it had not hitherto loomed large in their business, was to be the key to their London wartime success in the late 1790s.

The prosaic James also disliked the late dinner hour, and resented the way the long stay at table ran away with time. He met the daughters of Saule's friend Mr Cherry, and, ever practical, observed that 'I wish I had one of them with a good fortune'.[143] He was anxious to meet relatives of the Hennessy family in London, suggesting to Richard that he might get details of them from their cousin George, a captain in the trade between Cork and Bordeaux. A week later, in two letters, he reported meeting a Mrs Flanery, married to an absentee West Indian Irish planter and 'sister to the good for nothing young chap that was in Bordeaux and who has the estate of our family in Ireland'.[144] James's comment suggests that the nephew who had inherited the Ballymacmoy property visited Richard (very likely coming out on cousin George's vessel). George, son of Richard's deceased brother James, was master of a large Cork vessel on two occasions in 1788; as he did not appear as master on preceding voyages, we may assume that he had just reached this position, and that the voyage (the return leg of which was recorded in the *congés* for 3 July 1788) was his first visit to Bordeaux. The heir at Ballymacmoy may have taken the opportunity of coming out either on that voyage or on the succeeding one in October, and James presumably met him.

In any event his enquiries in London were prompted not by an interest in members of the family for their own sake, but by the purpose of getting more proof of the social standing of the family. He had already asked his father for the name and place of abode of the family in Ireland and 'to find our arms at the herald's office'.[145] By the end of the year, writing from Boulogne on his return, he remarked that he was en route to Paris where he was to dine with the brother of the 'famous Mrs Herbert'.[146] Gentry pretensions might help in making a good marriage, a subject on James's mind because of the capital it would bring into his hands. Richard on the other hand had seen members of his family simply as individuals or friends. He was neither snobbish nor calculating, and he had never been interested, despite his obsessive interest in friends and in his home region, in the family pedigree either in itself or as a basis for a higher social standing. Obsessions with their social standing were widespread among the Irish abroad as in French society around them, and they were having recourse to the herald's office in Dublin extensively from as early as the 1760s. As far back as 1776, James Nagle, an officer relative in the Irish Brigade, had advised Richard not to use the word 'bourgeois' or '*négociant*', and to describe his sons as 'fils de Richard Hennessy écuyer et de dame Elène Barret'.[147] While the advice seemed lost on Richard (apart from a perhaps half-hearted genealogical enquiry in County Cork in 1784), it or other advice of the same ilk thirteen years later was much on James' mind from the time he achieved independent business status in 1789.

The relationship between James and Turner was to prove a close one, and despite disharmonies it lasted for many years. Nor was Hennessy *fils* dependent on a new partner for shrewdness. Even before the new partnership came into being, 'pestered all the morning by brandy sellers', he offered a low price on the ground that 'as they are Mr Augier's and Martell's customers they would not come here if them gentlemen gave them more'.[148] The house was now to be dominated by two ambitious and capable young men, quite in contrast to the unworldly Richard Hennessy or the less single-minded Jack Saule. A secondary house in the business until the 1780s, it featured as the major buying force only fleetingly at the end of 1787. Hennessy & Turner, while strengthened by Saule's new contacts in London, hardly seemed set to challenge Martell Lallemand, more securely established than ever in 1789, for the leading place in the trade. Despite the accidents of death, the vagaries of London houses, and the advent of direct shipping to London, the trade looked as if it would remain unchanged in its essential features in the new decade. Revolution was to change that.

8

Business under the Revolution

The last two years of the 1780s unfolded in the shadow of uncommon weather and market conditions, and of an unsettling political
momentum. The year 1788 had already been an extraordinary one:
London buyers held off, and finally a great frost brought commerce
to a total halt from the outset of December. Distilling was disrupted
within the first week because the streams were frozen, and by the end
of the third week of the month the river was 'lower than ever remem-
bered and near entirely frozen'.¹ On 17 January, at the end of a
remarkable six weeks, a thaw set in and rivers in spate and flooded
or impassable roads had a more devastating effect on inland traffic
than the freeze-up itself.² An upward price trend in February was
reinforced by the tardy presence of a number of English vessels in the
Charente.³ By June correspondents in London abandoned their reluctance to order, thus ensuring that prices would soar. In August
exports were estimated at 5000 puncheons.⁴ This was a huge export
figure for so late in the season, helping to swell Martell invoices for
1789 to the unprecedented level of 16,000 barriques.

The Hennessys had returned in December 1788 to Cognac, though
the sociable Richard lost no time in returning in February for the pre-
Lenten festivities in Bordeaux, reporting from there that 'there is no
time to talk to anyone of business. Balls, parties and dinners are all
that is spoke of.' He took his daughter Biddy to the factory ball in the

Hôtel d'Angleterre. The timing of the sociable Richard's visit had a serious purpose: the need to arrange the negotiation of bills to ensure an immediate supply of specie for an improving brandy trade.[5]

Credit conditions worsened further in the autumn when the removal of specie from Bordeaux was prevented. The crisis eased somewhat by November, when MacCarthy *frères* told Hennessy & Turner that 'money is grown more plenty with us, and the exchanges are falling in consequence. Probably the very powerful prohibition of violent placards which prevented our sending money out of the city will not long remain in force.'[6] In Cognac, with the market in 1789 geared to a vigorous London demand, and hence to a degree insulated from the credit crisis, prices soared in the second half of 1789; in Bordeaux they stagnated between August and November in a band of 150–165 livres. In late October the price in Cognac, reflecting external demand, was 225 livres compared with 160 in Bordeaux.[7]

At the outset of the year political crisis had overshadowed even the singular business conditions. In January 1789 Delamain, advising a correspondent about legal business in Bordeaux, noted that 'all private business is suspended on account of the present commotion in government affairs'.[8] Events in July in Paris were to add to the unease, which itself was linked also to the celebrated *Grande Peur*, the vague fear of brigands, sweeping rural France in the same month. The weather of the preceding winter had already caused an ominous foreboding. The ice and snow, a calamitous thaw and a cold, wet summer heightened cumulatively the unprecedented mood of expectation and foreboding with which Frenchmen viewed their political and fiscal problems. This comes across hauntingly in Delamain's letters. Long before the grain began to ripen thinly and belatedly, the elements had become an actor in the unfolding political drama. However, in August a false confidence set in that political stability had been established. Famine had not occurred, brandy demand was reassuringly high, and foreign trade, less affected by acute credit crisis than inland trade, remained relatively buoyant. True, in 1790 one of the Roches had colourful adventures in Montauban and had been in danger of being 'lanterned'. But the experiences of this boisterous character hardly represented the norm, and he made off from his adventures to his friends 'who he always finds more inclined to drink than fight'.[9] Even a year later, after the king's flight to Varennes, Delamain observed to a London correspondent, Gorman, that 'the public papers will have fully acquainted you [with] the great political event in this kingdom, the king's evasion and return, which it is generally thought will more tend towards consolidating the constitution than enfeebling it. The people have behaved on the occasion with incredible moderation and firmness which proves they would not easily be terrified.'[10]

Social life, bright in the midst of political crisis in 1789, was still so in 1790 and 1791. Letters from Bordeaux to Cognac were full of news of the Irish colony, and, while harping on the credit crisis, were reassuringly devoid of political fears. Thomas Knight in February 1790 reported the alliance of Dowling to Miss Casey. Dowling's prospects in trade – he was a distiller – were thought to be good, and the occasion was celebrated by a supper and ball for 150 persons given by the Johnstons.[11] Knight himself, with backing from the Galweys, was to take premises on the Chartrons for two years for both retail and wholesale trade, and the senior MacCarthy, MacCarthy *oncle*, now retired from trade, recommended the bottle wine trade to Richard Hennessy. A year later – 1791 – the eve of the Lenten season was no less carefree. We can follow it through the eyes of Samuel Turner who happened to be in Bordeaux. He had been entertained by John Galwey. The next night there was in prospect 'une superbe fête que donne Mr Johnston où le monde entier est invité. Des préparatifs depuis 15 jours'. On Monday, Knight 'nous donnera un pied de boeuf irlandais'; on Tuesday he would be at the MacCarthys, on Wednesday at Bonfield's, on Thursday at Gernon's, on Friday at Barton, Johnston & Barry's, on Saturday at home 'à moins de quelque bonne fortune', and on Sunday 'chez Mr Dowling'.[12] Dowling's soirées were apparently very gay. Present on another occasion, and not having to rely on others' accounts, Richard Hennessy wrote on a Sunday morning in the wake of an entertainment: 'you see I can scarce hold my pen. We quitted Dowling this morning at 6 o'clock. He gave a most elegant ball and super. We were at least 200, most splendidly entertained with all the luxuries of nature and art of man.'[13] In the autumn even the revolt in St Domingue seemed remote: the complacent view of the Galweys as reported at second hand was

of 'the revolt at St Domingo as a matter of little consequence'.[14] The
setting up of the National Guard itself had at first added to reassur-
ance, a fact reflected in the making of portraits in uniform whether of
James Delamain as colonel of the force in Jarnac, or of Richard Hennessy, who was a lieutenant of the force in Cognac. It seemed lighthearted, as suggested by the frolicking detail in the background of the
Hennessy portrait or the entry of the name of a young London guest
of the time, the son of Richard's close friend, John Shoolbred, on the
regimental role.

RICHARD HENNESSY IN LONDON 1791–2

Domestic prices had risen more rapidly than the exchanges depreciated, creating an obstacle to the successful maintenance of foreign
trade by making brandy and other goods dearer to foreign buyers.[15]
This helps to account for Richard Hennessy's London visit. That visit
also cemented close ties with the house of Shoolbred, who were to be
of vital importance both in the English trade and in the conduct of
the Hennessys' Hamburg speculations later in the decade. At the
request of Turner and Jemmy Hennessy, the visit was extended until
after Christmas. The price of a successful business stay was that Hennessy had to abandon his intended journey to Ireland, 'returning to
you by land, rather than proceed to Ireland, which I think would be
attended with more pain than pleasure'.[16]

Hennessy was now sixty-three, already, as described in a Dunkirk
letter in early 1792, 'ce respectable vieillard'.[17] He had last been in
Ireland in 1768, and the passing of friends and relatives must have
been on his mind. Inevitably his thoughts from the time of arrival in
London turned to his cousin and former schoolmate, the most
famous of all his Irish acquaintances, the mighty Edmund Burke, now
bathed in the greatest celebrity of his life. Almost as soon as he had
landed in England, in his letters to Cognac he had mentioned Burke.[18]
By 6 October he had established that Burke was at his country house,
and he had sent a copy of *Reflections on the Revolution in France* to
Cognac. On 6 December he reported: 'I purpose seeing Burke if you
do not send me to the North. I told you I saw his son, who invited me

to go to see them'. Almost three weeks later he advised his firm that if he missed a post 'you may conclude I am on a visit to Mr Burk [*sic*] who I suppose will remain longer than he purpose as parliament does not meet until the end of next month'.[19] On 13 January 1792, back in London, Richard described his visit:

> I set out that day [Tuesday] for Mr Burck's [*sic*] where I arrived at 5 and was most kindly received by his worthy good lady and niece Miss French. His son is now in Dublin. Captain Nagle of the Marines, who is one of their family, Monsieur de Cazeles who has mostly lived with them since his arrival here above 2 months ago from Coblentz and much caressed by them and all those of his party here, and when in town lodges at Burke's. He came to town yesterday morning with three other gentlemen I found there, and before dinner were rein-forced by two others of their acquaintances so that we mustered 16 at dinner. All slept there except the Earl of Inchiquin who gave me a gracious invitation to his house in that neighbourhood. I took leave of the family last night.[20]

The letter says nothing of the conversations in the house or at the table. One can only wonder what they spoke of, meeting for the first time in twenty-six years, or whether their conversation strayed into the Catholic question, which had already brought Burke's son to Ire-land. As a Nagle was present as well, and Burke like Richard was ever haunted by recollections and friendships, the little world of Bal-lymacmoy and Ballyduff, old times and old friends, must have come alive and glowed for a fleeting hour.

The only topic we know for sure was discussed between the two men was the plight of James Barrett, son of the first cousin of Burke and of Hennessy's wife, whom Burke had tried in the past to help. A reference in one of Hennessy's letters to Burke having told him 'repeatedly' of his inability to help suggests that Hennessy may have met Burke on other occasions. Edward Barrett, James's father, had been a link between Hennessy and Burke in the 1760s, and again in 1772 and 1782. Barrett *père*'s misadventures and death in 1783 had left his son and family badly provided for. Barrett was one of a long line of Nagles, Hennessys and others either advanced by Burke or living in hope of advancement, and in 1791 he had just obtained for a Hennessy 'a very fine employment'.[21] Barrett had already been in Bordeaux in 1791, counting on help from the Galweys, but the Galwey failure in December meant that the family had no occasion for his services. He then proposed going to England, 'occasioned by my very great expectation of getting a good place, through Mr Burke's interest'.[22] Barrett had set off from Bordeaux more than a week before the end of January, apparently hoping to see Hennessy in London.[23] He arrived in London on the day before Hennessy left, Hennessy reporting that 'I omitted telling you that I saw Barrett for about half an hour the day I parted London where he arrived the day before. I was sorry to tell him that Mr Burk had repeatedly told me he had it not in his power to do anything for him'.[24] After his fruitless visit, Barrett must have returned to Bordeaux, as he was apparently there as late as 1793. Friends then made up 20 guineas, and he went to Ostend, where he entered a 'prince's' army. There had been no good news of him even two years later as Woods lamented news of 'poor Barrett's fate and disagreeable situation'. From Woods yet another two years later came news from a traveller from Spain that 'he left your poor nephew James Barrett about three months since at Barcelona. He had undergone every species of misery and had been these two years past deserting from one army to another …'.[25]

CHANGING BUSINESS FORTUNES: WAR, TERROR AND LAW OF THE MAXIMUM, 1792–4

Hennessy dallied for a while in Dunkirk, and then visited Ostend where he still was on 3 March. By mid-March he was in Paris, and from Cognac he visited Bordeaux in June. His Bordeaux letters painted a reassuring picture of the Irish circle. As usual there was a social round of dinners. His old friend Thomas Knight too seemed to be doing well. He had become an 'English ship broker' and 'had already ships to his address and of three that arrived yesterday afternoon from Cork and Waterford he got two and a chance of the other. You never saw a man in higher spirits. His wife in Ireland making friends for him.'[26]

Yet behind a still reassuring façade in France's greatest port, all was changing. From 1791, an inevitable consequence of credit crisis, business failures were occurring. John Galwey's house, one with many ties with Hennessy, failed in December 1791 for 800,000 livres, half of it due to four houses in London, and assets were few.[27] The failure had been coming on for some time, as Richard Hennessy observed: 'I saw these many years he was not at his ease'.[28] War from April 1792 added to the problems on all fronts. Even big houses were becoming very cautious. The house of Val & Patrick French & Nephew advised in November that 'in these difficult time we dont chuse having bills drawn upon us direct'.[29] Above all, the Convention in August 1792 initiated sweeping political change, and the contentious phase of the Revolution for the first time closed in on the Charente. At Jarnac the comte de Jarnac, Delamain's patron, joined the emigration. In Cognac in December James Hennessy was *commandant* of the Garde Nationale. The execution of the king in January 1793 meant that the revolutionaries finally crossed the Rubicon, while after the declaration of war by England a month later France was encircled and menaced by a coalition of external and internal enemies. In the wake of the Vendée rising the internal tensions unleashed by revolution came violently to the surface. By March 1793 the post had become irregular, and Delamain noted that in his role of 'administrateur du département, notable dans la commune, chef d'une légion du district, chargé de recrutement', political demands on his time had escalated. His son and his clerk were both in Poitou 'avec la jeunesse de ce pays à cause d'une insurrection qui s'y manifeste'.[30] In Cognac James Hennessy himself had gone off to the Vendée at the head of a detachment of 150 men.[31]

At the outset of the war with England in early 1793, trade was not permitted with the neutral port of Hamburg; this meant that the port could not play the role it had often played of an entrepôt base for trade between belligerents. By August France prohibited the export of brandy, a prime item in military provisions: Hennessy & Turner had to confess that 'our trade here is now quite at a stand'.[32] Increasingly business was done in paper money, *assignats*, which by the summer of 1793 had depreciated to a quarter of their value.[33] At this stage on 29 September the famous Maximum, first introduced in

May for grain, was extended to other commodities with the purpose of halting the inflationary spiral.[34] Under its terms prices were settled on the basis of the 1790 level increased by one third. In the case of brandy this meant setting the price at 300 livres, whereas market prices were already as high as 650 livres.[35] After offering 300 livres for fifteen days without getting any brandy, Delamain was outbid by less scrupulous buyers who offered more.[36] At an earlier date he had already noted his neighbours in Cognac becoming tired of trade (an implicit reference to the Martells).[37] The Martells and Augiers who had been prominent in public office in Cognac in the early Revolution seem to have run for cover at this stage:[38] this, combined with the fact that Hennessy and Turner were not put off by the challenge of transforming their business from orthodox trading to government orders, altered the relative fortunes of the houses decisively.

By November 1793 the Revolution threatened Delamain personally: 'Some of our strong citizens seemed to disapprove the two syllables by which my name begins, De and La. As I dont care a button by what appellation I am distinguished, I will hereafter sign Mayne instead of Delamain. Several of my family wrote theirs Delamayne, and I am therefore authorised in that choice.'[39] The Maximum, which profoundly perturbed Delamain, caused him to reduce his trade greatly. In reflection, two years later, he wrote that 'our property has suffered by being obliged by the maximum here to give at a low price goods which cost us dear, and losing totally some feudal rights, and we could not as many have done, prevail on ourselves to make up our prejudice by what we thought undue speculation ...'.[40] Even Hennessy & Turner 'thought it better to drop as much as possible all correspondence, for our little place felt the year of tyranny as much as larger theatres', and, their government business apart, correspondence was thin.[41]

In contrast to Delamain, overwhelmed by events, or to Martell Lallemand, equally running for cover, Hennessy & Turner profited from government orders. Turner was in Paris and Brest in 1794 and 1795. Whatever the fears of men like Delamain, merchants in Cognac and Jarnac did not suffer in the way they did in Bordeaux. There, Théodore Martell, as a successful merchant fell under suspicion, was twice arrested, and finally cleared with a heavy fine.[42] The Irish community was doubly suspect – both as merchants and as foreigners.[43] News of the survival of the Irish came to Hennessy from the pen of a single man, James Woods. Woods and his brother had both been clerks of the Galweys. James Woods reported in June 1793 that his brother 'by advice of Mr H. Galwey goes to-morrow in the counting house of Mr Fenwick the American consul'.[44] The brother was exempt from detention by virtue of his employment by a functionary for the Americans: James Woods himself, according to a later letter, owed his early release to the fact that he had been resident twenty years in Bordeaux. All the Irish, at any rate those who could not prove naturalization, were at one stage thrown into prison. Woods and some others were released well ahead of the rest:

> Most of the English are still detained here in prison. It is reported that those at Havre, Rouen, Paris and Nantes are set free. We hope it may soon be the case of my late fellow prisoners. The physicians are to be released very soon. Skinner, McDaniel, O'Connell, my wife and I, Dowling, Jacob, Casey and Jordan Mead are out – all the others remain at the Carmelites – the MacCarthys were under arrest in their own house until their letters of naturalisation were examined: they saved them from further confinement.[45]

James Woods later recorded that they were five months and three weeks with the Carmelites: 'there were some wet souls among us who amused us much in general from time to time'.[46] As well as the Irish medical men, Galwey and Fitzgibbon and another physician Langhorn, Nathaniel Johnston, Hugh Barton and their families were released in November.[47] Some thirty others, including three women, one 'a poor old servant woman', still languished in confinement.[48] In May 1794 Woods was still 'chiefly attending at our comité de surveillance entirely for friends'. They were finally released by Ysabeau, the Revolutionary *commissaire* from Paris on the famous occasion in September in which he embraced them individually. The students among them were given passports for Hamburg.[49]

Even naturalization of itself was an uncertain protection for the rich and influential. Thus, MacCarthy was at risk: 'his worthy family had been so particularly pointed out, in the days of terror, for their religious sentiments, that perhaps nothing but their absence saved them'.[50] Others who returned, like the two sons of Kirwan, did not fare well and had to quit. As for the father, 'It seems the poor man himself was on the list although he never quitted his estate in Médoc'. The Terror left its traces: Henry Galwey, who was excessively timid, was even 'afraid of his shadow'.[51]

Woods thought that the alarm among the community, as they were released, was excessive as clerks and those doing trades recognized as useful to the Republic were exempt from a new requirement to reside outside the commune: only three merchants (of whom two were Irish, James Roche and Child) suffered under its terms.[52] But an official decree, ignoring that the impediments on exporting their goods left houses unable to convert goods which they had bought into cash and requiring them to satisfy claims against them by their creditors, left them in a 'very disagreeable situation'.[53] The effects of the ban on brandy exports was serious for brandy houses in Bordeaux. Casey, a distiller, handed in his *bilan* (i.e. conceded bankruptcy) in May 1794, and his son-in-law was in the same predicament.[54] Andoe left by 1794. In the Hennessy letter books, there are remarkably few foreign letters even to Hamburg, and an interest in the foreign market among brandy exporters began to reawaken only in July 1795.

THE ENDING OF THE 'MAXIMUM', AND THE COMMODITY BOOM 1794–5

The Maximum was 412 livres in November 1794, but brandy was being bought by less law-abiding traders at 700 and 800 livres,[55] and under the adjusted Maximum of Frimaire when it was set at 500, the black market price was 800 and 900 livres.[56] In November the Maximum had been altered, and it was finally abolished on 24 December 1794.[57] The ending of price controls at a time when a flood of paper money existed led to a hectic but speculative and unhealthy business boom. By April 1795 the Hennessys were said to be buying brandy at 2000 to 2200 livres.[58]

Théodore Martell already acted in Bordeaux for Hennessy & Turner's house. The letters from Theodore to James Hennessy were frank and warm. He effected purchases and sales for them in Bordeaux, chartered vessels to come round to load in Charente, and also dispatched *assignats*. A Bordeaux base made it much easier to speculate in colonial commodities. Many of these ventures were on joint account, or even brought other associates into the field. While Hennessy & Turner dominated brandy requisitions, Théodore Martell was involved in large purchases of foodstuffs for the land armies worth two million livres on a contract secured through his close and long-standing ties with the Paris house of Girardot (Necker's old house). One consequence of the Hennessy association with Theodore was that the Martell family, casting aside their traditional hostility to the outside houses in the region, married a daughter to James Hennessy in February 1795. On receiving news of the marriage, Théodore Martell welcomed it (hinting at his own role in the affair): 'j'approuve beaucoup cette union et il y avait longtemps que je la désirais'.[59]

In the course of 1795, in the first year of his marriage, James was unwell, recovering from what was probably jaundice, and was advised to take the waters in the south of France. On his way he halted in Bordeaux, reporting to Cognac: 'I have seen Mr Stroble and made acquaintance with one of his partners a Mr Martini. Since Stroble's establishment its said they have made an immensity of money.'[60] From Bordeaux he proceeded to Bagnères, accompanied by his wife and sister-in-law. In Bordeaux he had made the acquaintance of General Arnaud, the military officer commanding the port. Through Arnaud's recommendation to the good offices of his wife in Bagnères, he got the ground floor of the house adjoining Arnaud's lodgings in 'the best house on the place du Couston: 4 rooms, 2 servants rooms, kitchen, yard, cellar and all things therein necessary for 40 livres per day'.[61]

Even in convalescence his letters were full of business comments.[62] By October he had left Bagnères, proceeding on his way home, to Bordeaux where 'we arrived here late last night and went to every hotel in town without finding any place to lodge not even au quatrième. At last we put up in a black nasty inn behind the Quai des Farines but Mr Beyerman no sooner knew us there than he came and brought us to his house.' Prices were very high: 'all is out of price here, bread 16 livres per pound, loaf sugar 100 livres per cwt etc etc'. Such prices meant that there was no scope for speculative purchases, and James was therefore keen to press on home 'as I have nothing profitable to do here, but I must give the ladies a few days to see their friends'.[63] His letters reveal his lack of talent for social life: 'For my part I think I pass my time very disagreeably here for paying duty visits and getting invitations to dinners is my death and I dislike it very much. I brought my wife to none of our English friends nor dont intend it.'[64] The contrast with his father could not be greater. Three days later he wrote that 'these women cannot be got out of here, though I dont see in what consists their great amusements'. At this stage, his visit was prolonged involuntarily as his wife, seven months pregnant, gave birth prematurely. He was to remain in Bordeaux until Nivôse, a stay that proved frustrating. To Samuel Turner he wrote, 'Je n'ai rien fait si ce n'est de m'etre ennuyé beaucoup. Plus je reste et plus cela augmente car je ne vois que des gens qui travaillent tandis que je ne fais rien.'[65]

Government orders and the termination of the Maximum had produced a very active market in 1795. In June brandy prices were 3200 livres, and even the cautious Delamain was tempted into trade quoting 3100 to 3600 livres.[66] A few days later brandy reached 4000 livres.[67] In July Hennessy & Turner declined an order from Delaps in Bordeaux as 'a very extensive order from Paris by orders of government puts it entirely out of our power to transact any other business'.[68]

Merchants lamented the rise of new houses. Even a successful house like Hennessy & Turner complained that 'a thousand people style themselves merchants who before the revolution never handled a pen. These men purchase at all rates and send to different parts of France for their accounts.'[69] Their origins were traced to the sharp practice of brokers taking to their own account commissions that came into their hands:

> Its discovered that there have been some handsome, not to say criminal things, done here in this way for some time past. A good deal of this came out, when your friend Knight and Sauvage quarrelled, such as letters to different houses being suppressed by Sauvage and the business done by him etc. ... Messrs Forsters, Messrs Coppingers, Fenwick, Stroble, Jonathan Jones, and MacCarthys complain loudly and justly of the unfair means that have been used to take away their friends.[70]

Thomas Knight, who had originally worked with Sauvage, and then became a broker, made, according to Woods, a good deal of money.[71] Woods himself, correspondent of Richard Hennessy, long a mere clerk in a merchant house, was now trading on his own account, and his letters from the autumn of 1794 breathe the new confidence of the business community. Bloomfield, formerly a clerk to Isaac Morgan, and who was about to marry Lucinda Byrne,[72] in turn also became a merchant. Houses like Casey's that had failed got back on their feet quickly. Woods reported hectic buying in April 1795, including 'wines at a very exorbitant price by Mr Delap for account of two Americans. Many of the English bid highly for some of the best but did not get any part.'[73] In June the Irish community was on the crest of the wave:

> Knight I believe has done and is doing handsomely exclusive of his share in the brokerage. He has rubbed off some old chalk and is daily doing so. All our brokers are become merchants. Captain Murphy and Comyn are partners and have a share of whats going. Your friend Casey has also made some very good hits. He has settled his affairs, and I believe purchased an estate yesterday for 100,000 livres and odd.

Thomas Gledstanes, a Dublin man long settled in Bordeaux, was to marry his eldest daughter, Nancy, to an American Adams, 'a very sensible man of about 30 years of age and as handsome a man as any in this province. He is an American who has been here 3 or 4 months, well recommended. He has dispatched a vessel of about 600 tons hence for the Isle de France and has purchased another, destined equally for there.' [74]

In this situation of easy and speculative gains for some, Bordeaux mercantile life resumed the ostentatious style that had struck Arthur Young on the eve of the Revolution. Woods himself had an order for 1000 tons of wine for the Conseil in January 1795, engaged cellars for their reception, and took the house next door to the Frenches: 'the house is one of the most elegant on the front'.[75] Though a new recruit to merchant ranks, he entertained many of the merchants: Henry Galwey, Daniel MacCarthy, West and Gledstanes: 'they will certainly remember the warm reception they met with for Mr Galwey was scarcely in the house when the chimney took fire'.[76] While business looked promising in 1795, political uncertainty still lingered. The Comité de Surveillance in the words of Woods was 'so well composed that you can not say with propriety to a member of it – Black is the white of your eye'.[77] However, things were moving decisively against the *terroristes*. James Hennessy in Bordeaux in October 1795 had a chilling tale to report: 'one Parmatier a terroriste who was set at liberty appeared at the play house the night before last. The young men turned him out and killed him at the play house door.'[78]

HYPERINFLATION, SOCIAL UNREST AND BUSINESS CRISIS

Business success led to popular resentment, especially when soaring prices were reducing living standards. In July 1795, when a bad harvest outlook added to the problems, the canny James Hennessy had observed: 'You must know that its the public opinion as its also mine that the excessive price of everything will bring on troubles and perhaps plunder.'[79]

His conclusion was that 'we must pay off all we owe and see to stand in a situation that may get us at our ease and out of all fear',[80] and somewhat later he observed that 'all is out of price'.[81] Hyperinflation was setting in. By October there were two exchange quotations on Paris – one for government bills, the other for private ones.[82] Brandy had reached a vertiginous 15,000 livres per puncheon and it had become difficult to purchase at all with *assignats*.[83] In late October instead of a regular fifty merchants from Pons, Saintes, St Jauc, Angoulême and Jarnac who attended the Cognac weekly *canton*, there were only three.[84]

With famine or near famine after the bad harvest and a flight from paper money, business deflation pricked the bubble of speculative prosperity, and unemployment added to the existing serious social problems. More than a year later a situation still existed of 'breaking and robbing – no man who has either plate or money is in safety'.[85] In Bordeaux the anti-*négociant* feeling seems to have peaked at the end of 1795:

> La semaine dernière plusieurs vendeurs d'argent furent cruellement
> batonnés à la bourse. Le lendeman on placarda plusieurs affiches avec
> les noms de 10 ou 12 négociants qu'on disait etre agioteurs etc.
> Peters, Martell, Boyer-Fonfraide, Bateman, Beyermann, Coppinger etc
> y ont figuré. Ces deux derniers ont répondu à cette dénonciation par
> des affiches.[86]

As a result of the flight from paper, an increasing amount of business
was transacted in specie, although it was not yet legal to use it in
transactions. Brandy quotations in hard cash ('which is scarce beyond
expression') emerged. The introduction of a new paper money, *man-
dats*, in place of *assignats* in March 1796 did not alter things and on
5 May 1796 the Paris Assemblies, forced to recognize the harsh realities of business, now devoid of the instrument of the Terror to bend
merchants to their ways, had to allow people to hold gold, and on 17
July to engage in cash transactions.[87] In the dire economic situation
of 1796, Théodore Martell's correspondence with his relatives
afforded little evidence of speculation, and the concern in his Cognac
business interests was increasingly confined to brandy. Even a great
Irish house like the Frenches had in early 1797 'scarcely sufficient to
support or pay the daily expenses of their house'.[88]

The 1795 brandy vintage, like the harvest, was not a good one,
and led to a joint interest by Hennessy & Turner and Théodore
Martell in a shipment of Languedoc brandy.[89] With demands from
the Brest expedition for Ireland (i.e. the fleet destined for Bantry Bay)
and Turner having already spent much time in Brest, government
demand helped to support prices. Despite deflationary forces, brandy
more than held its own in price: 230 to 270 livres in February 1796,
it was 260 to 280 in September. In December 1796, despite a new
vintage, a famine of brandy was reported.[90] The establishment of the
grande armée d'Angleterre in 1797 presaged future military orders.[91]

FOREIGN TRADE: THE HAMBURG AXIS, AND THE RISING PROMINENCE OF TURNER

In the period of large brandy sales to government in 1794 and
1795, both Turner and Hennessy were able to invest in property,

fitting rather neatly into the pattern of men who did well out of the Republic, then added further to their gains by acquiring confiscated property at the low prices at which an indebted government sold it. Hennessy enlarged his property stake; Turner started his. For both men, it was a signal of their new and secure position. In 1796 the capital of the house was already 150,000 livres (*valeur métallique*). Turner was the driving force of the first partnership. In 1796, when the original partnership of 1789 came up for renewal, Turner's portion was increased to seven sixteenths. Two sixteenths of this may have been held in trust for Biddy (or at least this had been proposed at the outset of the negotiations), but they were in Turner's name in the actual articles of the new agreement, which formally at least gave him the leading interest in the partnership. Moreover, the proposal which initiated the renewal of the partnership came from him.

> As our partnership my good friends finishes the 15th of next August, its necessary to know on what footing we should renew it. I hope you are both well convinced of my constant will and attachment to everything that can contribute to your advantage and how much your happiness influences on mine and was I to think but of myself most undoubtedly the ideas of any alteration in present state of matters would have never struck me, but I have the duty of a father to fulfil and the task is sacred. At same time it by no means suspends the ties of affection and by uniting them I propose the following plan for your mediation: to continue the partnership for five or seven years more; Richard Hennessy to have 4/16ths, James Hennessy 5/16ths and Turner 5/16ths by which means James and me would be on an equal footing and there would remain 2/16ths for Biddy as the constant solicitude of Mr Hennessy is justly concentrated to that point, and I confess I feel myself interested in the pursuit of everything that may render her happy.

Turner's portion appears as seven sixteenths in the final contract and is in no way qualified by reference to a share for Biddy's benefit. Either a trust was created by another document or she was in the end provided for in some other way. Turner had already spent two years away from Cognac and article 16, which regulated 'les frais de commerce et de voyages', suggests that he had it in mind to travel again.

The new agreement was signed on 23 June and Turner lost little time in departing from Cognac.

He left Jarnac on 2 July, arriving in Hamburg in August. Brandy prices almost doubled in 1796–7, reaching 420–440 livres in November 1797.[92] The pessimistic Théodore Martell commented in 1798 that 'c'est aujourdhui le seul commerce qui nous reste'.[93] Martell, a big-time speculator, his fingers burned by the business downturn in 1796, was too overstretched to get involved in brandy business with Hamburg and declined the attempt of the Martell house in Cognac to draw him into it.[94] The decline in his fortunes was permanent, and he retired to Paris by 1802. For the first time in normal civilian commerce (apart from Saule's short-lived flourish in 1787) Hennessy's had the largest turnover of any house in Cognac. In May 1797 Delamain paid tribute to Hennessy & Turner's success in saying that 'any commercial lucrative concern is the property of our mutual good friend Dick'.[95]

The Otard house in Cognac grew into a new venture by 22 June 1796, when a partnership was created of Otard *jeune* and Léon Dupuy in Cognac. An arrangement with Gramagnac their Paris banker had already led to regular business in brandy on joint account as early as August 1796. Three years later Dupuy, the driving force of the enterprise, visited Paris, and this was followed up by circulars to seven Paris houses.[96] While Otard *jeune* had envisaged in 1796 going to Hamburg, it was his partner in 1799, Dupuy, who finally took up residence there. While rumours in 1797 of peace could have halted the ascent of Hennessy & Turner, the collapse of peace prospects helped them. Speculation in Spanish brandy was a sure sign of demand exceeding supply. The sour view of one Dunkirk house was that Barcelona houses delayed executing the buying commissions given to them until their own brandy speculations had flooded the market.[97] Turner's business in Hamburg reached its heights in the period 1798–1800. Otard had noted in 1798 that their own business was almost all overseas, especially with Hamburg.[98] However despite optimism in the early spring of 1800, undercut by five livres by Hennessy & Turner, they observed at the end of May pessimistically that 'le plus prudent est de ne rien faire; d'écouler peu à peu pour l'intérieur'. In four months they wrote only two letters to de Katter.[99]

We know very little about Turner before he became a member of the Hennessy house. The only firm evidence – apart from the fact that he was a nephew of Delamain – lies in an early passport or *carte de sûreté* from the commune of Paris, dated 26 Frimaire an 2, which gives his height as 5 foot 4 inches, age as thirty years and place of birth as 'Blaw [*Bray?*] en nirlande'. This might suggest that he was born in 1764, not 1761 as suggested in family accounts. However, family tradition is supported by a statement by Turner on 6 October 1793 for an *acte de naissance* of a son to the effect that he was thirty-two years of age. He seems to have arrived in Cognac in the early 1780s – the earliest surviving letter from him is in 1783 – and under the patronage of his uncle, no doubt, to have got a partnership with a local merchant. He had little formal education. Later in Hamburg, a letter giving instructions for the education of his children to James reveals an awareness of his limitations: 'j'ai la seule ambition mon cher ami de donner à mes enfants de l'éducation et je sens tous les jours que la mienne a été negligée, et qu'il faudra absolument éviter ces désagréments à mes enfants'.[100] In 1793 he acquired the works of Voltaire in sixty-eight volumes, and was apparently seeking a copy of the *Encyclopaedia*.[101] He was quite well established in 1789, though 'I'm in partnership with a man a little near his interest'.[102] His rapid integration into local life had been reinforced by his marriage on 10 December 1787 into a local Protestant family, the Guédons, who were, to use a term which came into vogue during the Revolution, *agriculteurs*, at Juillac le Coq.[103] How wealthy were the Guédons? We do not know. A brother-in-law of Turner's, also described as an *agriculteur*, in 1794 purchased the domaine of Mazotte for 61,000 livres. This might suggest that they had considerable resources but it is more likely that he was acting as a cover for Turner in the purchase.[104] The marriage itself was from outside the *négociant* circle. Thus it conferred no special commercial advantage, though an alliance with an established family in the Grande Champagne district may had added to his perceived success as a brandy buyer. We get then a glimpse of what Turner was like in a letter from Richard Hennessy in London in 1791 which mentioned that he had been told that 'Mr Turner is too eager to get rich'.[105] Turner's own view of himself might not have been that much different. In March 1800, significantly to Richard, who was every man's friend, he admitted, speaking of himself, that 'I confess my dear friend that our ambitious spirit often leads us beyond the bounds of prudence'.[106]

The government contracts were in Turner's hands, as the long absences in Paris and in Brest suggest. Later the idea of going to Hamburg originated with him, and when he was there he resisted in 1798 the proposal of coming back to Cognac. A hint of strong disagreement on this point with James occurred in March when under the assumed name of Johnson (which occasionally appeared in the correspondence in the full form of Thomas Johnson) he wrote referring to himself as a third party ('votre associé'):

> Votre associé est maintenant très décidé à partir le plus promptement possible, regrettant toujours que ses efforts pour augmenter les interets de sa maison soyent toujours payés d'ingratitude; non, Monsieur ce n'est pas pour son plaisir qu'il s'est constamment tourmenté depuis plusieurs mois et vous auriez pu, il me semble, lui dire, bien plutot que vous n'avez fait, que son retour était attendu.[107]

The threat of returning was not serious. A month later, he made it clear that he had no intention of returning before the end of the war, referring ironically to his alias in the course of his assertion: 'vous savez que rentrer en France dans ce moment seroit tout fermer la porte à toute operation ... Johnson attend toujours la fin de la guerre avec l'espoir de retourner en France et comme à mon retour je vous promets de l'augmentation dans mes affaires nous aurons de l'occupation pour tout le monde'.[108] He was still strongly against it on 10 August: 'Si on exige mon retour en France, adieu à toutes les affaires et peut-etre pour jamais'. It remained a theme of his letters, and in the last months of 1798 the relationship between the two men, judging by the tone of Turner's letter at that time, was under considerable strain.

A renewed deterioration of international relationships, after the short-lived thaw of 1797, had of course one unpleasant consequence, a growing suspicion of foreigners. What was described as the 'second arrestation' occurred in March 1798.[109] If foreign merchants in France were under detention, it was even more certain that French merchants overseas would fall under suspicion. In Cognac, with a sharp political divide between two factions in the town, the five or six large houses were vulnerable to charges of royalism and fanaticism.[110] It is hardly surprising that suspicion fell on Turner, who spent all this time since 1796 out of France. Under his alias Johnson, in March he wrote:

> Comment est il possible que les authorités constitués de Cognac songent seulement de mettre sur la liste des émigrés, un négociant sorti avec des passeports en règle qui n'a séjourné en pays étrangers que pour les affaires de sa maison? Votre associé vous enverra vraisemblement de Hambourg le certificat que vous lui demandez mais ayant voyagé dans plusieurs parties de l'Allemagne il lui sera difficile peut-etre d'obtenir de Hambourg une attestation convenable pour faire fermer la bouche à ses ennemis ... Je soupçonne plus quelques personnes qui se disent ses amis que celles qui se disent ouvertement ses ennemis.[111]

One of the reasons for his embarrassment is very evident. He had been out of Hamburg continuously from mid-January to the end of March. His absence started with a visit in January to London. From London he went to Holstein and he seems to have intended to proceed to Copenhagen, as de Katter forwarded letters in March to that city. In such circumstances a demand from the municipal authorities in Cognac for certification of residence raised awkward questions, the more so as the absences included visits to two belligerent countries.[112] In fact, he does not seem to have proceeded as far as Copenhagen. As late as 10 April he expressed the intention of going to Copenhagen 'à moins que des raisons de prudence exigent un séjour constant ici'. Fear of being declared an émigré in Cognac led him to curtail his travels and abort his visit to Copenhagen. He later spoke of his 'retour précipité de Holstein', and the question of certification crops up repeatedly through the year.

Turner's letters in January and February, though economical in content, and invariably failing to give his location, were all signed

Turner. In early March, several weeks before the Cognac demand came to his attention, he seems to have decided to use an alias in signing his letters when away. The tone of the letters changed somewhat and the habitual 'tu' Turner employed with Hennessy was changed to 'vous'. The purpose was clearly to conceal Turner's absence, and even to imply that he was still in Hamburg: thus on 8 March Turner under the alias Johnson sought a response from Hennessy 'd'une manière claire que je ne puis me tromper dans mes avis à Mr Turner'. Even before March the alias Johnson was in existence, and it would seem that it was used in England at that stage, with Shoolbred's awareness, as a post box for some sensitive communications to or from Turner. The fact that Turner used Johnson as an alias for correspondence on his travels became explicit on 19 November 1798 when, in advising Hennessy of a coming absence, he gave the instruction that that 'tu écriras ensuite à Johnson pendant un mois ou six semaines, car il espère ne pas demeurer plus longtemps ici'.

The papers he eventually put together seem to have satisfied the authorities in Cognac, though all danger had not been removed as on 10 August Turner wrote that 'vous aurez tous les trois mois si vous l'exigez un certificat de résidence et je vous préviens que mon retour précipité du Hostein demande au moins encore trois mois d'absence avant que de pouvoir mettre tout en règle quand meme la municipalité exigerait impérieusement mon arrivée en France'. Turner later observed that he had been told by 'républicains' that there was no law which authorized a municipality to demand such a document, and that merchants were exempt from such a formality.[113] It is significant that Shoolbred, the London correspondent of the house, had followed the issue closely. He expressed the wish 'that I could congratulate you on the full success of the papers you have sent to Cognac, to be the advocates of your emancipation from local inconvenience, in respect to your family and fortune.'[114]

The Shoolbred correspondence, departing from the usually restrained tone of business correspondence, strayed from mercantile observations into an expression of anti-French views which the writer assumed were shared by the recipient. Thus on 2 October Shoolbred wrote:

> The ladies of this family are well and join me in their best wishes for your health and happiness; they were wishing last night at supper, to have your assistance for a few evenings in Sloane Square, to help forward the illuminations expected to be *exhibited* and *repeated*, in consequence of Nelson's success, which according to report is even more brilliant than any that has preceded it since the war.

The underlining by Shoolbred of the word 'repeated' seems significant because it implies a role by Turner in events, both present and future. The letter confirms, from the implied intimacy with the family, not only that he had visited the family but had spent time in their company when he was in London.

Shortly after his return from England, a letter from Shoolbred to Turner broached the question of some articles to be sent from London to him: 'am I to procure these articles? or is Johnson to send them to me'. It would seem to be some form of hint at existing channels of communication, and although Turner was now back in Hamburg these comments were preceded in the letter by the statement that 'I can not inform you from what cause it proceeds that nothing has been received from Mr Johnson since you left London, indeed I have not seen him above twice since that period'. This would seem an explicit reference, for the interval since Turner had left London, to a person in London assuming the name of Johnson (the name which Turner used in his absences from Hamburg). The cloak-and-dagger dimension becomes even more curious in a further paragraph of the letter:

> Your servant William has applied to me for a character – but I could give none to the gentleman who was desirous of taking him. He now tells me a cock and bull story about the lost parcel you brought from Ireland: first, it was left at a house whose number he could not recollect, now he says it was delivered to the servant of the gentleman for whom you brought them over, and as he changes his servants often, he cannot find him out. It is in short a most mysterious affair, and I fear all may not be in the exact order it should.[115]

This obscurely worded letter is not necessarily to be taken literally. Turner cannot have visited Ireland (given the lack of business with Ireland, it would in any event not have warranted a visit). It seems a simple message about some breakdown in the transmission of information through regular channels, spelling out the last link in the chain, designated as 'your servant William'. A person using the name Johnson may have been a post office for communication. Shoolbred's business with Hamburg could have led to an official request for his good offices in securing regular communication with Hamburg, and Samuel Turner would have been his obvious Hamburg contact: letters could have been addressed to Johnson rather than to Turner in Hamburg in his own name. However, the individual described as 'your servant William' is not to be confused with the W. Williams from whom a long letter survives dated 29 April 1800. Williams was decidedly not a servant, and the letter begins 'My dear Turner'. The long and rather obscure letter does make it clear that Williams was under an obligation to Turner from the time he had been in London, and is probably the man whose name occurs in the styling of the house as Shoolbred & Williams at the end of the 1790s. Whether he is the Williams referred to elsewhere as travelling from Dublin to Hamburg in mid-1798, it is impossible to say.[116]

It has been necessary to go at some length into the possible role of Samuel Turner as a purveyor of information between Britain and Hamburg, less for its importance in the context of the Hennessy – or brandy – story than because of the remarkable coincidence of another Irishman with the same name residing in Hamburg from 1797 onwards. Contemporaries, unlike the historian, were at least free from the dilemma posed by the presence of two Samuel Turners in Hamburg. Samuel Turner of Cognac, despite his employment of the alias Johnson, in Hamburg itself publicly used his real name without interruption. The second Turner, according to a letter signed over the *nom de plume* of 'a sincere convert', was on the other hand 'a fellow here who goes by the name of Roberts, but whose real name is Turner'.[117] This latter Turner used a further alias, Richardson, for his communications with government. Indeed the letter from 'a sincere convert' was in Turner's hand and, intended for Lord Downshire and surviving in the Downshire papers, was endorsed 'Mr Richardson from Hamburg'. The information about himself was simply a bit of laboured humour, as he had been recruited by Downshire.[118] As a means of buying immunity in the Downshire-inspired crackdown in

County Down, Turner, a prominent member of the county's United Irishmen, fled from Newry in the early autumn of 1797. This appeared to be in order to escape arrest (and in fact his name was to remain on the list of proscribed rebels), but in reality his departure was a cover for his new role as an informer.[119] The key figure in penetrating the United Irishmen in south Down in 1796–7 had been the great County Down magnate Lord Downshire. Samuel Turner called on Downshire in London in November 1797 in a cloak-and-dagger visit. Going to Hamburg, after his recruitment in the wake of this visit, he consorted with the United Irishmen, had access to the French minister there, and regularly reported to London. He was very successful in maintaining the guise of a determined United Irishman, and letters even survive reporting suspected sights of him on alleged return visits to Ireland.[120] These reports are incorrect, but the Scarlet Pimpernel quality which they imply (and which the real-life Turner of Newry sadly lacked) illustrate Turner's success in maintaining an image of a dedicated United Irishman in Hamburg.

The remote possibility that the two Samuel Turners were one and the same person (given an Irish background to both men and an alleged visit to Ireland in or before 1798 by Samuel Turner of Cognac), afloat on a sea of aliases, has to be excluded. It would have been very difficult for a Cognac merchant, in 1797 already at least fourteen years out of Ireland, to have insinuated himself into a position of confidence among the political exiles in Hamburg and to have played the part of a Turner whose bona fides to political exiles was his former prominence in the movement in south Down before the mass arrests of leaders began. Most decisively of all, the handwriting of the two men is quite different – as is made clear by one of the very few letters written over the real signature of Samuel Turner of Newry, one from Hamburg admitting his government role.[121]

There is also a sharp difference of style between the sometimes fawning and laboured letters of Samuel Turner of Newry and the almost obsessive single-mindedness of the letters of Samuel Turner of Cognac. The only window into other thoughts comes out not in his letters but in the replies from Shoolbred. Shoolbred's link with the Hennessys was very close from the time of Richard Hennessy's visit to London in 1791–2. At that stage he emerged as a regular correspondent for the house, and it is one of the ironies of the story that although Richard was a poor businessman, his capacity for friendship secured for the house the key commercial contact for its dominant role in the London brandy market in the late 1790s. The friendship had long preceded Richard's visit in 1791. They made contact anew when Hennessy was in London in 1768, and years later in 1784 John Saule, at the time in London, reported meeting 'your friend Mr Shoolbred'.[122] The following year, Shoolbred wrote to Hennessy 'to look back to those happy and agreeable days we spent at Ostend (22 years ago) when I first had the pleasure of your acquaintance'. Shoolbred was already a man of considerable substance, and seems to have had £150,000 in post-war American debt.[123] The fresh contact between the two houses in the wake of Richard Hennessy's visit in 1791 was further cemented by Shoolbred's son spending time in Hennessy's counting house in 1789-90, before getting a place in a house in Smyrna.[124] Hennessy's friend James Delamain, faring very badly in business in 1797, wrote to Richard seeking a letter of introduction to 'your friend Mr Shoolbred of London, I know he is a man deservedly of influence and I much want the protection of such at this moment'.[125] Turner can have made Shoolbred's acquaintance only after he arrived in Hamburg, whence he made, as far as can be told, a single visit to London.

What advantage would there have been for a well-established merchant such as Shoolbred or an ambitious one like Turner engaging in some secret communication? And what could the content of the communications have been? Even before Turner went to Hamburg, Shoolbred had business interests in the Hamburg trade and had visited the port in 1795. One guess would be that Shoolbred, very much an establishment figure in London and the linchpin of Hennessy & Turner's London business in the late 1790s, in response to official overtures, provided through his good offices the cooperation of Turner in passing communications between London and Hamburg without necessarily having any concrete knowledge of their contents. However, as Shoolbred referred to the fate of French naval expeditions, assuming a shared view by Turner, it is probable that there were other communications in which both men had a common purpose. Turner, it should be recalled, had the largest trade in brandy of any house in Cognac, and his main customer in Hamburg, de Katter, had the largest Hamburg business with the south-west of France. Turner would also have had frequent contact with masters of vessels arriving from Charente, a few miles upstream from Rochefort, one of the two French Atlantic naval ports. Eighteenth-century governments attached much importance in determining the timing of enemy fleet movements to intelligence of activity in naval arsenals: in Hamburg this would have been readily available from the masters of commercial vessels arriving from Bordeaux and from Charente. The Rochefort arsenal in particular would have been in their sight, literally a few yards away, as they sailed down the Charente bound for Hamburg. Such intelligence could have been forwarded to London under cover of Turner's Johnson alias.

Shoolbred referred frankly to English victories in engagements with the French navy. In one letter, dated 23 October for an unstated year (but clearly 1798), Shoolbred concluded 'with my hearty congratulations, in the entire defeat of a second expedition to Ireland, consisting of 3 or 4,000 troops, a new 80 gun ship, *Le Hoche*, and 8 frigates, and I have the satisfaction of telling you have been nearly all brought in by Sir Borlase Warren's squadron ... That country cannot be expected to continue quiet under such a series of disasters and misfortunes.' The major part of that fleet had sailed from Rochefort. Shoolbred counted on Turner as a sympathetic audience for such news, and on 20 April 1798 had written:

> We are making daily discoveries of the traitorous conduct of concealed enemies to the country in every quarter and by means of the great vigilance used by the executive and the general disposition to train all descriptions of men to the use of arms, I hope the *Army of England* will meet a warm reception on her coasts.

He expressed himself strongly again a fortnight later 'on the spirit of becoming useful in case of invasion that every man, young and old, rich and poor, throughout the country are learning the use of arms'.[126] For Turner, while war had created the lucrative business of Hennessy & Turner in Hamburg, successful French expeditions would have thrown uncertainty over the continuance of all foreign trade with England. It is likely that a cold and detached figure like

Turner was moved, in so far as he could be moved by any consideration other than ones of immediate commercial advantage or of obliging his profitable London correspondent, by such a calculus.

BRANDY BUSINESS IN HAMBURG

Hennessy & Turner was not the only house that supplied brandy to
de Katter. Signifying the effect of the Revolution in deepening commercial networks, some was even consigned by Bordeaux houses and,
in very novel fashion, by Nouel of Angoulême.[127] The houses of
Broussard and of Salignac & Babin also entered into the Hamburg
market in 1799. The correspondence between Turner and Hennessy
is replete with references to enemies, and to friends concealed as enemies which are said to be even more dangerous. Turner regarded the
problem of documenting his absence with the Cognac municipality as
having its origins in doubts sown by Cognac rivals.

In the autumn of 1798 Turner, again under pressure to return, had
observed that 'il semble verité à lire vos lettres que je dois, en outre
des commissions que je vous ai procuré, avoir fait une fortune. Si c'est
la votre idée je vous remercie de votre bonne opinion de mes talents,
mais n'allez pas batir des chateaux en Espagne. Tout ce que j'ai pu
gagner sera mis sur un petit tableau qu'en cas d'accident vous sera
envoyé et vous ne perdrez rien'.[128] His speculative interests mainly
concerned commodities other than brandy.[129] He lost heavily in sugar
in 1799 as prices fell unexpectedly. The sugar seems to have been on
the joint account of the house, as he accepted blame.[130] The source of
future tensions between the two men was thus evident. It was also
clear that Hennessy, now becoming more experienced, was asserting
himself more. It seems that he did not trust the speculative flair of
Turner, and the belief that Turner was extending his stay for private
profit came up in the correspondence.

Turner was strongly opposed to coming back to Cognac. On 6
April he resisted the idea, because, as he said, 'j'ai encore devant moi
le moyen d'augmenter notre fortune qui serait perdue si j'étais à
Cognac et il ne faut de votre coté qu'agir avec prudence dans les
achats pour que tout aille au mieux. Maintenant que je ne cours plus,

je serai plus régulier à vous écrire et plait à Dieu je vous ferai faire de bonnes affaires'. De Katter's orders in particular depended on sureness of supply. Turner insured in Hamburg and arranged Hamburg vessels for shipments. No one else in the brandy trade was doing this. He paid every attention to detail: if prices were falling, he worried about costs in Cognac; if quality were poor, though he thought some of the brandy coming on the market not cognac, he stressed the necessity to pay attention to quality. On 8 May he asked rhetorically: 'ne t'ai je pas procuré de bonnes affaires. Nos spéculations ont-elles été mauvaises? N'ai-je pas rempli tous les buts de mon voyage. Qu'est-ce que tu veux?'[131]

RICHARD HENNESSY: LAST DAYS

Richard Hennessy comes up scarcely at all in this correspondence. From the time of its acquisition, La Billarderie became both Richard's residence and his concern. James's comments in a letter in October 1795 hint at the situation: 'we may be able now and then when winter allows to pass a day there and trust and hope that little place will afford you some agreeable days and that certainly is what I can wish the most'.[132] For almost the first time perhaps in his life, a fleeting period in 1784–5 excepted, Richard was free from preoccupation. Delamain, who remained in touch with him, proposed in February 1797 'going to keep you company a couple of hours', and three months later referred to him 'in health and spirits manually cultivating a pleasant property sixteen hours in the twenty-four'.[133] That it was close to Richard's heart and that he talked freely about it is suggested by Madame Byrne's letter in 1797 in which she referred to 'your own estate a new little Ballymacmoy ... why not give it that name'.[134]

A chilling insight into Turner's disposition arises from an episode in 1798, when a friend of de Katter who held Andoe's old distillery proposed to set it to work if an associate with a knowledge of brandy could be found on the spot. Turner suggested that 'si l'association a lieu Papa pourrait aller passer quelque temps à Bordeaux et à fin de mettre tout en train, acheter pour le compte des intéressés des eaux de vie faibles qu'il ferait rectifier à la preuve'. For Turner this would be a good opportunity 'pour nous lier très étroitement avec un homme aussi intime avec Katter'.[135] Turner came back to the subject several times.

The old world was dying. The abundant correspondence from Bordeaux was waning, and the letter books contained at times few letters to old friends, and none at all to the Bordeaux Irish. Perhaps that world, not only the Franco-Irish one but the *ancien régime* universe of commerce in which Cognac was a satellite to Bordeaux, expired with, or even before, Richard. He had not long to live. He died on 8 October 1800 'après quelques jours de maladie accompagnée d'intolérables douleurs'.[136] The duration of his illness was fifteen days.[137] He had outlived almost all his contemporaries. In recent years, James Woods' letters to him had catalogued the deaths of old Bordeaux acquaintances: John Galwey in 1793, Daniel MacCarthy (one of Bordeaux's greatest *ancien régime* merchant princes) in 1795, Knight in 1797, Robert Forster in 1799. For a man much attached to his friends these must have been painful years, softened only by the good relationship with his son James and by his rustic occupations at La Billarderie. Delamain, patriarch of the brandy trade and his friend of thirty-five years from the first days of arrival in the Charente, preceded him by a few months, dying in May on the way to take the waters.[138]

Few men can have been loved as much as Richard. He was not well educated, but he was warm and kind, able also to hold simultaneously the friendship of his contemporaries and of young people, whether John Saule, little more than a third his age in 1768, or the young merchants who joined with him in the carefree club in the Lormont hills in 1785. Thomas Knight in 1790 had spoken of his heart as 'unequalled'.[139] John Auguste Byrne went even further, stating that 'I am convinced you have a number of friends and not one enemy'.[140] Many years later in 1797 Madame Byrne wrote: 'I often thought of you and as often reflected on the generosity of your heart. I said Dick Hennessy will advance me one or two thousand livres. Am I presumptuous in the expectation ...'. She was not: Hennessy provided 1200 livres. Woods, writing from Bordeaux, provided in a letter of condolence to James the longest and the most moving testimony:

You have not a relative in the world who was more particularly affected than every individual under roof were at hearing the melancholy event that happened in your family, nor does any person condole with you more sincerely thereon than I do. If it can be any consolation to you, you may also rely, there never was a man more universally regretted here by all those who had the pleasure of knowing him, which is not at all surprising as it may be said with propriety that his amiable character and sentiments were peculiar to him.[141]

DECLINE OF THE DELAMAIN HOUSE

Over the 1790s the Delamain house passed from a major to a minor place in Cognac business. In 1798, for instance, it was a poor fourth in the size of its of shipments ready for dispatch, and its total was far short of the figures for the larger houses.[142] Even if a separate business by a son, Delamain *fils*, was included, the rank order would not have altered. Thus while Delamain held a place in the trade in and through the 1780s, even in the eddies of the late 1780s, the house faltered decisively in the following decade. Why was this?

To understand the reason, we have to turn to the history of the 1790s. As a prominent citizen, indeed Jarnac's most prominent *roturier*, Delamain may have been distracted by political life. Also, Delamain was ageing: James Hennessy and Samuel Turner were young, ambitious and more likely to take risks. Moreover, openminded though he had been in the 1780s, he was in the last analysis a liberal man of the *ancien régime* who had known the comte de Jarnac and had met the great aristocrats of the region at Freemason assemblies, and his letter of 29 June 1795 breathes his caution:

Not long since I had a tolerable share of business not so much as I might because I did not encline to be adventurous and undertook only what I deemed entirely safe and such maxim I intend to be the rule of my future conduct during the strange situation in which commerce has been for some time past in this country. I in a manner retired and did little or nothing at which I have not the smallest regret and observe with pleasure the success of those who in my opinion underwent some danger in obtaining it.

All that may explain why he did not pursue business ends ruthlessly, but not why the firm did not find its feet again. A more likely explanation is the inadequacy of his sons. Delamain himself in 1797 regarded his family as failing him.[143]

The eldest son had been apprenticed to a merchant's house in Rotterdam in 1781.[144] All the children were well provided for: fortunes of 20,000 livres, in other words on a scale almost rivalling the Martells, were to be given to each of them.[145] Jean Isaac married the youngest daughter of Philip Augier the elder in 1787.[146] This is the Delamain *fils* who was in business on his own account in the 1790s. However, the fact that he was not heir to Delamain's own business was one of the consequences of the disillusionment which he described in 1797. While the grounds for his disappointment in his eldest son are not clear (the letter books thrown light only on members of the family abroad), disappointment with a younger son, James, is well documented. James had been dispatched in 1788 to Hull, a city with which his father enjoyed close connections.[147] The father expected his son to return to Jarnac; in other words, with Jean-Isaac provided for (or metaphorically banished), he may have seen James as his successor. But James seems to have been prevailed on through 'his ridiculous inclinations' and by an associate – 'he who thus wheedles him must be a great villain' – with the consequence that the course which he followed was, in Delamain's words, in 'total opposition to our plans'.[148] Shortly after his arrival the son married the daughter of one of his new acquaintances in circumstances which drove the father to fury: should the son return 'he shall be received as company in a civil manner but with his companion he must not attempt to approach my door'.[149] When the son had borrowed money from a Hull merchant, an exasperated James Delamain had written in January 1789 that 'we now declare we have done with him'.[150] But a month later when the son loaded a cargo of wheat for Rochefort and Bordeaux, in a milder tone he wrote that 'his welfare can not be a matter of indifference to me and any opportunity that offered of setting him forward in the world I should gladly embrace'.[151] Somewhat later, he guaranteed a credit of £500 for him at the London house of Thomas Gorman, somewhat untruthfully telling Gorman: 'we hear he is careful therefore he may probably succeed notwithstanding our great reason to complain of his conduct'.[152]

Complaints in the 1790s from the father about the son were a constant refrain.[153] As late as May 1801 the son made an offer to MacCarthy *frères* to act as a factor in the sale of prunes, suggesting wildly that he could execute orders to the extent of ten cargoes a year.[154] Shoolbred, correspondent of Hennessy & Turner in London noted in April 1798 his incapacity to honour a bill, and a few months after observed that 'he does not appear to merit your friendship, having no sense of it'.[155] Another letter by Shoolbred referred to 'his cringing letters', and in 1800 he went so far as to say that 'I wish never to have any correspondence with a man so unworthy of the name of merchant'.[156]

Delamain's health was probably declining, and in 1797 he complained of gout in one of his hands. As long as Richard Hennessy remained alive, the close contact with the Hennessys continued: letters from Delamain were regular as late as 1799. The absence of comment on his death in the Hennessy archives is a mute testimony to the small weight of Delamain's business in the Cognac of 1800. The story hints at a family which fell short of expectations, riven by conflicts between children and an authoritarian father and even jealousies between sons. While the eldest son was married in 1787 to a daughter of Philippe Augier, with a very good dowry of 23,000 livres, her husband's contribution to the marriage probably consisted of his portion from his father to set him up independently in business. He made no mark as a merchant. It was somewhat unusual to set up an eldest son in this fashion in a separate business in the home locality. The other marriages did not greatly advance the standing of the house. Anne Marie Esther was married to Paul-Frédéric Roullet, a merchant member of a family very much of the second order in business, and another daughter, Jeanne Esther-Adelaide, was married to a La Rochelle merchant, Gabriel Garreau (though hardly one of great prospects because his future was to be tied up with the house).[157] A further daughter married a young Englishman, Thomas Hine from Dorset. He had first appeared as a clerk in the house in 1791, recruited apparently through the good offices of James Ireland, a customer of Delamain's in Bristol.[158] Hine then retired to England either because business turnover fell or because the Terror suggested, for a recently arrived young man, a more prudent course of returning home. He was lured back, as soon as conditions got better politically and economically in the course of 1795, with the promise of an interest in the house and the prospect of marriage to a Delamain daughter.

Delamain's letter to Hine's father on 29 June 1795 made the offer of an interest in the house. He envisaged Hine executing 'such excursions which contribute much to the success of business, such is the constant practice of the merchants in Bordeaux from which it appears they reap a great benefit'.[159] The partnership was for a small interest, one fourth. It took effect from 1 January 1796, though the formal articles of partnership were not drawn up until 1 May 1796. The articles even envisaged the possibility of changing the style of the house in a year's time. His abrupt progression to partnership and to marriage to Delamain's daughter Françoise-Elizabeth suggests that the idea of marriage may even have preceded the offer of a place, more particularly because of the hint at changing the style of the house.

Business was neither easy, given the difficult business conditions, nor smooth within the family circle. Hine's introduction to the business and to partnership, a position held by none of Delamain's sons, may even have sharpened the divides. For Hine's own role we have only his own words in his out-letters. The fact that renewal of the partnership proposed in 1800 on the death of Delamain saw the appointment of a clerk as something to be envisaged if there was an 'extension des affaires' suggests that turnover had been so small that the partnership had been getting by without one.[160] Resentment at Hine's place is hinted at in article 20: 'il demeure convenu que le citoyen Thomas Hine pourra conserver dans la maison de commerce l'intéret que lui donne le présent act social sans que le citoyen H. Delamain puisse le lui disputer'. The fact that in the event of wishing to retire from the house on the death of his partner (Delamain's widow) he was held to give six months' notice to Henri – or Harry – of his intentions suggests that Henri was expressly kept out of the house. Strikingly, two draft articles providing for replacement of the widow in the event of her death by Henri had been struck out in favour of vaguer clauses. A further clause provided that while the widow could cede her interest to Henri, he would have no managing authority in the house without the consent of Hine. When James

Hennessy went to London in 1800, Henri was sent with him: 'our Mrs Delamain has obtained of him to conduct on the journey her youngest son Henry Delamain formerly at Lausanne for his education, which she wishes he could continue in England'.[161] Some business orders seem to have been solicited by him. However, he was on bad terms with his own brother James, who in turn did not get on well with the parent house. Hine wrote on 1 June 1805 that 'we really believe he has great reason to complain of you, but that at same time he acts very ungenerously if he has made reports injurious to your character'.[162] In considerable exasperation with Henri, Hine wrote a year later that 'we have had too many specimens of his harmful and scandalous conduct', and expressed the view that 'the sooner will be the better' for Harry's departure from England.[163] Harry returned by September, and Hine was reduced to writing to James of the jealousy between the two brothers: 'the letter he wrote you on the subject, the copy whereof you sent us, we shall keep as masterpiece of refined [*word missing*]'.[164] Three month earlier, before Harry's return, Hine had observed to James:

> Tho' true enough, we are very awkwardly situated with your brother Harry and it will not be an easy matter to argue, as long as he will persist in spending more money than the house can afford to allow, especially that he will not meddle with our business, indeed he has left it aside for several months past. His mother has wrote him very lately expressing her wish that he would immediately return to Jarnac and we take the opinion of his regard for his mother that we make no doubt but he will comply therewith without loss of time; as such the arrangement you propose, cannot suit us and if you have an opportunity of connecting yourself with another house, we would [*word indecipherable*] rather in your interest, that you would embrace it than to wait the issue of our debates with Harry. You say the reason why our share of business is so much reduced of late, is owing to several irregularities in our correspondence and to the inferior quality of some brandies of our shipping.[165]

This letter shows how James as well as Harry remained difficult. Not only was James Delamain in Hull a wretched businessman, but what Hine described delicately as 'our debates with Harry' were an added problem. Though the partnership was one of the widow and Hine, the house seems to have been intended to keep both sons and married daughters and their spouses afloat. In 1801 the deed of partnership was for five years. In 1807, while retaining the style of Delamain Ranson & Co., both Henry and Garreau, who was married to a Delamain daughter, were brought into a partnership for ten years, each for a one-third interest. What this meant was that the widow Delamain ceded her interest to her son Henry, something already envisaged as a possibility in 1801, subject to the consent of Hine. A deed of 19 July 1810 suggests that conflicts must have arisen and that it was intended to clarify matters. It limited withdrawals by any partner to 6000 francs per year. In other words Harry was almost certainly up to his old tricks again, and a further clause prohibiting any of the partners from putting a legal stay on papers or effects of the house suggests that there had already been notarial actions and threatened litigation.

In 1817 family conflicts finally led, at the insistence of Henry, to the liquidation of the business, and to the emergence of two new but separate houses, a Delamain house (including Henry – 'Harry' – and a nephew, another Henry, son of Jean-Isaac Delamain) and the house of Thomas Hine & Co., in which Hine and Garreau each held a half share.[166] James Delamain's widow died at the end of the year, Hine himself in 1822, and Gabriel Garreau withdrew by deed of 14 February 1823. An act of the same day's date created a new partnership for five years with Hine's widow as a *commanditaire*, while her son Thomas-George ran the business. Another son, Thomas, was added to this arrangement in a new five-year contract in 1831. No deed survives for 1828: the presumption is that the old partnership was extended until Thomas appeared in 1831. The pattern was repeated in the next decade; no act survives from 1836, but a third son, Auguste, appeared in new articles in 1841. These were terse agreements providing for a house exclusively of the widow (a Delamain daughter), and of the offspring of her marriage to Hine.

The second of the two new partnerships, the Delamain one of 1817 (containing the two Henris, son and grandson of James Delamain), was at first styled Delamain & Co., becoming in turn Roullet & Delamain in 1822, and, recruiting a Roullet cousin in 1824, the partnership of that year is in legal terms the present Delamain &

Co.[167] Conflicts among Delamain's sons in large part explain the slide in the position of the Delamain business in the life of the Charente: failures to control expenditure, family disputes, and, in the wake of changes in 1817 and 1823, a haemorrhage of capital. James Delamain's great residence itself was to have a chequered history. It had been made over to the eldest son, Jean-Isaac, in 1795; his widow sold it in 1812 to Garreau, a partner in the business. After Garreau left the partnership in 1823, the house passed though many hands before it was finally purchased by Hine's in the 1930s. The Ranson & Delamain business papers from 1778, deposited in it by Garreau during his early tenure of the house, remained undisturbed in the lofts until modern times. The fact that they were left there in 1823 when Garreau withdrew from the partnership is as much a testimony to the rupture in or loss of old business relations as to the family divisions. The decline of Ranson & Delamain was a parallel to that of Augier's. Etienne Augier's resources in 1827 were modest: property worth 37,000 francs, and liquid assets worth 4960 francs.[168] Like the Augier house – the oldest in Cognac – the Delamains, even more steeped in the business history of the Charente through the Ranson association in Jarnac, had ceased to be a business force in a changed world.

TURNER'S RETURN FROM HAMBURG

While Dupuy had returned from Hamburg in May 1800, Turner, whose determination to remain on had already been a source of friction with his partner James Hennessy, came back only at the time of the peace of Amiens. His personal standing and his place within the house of Hennessy & Turner led to his immediately becoming mayor of Cognac, an office he held until 1804. The partnership with Hennessy was dissolved at the end of 1812. The recollection of the grandfather of one of the present generation of his descendants is that it arose from differences between Turner and Hennessy.[169]

Turner's world had changed radically in the course of 1812. His wife had died in February, and at the end of the year he left for the last time what he and Hennessy had turned into the largest brandy business on the banks of the Charente. The parting was at least amicable enough for Turner's letters to Hennessy after the event to have a personal ring. There is a tone of melancholy, however, as he was worried about the fate of his sons serving under the *levée en masse*: 'les peines de l'ame me sont bien familières depuis longtemps, mais l'ame ne s'y habitue point, et chaque jour reprend ses droits'.[170] There is a hint too in this letter at deep and continuing grief at the loss of his wife. He continued a business in a partnership – Turner Fioulet et Cie – at Vinade, where he also lived, presumably in the Logis de Vinade, in the commune of Saint-Meme les Carrières, Bassac. His property was worth 97,000 francs and movable property 39,000 francs, modestly large but less than the high expectations of his earlier life.[171] He died in 1822. There were seven children of the marriage; they married well in conventional terms, but none married into the *négociant* milieu in which for twenty-three years Turner had loomed so large. We are left wondering what precisely happened in the end to this single-minded and ambitious man's purpose and calculation in 1812, and what was the mood of his last ten years.

Old established houses like Augier, despite its social esteem, or Delamain, equally prominent, had already lost their place. The deaths of Richard Hennessy and Delamain, both very much men of the old world in personal style and business methods, also emphasised how the community had changed. They contrasted in methods and attitudes with Théodore Martell in Bordeaux, and with the approach of both James Hennessy and Samuel Turner, equally with that of Dupuy, who were men in a new mould. Superficially, the firms seem of foreign origin. Martell (a Jersey man himself) had come from Guernsey in 1718; Richard Hennessy had arrived in 1765; and the house of Otard & Dupuy, in essence a French house, claimed an aristocratic lineage through the Otards and later embellished alleged Jacobite ties. James Hennessy and Turner, even if of Irish background and Irish birth respectively, had no active Irish ties and no obvious Irish friends. Like Jean Martell, whose marriages ties with the Lallemand family turned the Martells into a French house, they were in effect Frenchmen, married to French women, writing in French more easily than in English (correspondence in English within the circle lasted only as long as Richard had lived), and only political opportunism in 1824 prompted rivals to taunt Hennessy with a foreign ancestry and nationality. The Delamains too were in essence a French house, through their Ranson ties, and French was the medium of conversation within the family.

The old world, one in which outside families set up relatively easily, had ended. The Exshaws might seem to suggest the reverse, but John Exshaw, nephew of a lord mayor of Dublin, and whose mother came from the Dublin branch of the Bordeaux Nairacs, was in a sense returning home, and settled in Bordeaux.[172] In the nineteenth century, business was dominated by a handful of houses, which had achieved status and scale by the beginning of the century. They often marketed on their own account, and in contrast to the old brandy houses in Cognac, which trembled at the displeasure of their foreign customers, they were more powerful than most, if not all, of their individual customers. The Revolution had speeded the process of change: unusual alliances, the daring social link between Hennessys and Martells through two marriages (James's in 1795 and that of Lucie-Hélène, daughter of James Hennessy, and Jean-Gabriel Martell in 1816), the movement abroad to Hamburg, and active business ties in Bordeaux and Paris (a process pioneered by the innovative Théodore Martell) all speeded the process. The old market was unstable, the houses numerous, their hold easily challenged by new arrivals with fresh ties outside, their prospects changing wildly over time. By contrast the nineteenth century was one of large, stable businesses, and of dominance by three giants: the Martell house, which enhanced its status in the 1780s, and the Hennessys and Otard-Dupuys, who achieved their positions under the Revolution and Empire.

NOTES
NOTE ON SOURCES
BIBLIOGRAPHY
INDEX

Abbreviations

AAC	Augier archives, Cognac
AAE	Archives des affaires étrangères, Ministère des affaires étrangères, Paris
ACC, La Rochelle	Archives de la chambre de commerce, La Rochelle
ADC, Angoulême	Archives départementales de la Charente, Angoulême
ADCM, La Rochelle	Archives départementales de la Charente maritime, La Rochelle
ADG, Bordeaux	Archives départementales de la Gironde, Bordeaux
AN, Paris	Archives nationales, Paris
CPA	Correspondance politique Angleterre
DAJ	Delamain archives, Jarnac
HAC	Hennessy archives, Cognac
HAJ	Hine archives, Jarnac
MAC	Martell archives, Cognac
OAJ	Otard archives, Cognac
PRO	Public Record Office

Notes

1. Archives départementales du Morbihan, Vannes, E2340-E2445, Lamaignère and Delaye papers. This firm acted as agents for Sutton, and the papers contain extensive correspondence from Sutton. On the poor qualities of both red and white wine, see also letter of 6 July 1757 from the Intendant of the navy in Brest to the Minister of the marine (Archives du port de Brest, 1E 531, ff.336-8).
2. W. Minchinton, 'The Canaries in the British trade world of the eighteenth century', in Francisco Morales Padron, ed., IX *Coloquio de historia Canario-Americana* (Las Palmas, 1990), p. 678, quoting figures from Ralph Davis.
3. See L.M. Cullen, 'Comparative aspects of Irish diet 1550-1850', in Hans J. Teuteberg, ed., *European food history* (Leicester, 1992), pp. 47-8.
4. A. Guimera Ravina, *Burguesia extranjera y comercio atlántico: la empresa comercial irlandesa en Canarias 1703-1771* (Tenerife, 1985).
5. HAC, 24 April 1766, Pat Nagle, Paris, to Richard Hennessy.
6. National Archives, Dublin. Wyche documents, 114/41, 'Some reasons demonstrating the prejudice that the importation of brandy occasions to Ireland'.
7. S. Madden, *Reflections and resolutions proper for the gentlemen of Ireland* (Dublin, 1738), p. 46.
8. W. Henry, rector of Urney, *An earnest address to the people of Ireland against the drinking of spirituous liquors* (Dublin, 1753), p. 31.
9. L.M. Cullen, *The brandy trade under the Ancien Régime: regional specialisation in the Charente* (Cambridge, 1998), pp. 30, 36.
10. MAC, letter book 1774-5, 19 March 1774, to Josias Cottin et fils, London.
11. ADLA, Nantes, Amirauté B4694[1]. Masters' declarations on departure give the destination of vessels. The total quantities of brandy shipped in the *Balance du commerce* statistics for each region divided by the number of shipments gives a figure for the average cargo size.
12. *Inventaire de la Série C*, Archives départementales d'Ille-et-Vilaine, vol.1, p. 21

2: BRANDY SMUGGLING

1. L.M. Cullen, 'The smuggling trade in Ireland in the eighteenth century', *Proceedings of the Royal Irish Academy*, section C, vol. 67, no. 5 (1969).

2. Archives départementales d'Ille-et-Vilaine, Bourde de la Rogerie papers, 5 J 74, notes on Warren correspondence, especially letter of 1 Sept. 1766; Archives départementales du Morbihan, Vannes, Warren papers, letters at various dates from Andrew Galwey of Nantes. See also Cullen, 'The smuggling trade in Ireland in the eighteenth century', *Proceedings of the Royal Irish Academy*, section C, vol. 67, no. 5 (1969), p. 155.

3. L.M. Cullen, *Anglo-Irish trade 1660-1800*, pp. 148-50; idem, 'The Irish smuggling trade ...', p. 153; PRO of Northern Ireland, Belfast, Black papers.

4. University College, Dublin. O'Connell papers.

5. L.M. Cullen, *Smuggling and the Ayrshire economic boom of the 1760s and 1770s*, Ayrshire Archaeological and Natural History Society, Ayrshire monographs (Sept. 1994).

6. DAJ, letter book 1767-8, 16 and 23 May 1767, to Robert Young; Irish Manuscripts Commission, *The Kenmare manuscripts* (Dublin, 1942), ed. E. MacLysaght, p. 232.

7. HAJ, invoice books and accounts.

8. HAC, 14 Dec. 1774, Luke Cassin, Dublin. See also Cassin, 20 Aug. 1774.

9. HAC, letter book 1771-5, 22 Nov. 1773, to Francis Kiernan, Dublin.

10. Ibid., 20 Aug. 1774, Luke Cassin, Dublin.

11. HAC, letter book 1784-6, 21 March 1785, Saule to Tallon. Other smugglers seem to have done so too. See HAC, letter book 1784-6, 23 April 1785, Saule to John Oram, Charente. See also MAC, letter book 1784-5, 12 Nov. 1785, to Hore.

12. National Library, Dublin, microfilm p. 928, nos. 5, 6, 7, 18, 24 May, 10 June 1783, Thomas Hutchins to James Peed.

13. HAC, 20 Dec. 1783, Brown, Bubbers & Co., Dunkirk.

14. Boulogne's business for England may have already been rising in the 1770s. A correspondent in Boulogne in 1774, seeking a place in a house in La Rochelle for a young man, noted that 'in this and our neighbouring towns there is no encouragement for young men as our trade is entirely confined to the brandy business'. HAC, 13 June 1774, John Walsh, Boulogne. See also letter of Isaac Brown, Dunkirk, 10 Feb. 1787.

15. HAC, 7 August 1790, Robert Murdock, Dunkirk.

16. See AN, Paris, F^{12} 1646-50, 'Rapport sur le re-établissement des ports francs', 9 Thermidor an 9; F^{12} 1666. For details of the ship sailings, see AN, Paris, G^5 81*, G^{5}85*.

17. HAC, 25 Oct. 1790, Robert Murdock to Richard Hennessy, Dunkirk.

18. HAC, 26 Jan. 1785, John Christian, jnr., to John Saule.

19. AN, Paris, F^{12} 1666. See Cullen, *The brandy trade ...*, p. 38.

20. HAC, 18 Oct. 1783, Luke Cassin, Dublin, to Saule.

21. HAC, 23 Nov. 1784, Richard Hennessy, Bordeaux, to Saule.

22. HAC, 22 Oct. 1784, Hennessy, Bordeaux, to Saule.
23. HAC, 30 Oct. 1784, Hennessy, Bordeaux, to Saule.
24. HAC, 9 Jan. 1784, Hennessy, Bordeaux, to Saule.
25. HAC, 26 Oct. 1784, Hennessy, Bordeaux, to Saule.
26. HAC, 1 Jan. 1785, Hennessy, Bordeaux, to Saule.
27. MAC, 31 Dec. 1785, T. Martell, Bordeaux.
28. HAC, 10 Feb., 25 Feb. 1786, Hennessy, Bordeaux.
29. HAC, 16 Feb. 1787, Hennessy, Bordeaux.
30. HAC, 31 March 1787, Hennessy, Bordeaux. Two vessels declaring for North Faro feature in the Bordeaux *congés* for late March and early April 1787. Very probably also two Cork vessels, though declared for orthodox destinations at the same time, were smugglers as well.
31. AN, Paris, G⁵ 47*.
32. HAC, 18 Dec. 1785, Hennessy, Bordeaux, to Saule.
33. HAC, 7 Oct. 1785, Hennessy, Bordeaux, to Saule. Hennessy, the recipient of many confidences from smugglers in 1785, had observed that 'the coast of Ireland was never so guarded as it is now'. HAC, 10 Aug. 1785, Richard Hennessy, Bordeaux.
34. On John Murphy, see L.M. Cullen, 'Smugglers in the Irish Sea in the eighteenth century', in *The Irish Sea: aspects of maritime history*, ed. M. McCaughan and J. Appleby (Belfast, 1989), p. 89.
35. AN, Paris, G⁵ 47*, 48*, 50*, 51*, *congés* granted in Bordeaux.
36. MAC, letter book 1783-4, 9 June 1783, Martell to Cassin.
37. MAC, 5 Feb. 1784, Vaughan & Litton, Dublin.
38. AN, Paris, G⁵ 62, *congés* for Charente. The *congés* for 1783, 1785 and 1788 are missing.
39. MAC, 22 April 1786, Luke Cassin. Payment for Hore's brandy passed through Cassin's hands to London, where Martell drew on Cassin's correspondent in the normal way. MAC, letter book 1784-5, 5 Sept. 1785.
40. See L.M. Cullen, *Smuggling and the Ayrshire economic boom* ...; idem, 'Smugglers in the Irish Sea ...'.
41. HAC, 12 May 1784, Richard Hennessy, Bordeaux, to Saule.
42. HAJ, Delamain letter book, 1785-7 (no. 1), 1 Nov. 1785, to Cassin; Delamain invoices.
43. HAC, letter book 1784-6, 7 May 1785, Saule to Tallon.
44. HAC, letter book, 1786-7, 22 Jan, 1787, to John Kennedy Saule.
45. HAC, 12 May, 28 Aug. 1784, Richard Hennessy, Bordeaux, to Saule.
46. HAC, letter book 1784-6, 20 Sept. 1784, to Tallon; 6 Dec. 1784, Robert White to Saule; Dublin, 2 Feb., 25 July, 4 Aug. 1785, Val Tallon to Saule. The vessel is listed in the *congés* for the Charente as departing on 4 September, where it appears as a tiny vessel of 20 tons, master William Christian. AN, Paris, G⁵ 62. The *congés* for 1785 are missing.
47. HAC, Dublin, 2 Feb. 1785.
48. HAC, Dublin, 6 June 1785.
49. HAC, letter book 1784-6, 23 July, 13 Aug. 1785, Saule to Tallon.
50. See HAC, various letters, especially from White, St. Martin's, 24, 30 July 1785.
51. HAC, Dublin, 27 Aug. 1785, Tallon to Saule.

52. HAC, 29 Aug. 1785, Hennessy, Bordeaux, to Saule, and later letters.

53. HAC, 7 October 1785, Richard Hennessy, Bordeaux, to Saule. See also HAC, 12 Nov. 1785, Hennessy, Bordeaux, to Saule.

54. See chapter 8.

55. See Priaulx Library, Guernsey, Carteret Priaulx papers.

56. See records of Hewitts for the 1790s in the Cork Archives Council for details of the market in the 1790s.

3: DOMESTIC, FOREIGN AND IRISH MERCHANTS
OF THE BRANDY REGIONS

1. L.M. Cullen, 'The Huguenots from the perspective of the merchant networks of W. Europe (1680-1720)', in *The Huguenots and Ireland: anatomy of an emigration* (Dublin, 1987), ed. C.J. Caldicott, G. Gough and J.P. Pittion, pp. 129-49.

2. ADG, Bordeaux, 6B 47, 6B 48, 6B 49, 6B 50, passports 1727-1750. See also Cullen, 'The Huguenots ...', p. 142. Christian Huetz de Lemps, *Géographie du commerce de Bordeaux à la fin du règne de Louis XIV* (Paris, 1975), p. 496, has figures for 1712-18.

3. ADCM, La Rochelle, Etude Cherpentier, 13 Feb. 1759.

4. A.G. Jamieson, *A people of the sea: the maritime history of the Channel Islands* (London, 1986), pp. 312-14.

5. MAC, letter book 1721-2, 28 Jan. 1722, to Jean Bonamy de Caches, Guernsey.

6. MAC, letter book 1724-25, 13 Jan. 1725, to Jean Brunet.

7. Ibid., 3 March 1725, to Le Mesurier.

8. For the marriage contracts of 1726 and 1737, see R. Firino-Martell, *La famille Martell* (Paris, 1924), pp. 17-21. The date of death of Jeanne Brunet is unknown.

9. AAC, letter book 1724-6, 5 Dec. 1725, to Martell.

10. Ibid., 26 February 1725, to Bucknell, Portsmouth.

11. Ibid., 3 April 1726.

12. AAC, letter book 1727-8, 25, 27 August 1727, to Elisha Dobrée, London.

13. AN, Paris, O¹ 231, f.47, *lettres de naturalité*, 1755. He was a signatory with other La Rochelle merchants of a petition to the Chambre de Commerce on 9 Nov. 1752. AAC, La Rochelle, no. 3592. He is also mentioned as a creditor of Daniel Galwey of Tonnay in a *procès-verbal* about brandy in Tonnay. ADCM, La Rochelle, *étude* Cherpentier, 20 Jan. 1753. However he also in turn failed in 1755. See ADCM, La Rochelle, Jurisdiction consulaire de La Rochelle, B398, 4 and 16 April 1755.

14. ADCM, La Rochelle, *étude* Cherpentier, *procès-verbal* of bankruptcy, 20 Jan., 19 March 1753.

15. HAJ, Delamain no. 2 letter book, 1 Dec. 1778, to Thomas Murphy, Dublin.

16. HAJ, Delamain no. 2 letter book 1778-81, 30 Nov. 1779, 12 Feb, 1780, to Greg Scurlog, Dublin.

17. HAJ, Delamain no. 1 letter book 1785-7, 21 Jan. 1786, to Hennessy, Bordeaux.

18. R. Firino-Martell, *La famille Martell* (Paris, 1924), p. 62.

19. J. Jezequel, *Grands notables du premier empire* (Paris, 1986), pp. 46, 81.

20. J. Royr, *Histoire de la franc-maçonerie en Charente* (Paris, 1994), p. 215.

21. MAC, letter book 1766-7, 6 Dec. 1766, 21 Feb. 1767, to Bruneaud *frères*.

22. HAC, Saule & Co., letter book, 1787-8, to Otard, 16 July, 27 August 1788.

23. From text of a letter as given in *Génealogie de la famille O'Tard de la Grange précédée d'une notice historique et chronologique sur le Jarl Norvegien Ottard et ses descendants Barons de Gournay de Dunnottard et de la Grange par le Comte de Valls, gendre du généalogiste d'Hozier, p. 12* (OAC). The letter, quoted by le comte de Valls, does not seem to survive.

24. Notarial *étude* Richon 3E 12848 (Libourne), 3-7-1704. I am greatly indebted to Monsieur Gérard De Ramefort, at the time managing director of Otards, for a copy of this document, and for showing me the evidence and discussing the uncertainties in the Otard genealogy documented by his painstaking reseaches into a fascinating question.

25. The Otard genealogy of 1882 indicated the parents as John O'Tard, baron de Dunottard, and Marie Drummond. The link of the Otard name to the place name Dunottard, associated with the 'De la Grange' fief name and the conversion of the real name Otard into O'Tard, are not very convincing. The marriage act of 1704 prosaically indicates Jacques Otard's parents as Jean Otard and a distinctly French-sounding Marie Chatard. If the Otard groom was Scottish, as was his bride's mother, given the name Oglethorpe, the expectation of Scottish witnesses would have been all the greater. Their total absence is not to be ignored, and the possibility remains that a slight Scottish connection through the Oglethorpe mother of his bride later prompted a creative approach to the genealogy. The effort to embellish origins by an emphasis on a noble foreign background was far from unknown. An extreme case is that of the Nesmonds, paper makers in Angoulême, two of whom rose to naval rank and claimed falsely to be descended from a family 'd'Esmond, originaires d'Irlande, descendants des Hamiltons, nobles anglais du XIᵉ siècle'. M. Verge-Franceschi, *La marine au XVIIIᵉ siècle* (Paris, 1996), p. 397.

26. Henry Jougla de Mornas, *Grand Armorial de France* (vol. 5, 1948), quoting from sources from the late 1880s and early 1890s, gave the name as O'Tard, and referred to them as a 'famille ancienne noble et originaire d'Irlande'. The detail in this source adds to the confusion about the genealogy.

4: THE IRISH CHALLENGE TO MARTELL, LALLEMAND & CO. IN THE 1760S

1. Aubry J. Toppin, 'The will of Henry Delamain the potter', *Transactions of the English Ceramic Circle*, vol. 8 (1942), pp. 158-9. James Delamain was a son of a younger brother, William.

2. See J.P. Poussou et al., unpublished list of Bordeaux passports. The original passport is in DAJ.

3. See DAJ, letter book 1767-8, 10 May 1768, to Bacot & Baire, Tours; 25 June 1768, to Delap, Bordeaux.

4. HAJ, Delamain letter book 1781-3 (no. 1), 22 March 1783, to MacCarthy Bros., Bordeaux

5. HAJ, journal of Isaac Ranson, Oct. 1758 to 16 March 1761.

6. DAJ, 23 Oct. 1760, James Delamain to Isaac Ranson, Rochefort.

7. HAC, Régnier letter book 1735-6.

8. HAC, Delamain no. 2 letter book 1787-9, 19 Sept. 1789, to Mallet.

9. HAJ, Delamain no. 2 letter book 1797-1801, 3 March 1800, to Hollerman, Gothenburg. To the end the house retained the style of Ranson & Delamain.

10. DAJ, contract dated 1 Nov. 1762, notary Gaboreau.

11. DAJ, letter book 1767-8, 17 March 1767, to John Kirwan, London.

12. MAC, letter book 1762-4, 15 May 1763, to S. Mitchell.

13. Ibid., 6 Dec. 1762. The reference to McDermott as their oldest acquaintance in Dublin is in a letter of 14 Nov. 1763 to McDermott. Correspondence with McDermott occurred again in 1775. MAC, letter book 1775–6, 19 June, 24 July 1775, to McDermott.

14. HAC, Saule, 12 Aug. 1773, John Saule, La Rochelle, to Richard Hennessy. See also file on the de Galwey succession in ADCM, La Rochelle, notaire de la Vergne, no. 177. On the origins of the La Rochelle Butler house, see L.M. Cullen, 'Galway merchants in the outside world 1650-1800', in *Galway town and gown 1484-1984* (Dublin 1984), ed. D. O'Cearbhaill, p. 66.

15. MAC, letter book 1762-4, 7 Nov. 1763, to Mathew Stritch.

16. Ibid., 13 June 1763, to Thomas Egan; 11 July 1763, to Barney Egan.

17. Ibid., 13 Dec. 1762, to Thomas Egan.

18. MAC, letter book 1766-7, 1 June 1767, to Stritch.

19. Ibid., letter book 1762-4, 7 Jan. 1764, to Jonathan Steel.

20. See ibid., 21 March 1763, to Thomas Egan.

21. Ibid., 8 Aug. 1763, to David Walsh.

22. Ibid., letter book 1766-7, 30 June 1766, to Mathew Stritch.

23. Ibid., 12 Jan. 1767, to Hutchinson, Leeds.

24. Ibid., see especially letter of 2 March 1767 to Morgan Rice, illustrating the importance attached to this point.

25. Ibid., 13 April 1767, to Morgan Rice, and earlier letter dated 30 March 1767.

26. Ibid., 18 Oct. 1766, to Didier, Dunkirk; 30 May 1767, to Didier, Dunkirk; 30 May 1767, to Stivel, Dunkirk.

27. T. Reynolds, *Life of Thomas Reynolds*, vol. 1 (London, 1839), p. 31.

28. W.J. Fitzpatrick, *Ireland before the union*, 6th ed. (Dublin, 1880), p. 199.

29. See entries in *Wilson's Dublin Directory*.

30. HAC, 'An account of sundry affairs left by Mr Laurence Saule in the care of Messrs Davys & Jennings to recover and receive on his account in virtue of a letter of attorney from said Saule to them dated this day of 1763' (receipted Davys & Jennings, Dublin, 1 Aug. 1763).

31. MAC, letter book 1762-4, 15 Aug. 1763, to Mathew Stritch.

32. Ibid., 12 Sept. 1763, to Christopher Boyle.

33. Ibid., 29 Aug. 1763, to Van Yzendorn.

34. Ibid., 12 Sept. 1763, to Thomas and William Clancy.

35. Ibid., 15 Oct. 1763, to Van Yzendorn.

36. Ibid., 23 Nov. 1763, to Gast Lallemand.

37. For example, ibid., 15 Aug. 1763, to David Walsh. Lallemand's comments on the Jennings-Saule threat were abundant in the closing months of the year.
38. Ibid., letter book 1766-7, 30 July, 2 Aug. 1766, to Gast Lallemand.
39. Ibid., 4 Oct. 1766, to Mathew Stritch; 20 Oct. 1766, to Richard Bennis.
40. HAC, 7 Jan. 1766, Denis MacCarthy, Bordeaux, to Richard Hennessy.
41. MAC, letter book 1766-7, 12 Nov. 1766, to Gast Lallemand.
42. Ibid., 2 March 1767, to Didier.
43. DAJ, letter book 1767-8, 9 April 1768, to Samuel Delap.
44. HAC, 29 Dec. 1765, Laurence Saule, Charente, to Richard Hennessy.
45. HAC, 20 Oct. 1766, Laurence Saule to Richard Hennessy.
46. HAC, 'Inventory of the effects of the Late Mr Saule deceased the 20th ult, 1 October, made in the presence of Mrs Bridget Saule his widow, Mrs Eleanor Jennings and Miss Catherine Saule his sister'.
47. DAJ, letter book 1767-8, 10 Dec. 1768, to Davys & Jennings.
48. Ibid., 29 Oct. 1768, to Isidore Lynch, London.
49. MAC, letter book 1766-7, 1 June 1767, to Mathew Stritch. Dublin failures were noted as early as 12 January in a letter of Lallemand to Stritch.
50. HAC, letter book 1765-9, 21 Nov. 1768, to Connelly & Arthur. See also DAJ, letter book 1767-8, 24 May 1768, to B. & J. Richard, Charente.
51. The sale of the interest in the lease is recorded in Registry of Deeds, Dublin, 227/416/148083, 1 July 1763. The original lease of the dwelling house, yard and warehouses in Eustace Street was dated 21 July 1759 (200/246/133032). The lease recorded his occupation as merchant. He appears in *Wilson's Dublin Directory* from as early as 1753 as a grocer in Fishamble Street, and is missing from the 1762 and later editions.
52. HAC, will (copy) dated 26 Sept. 1760, witnesses Theobald Jennings and Richard Kearney.
53. HAC, 27 April 1775, John Saule, La Rochelle, quoting from a Jennings letter dated 18 April. The quotation hints at the County Galway background. There were several Jenningses in Bath; as a result it has not been possible to identify the Irish family from the rate books in the Guildhall, Bath. Nor does the family appear in the records of the Catholic community, as do the Hennessys' relatives the Nagles, which suggests that the residence of the uncle was brief (J. Williams, ed., *Post-reformation catholicism in Bath* [2 vols, Catholic Record Society, London 1975-6]).
54. DAJ, letter book 1767-8, 10 Dec. 1768, to Davys & Jennings.
55. Ibid., 29 Oct. 1768, to Isidore Lynch.
56. HAC, 27 April 1775, John Saule, La Rochelle, to Richard Hennessy.
57. HAC, 8 Nov. 1772, John Saule, La Rochelle, to Richard Hennessy.
58. DAJ, letter book 1767-8, 10 Dec. 1768, to Laurence Saule & Co.
59. HAC, letter of 1 June from John Saule Kennedy, Dublin, quoted *in extenso* by John Saule, 27 June 1771, to Richard Hennessy. See also HAC, 8 Nov. 1772, John Saule to Richard Hennessy.
60. HAC, 3 Oct. 1771, John Saule to Richard Hennessy.
61. HAC, 13 March 1773, John Mehegan, Brest, to Hennessy.
62. HAC, 4 May 1775, John Saule to Richard Hennessy.
63. HAC, 27 April 1775, John Saule quoting from a letter from Saule Jennings.

64. HAC, 21 Dec. 1775, John Saule.
65. HAC, 3 Dec. 1775, Edward Saule Jennings to Saule.
66. On Charles Saule Jennings, or Kilmaine, see R.J. Hayes, *Biographical dictionary of Irishmen in France* (Dublin, 1949). Some of the detail in this account appears to be inaccurate, but in fact much of the early period of Jennings' life is obscure. The portrait is however reproduced in L'abbé Méderic Brodot, *Tonnay-Charente et le canton: étude historique, géologique, archéologique, généalogique, bibliographique, religieuse et commerciale*, vol. 1 (Rochefort, 1901), p. 562. Brodot's account states that Jennings entered the Royal Dragoons regiment in 1774 (though the correspondence in the Hennessy circle would suggest that his entry into the French army was somewhat later, and a letter from Jennings' cousin John Saule Kennedy in Dublin suggests that in 1789 he was in Lauzan's regiment of Huzzars, HAC, 30 July 1789), and is incorrect in its suggestion that the family had already been established in Tonnay-Charente before 1762. Hayes' own account of the family may be drawn from Brodot or from Léonce Grasilier's biography of Jennings or Kilmaine. The commune of Charente later had a portrait painted of him; it is now missing from the Hotel de Ville and unaccounted for. A security report much later, in 1797, noted that Kilmaine's uncle, Jennings, had kept a grocer's shop in Fishamble Street. National Archives, Dublin, 620/10/121/45, 11 January 1797, Leonard McNally.
67. HAC, 9 April 1775, John Saule to Richard Hennessy.
68. HAC, 30 Aug. 1772, John Saule to Richard Hennessy.
69. HAC, 7 Jan. 1773, John Saule to Richard Hennessy.
70. HAC, 'L. Saule's correspds. in 1768'. In John Saule's hand, attached to James Tuke's letter of 7 Nov. 1776. Delamain in the 1760s had 36 Dublin correspondents, Martell about 30, and Hennessy 24.
71. HAC, 9 May 1773, John Saule, La Rochelle, to Richard Hennessy. See also Saule to Hennessy, 8 July 1773.
72. HAC, 25 April 1773, John Saule, La Rochelle, to Richard Hennessy.
73. HAC, 8 July 1773, John Saule, La Rochelle, to Richard Hennessy. The Colebrooke saga is tied into a complex background network embracing both the Nesbitt interest and, for some of its speculative ventures, the Sutton interest. It was in this context that Burke engaged in the speculation in which his involvement is often denied. See L.M. Cullen, 'Burke, Ireland, and Revolution', *Eighteenth-century life*, vol. 16, n.s. (Feb. 1992), p. 36; idem, 'Luthy's *La banque protestante*: a reassessment', *Bulletin du Centre d'histoire des espaces atlantiques*, n.s. no. 5 (1990), p. 252; idem, 'Merchant communities overseas, the navigation acts and Irish and Scottish responses', in *Comparative aspects of Scottish economic and social history 1600-1900* (Edinburgh, 1977), ed. L.M. Cullen and T.C. Smout, pp. 165-6; idem, 'The Scottish exchange on London 1673-1780', in *Conflict, identity and economic development 1600-1939* (Preston, 1995), eds S.J. Connolly, R.A. Houston and R.J. Morris.
74. HAC, 7 June 1769, John Saule Kennedy, Dublin, to Richard Hennessy.
75. Saule made comments on his family on a number of occasions in the early 1770s, e.g., HAC, 27 June 1772, John Saule, La Rochelle, to Richard Hennessy.

76. HAC, 23 May 1778, John Saule Kennedy, Dublin, to John Saule. The letter refers to him getting his place in Plunkett's house three years previously.

77. MAC, letter book 1762-4, 31 Jan. 1763, to Michael Cosgrave.

78. HAC, 29 July 1782, John Saule Kennedy, Dublin, to John Saule.

79. DAJ, letter book 1767-8, 13 Oct. 1767, to Murphy, Dublin.

80. 'Test book 1775-6' in *59th report of the deputy keeper of the public records ... in Ireland* (Dublin, 1962), pp. 50-84

81. Catholic families from Waterford and its hinterland were very actively engaged in trade with Iberia. See L.M. Cullen, 'Merchants communities overseas ...', in A. Guimera Ravina, *Burgesia extranjera y comercio atlántico: la empresa comercial irlandes en Canarios 1703-1771* (Canary Islands, 1987), p. 170. This pattern was still evident at the end of the eighteenth century, and the archives of the Garvey sherry house in Jerez provide some interesting detail on this pattern in the 1790s.

82. The successor figure for Fitzgerald in the Irish international network (first identified as an agent for Fitzgerald in 1745), Thomas Sutton, comte de Clonard, relied on a new house, Selwyn & Foley in Paris, which gradually took over the business of the increasingly ineffective Woulfe/Waters business. Isaac Panchaud was a member of this house, and it was from this background that Panchaud made his mark, obscure but much commented on, in Paris banking.

83. HAC, 20 Aug. 1777, John Galwey & Co., Bordeaux, to Richard Hennessy.

84. AAE, Paris, CPA, vol. 440, Versailles, 4 March 1756.

85. See also file on the de Galwey succession in ADCM, La Rochelle, notaire de la Vergne, no. 177. On the origins of the La Rochelle Butler house, see L.M. Cullen, 'Galway merchants in the outside world 1650-1800', in *Galway town and gown 1484-1984* (Dublin 1984), ed. D. O'Cearbhaill, p. 66.

86. AAC, copy letters to English correspondents 1768-1782, 29 Oct. 1770, to John Galwey. See also letter to Edward Galwey, 22 Oct. 1770.

87. AAC, Broussard papers, 4 and 10 Nov. 1770, William Galwey, La Rochelle, to Broussard *fils*.

88. AAC, Broussard papers, 11 Nov. 1770, Madame Veuve de Galwey, La Rochelle, to Broussard *fils*.

89. HAC, 6 June 1771, John Saule, La Rochelle, to Richard Hennessy.

90. HAC, 5 Sept. 1771, John Saule, La Rochelle, to Richard Hennessy.

91. AAC, copy letters to English correspondents 1768-1782, 23 March 1771, 22 Aug. 1772, to John Galwey.

92. Ibid., 2 Aug. 1772, to John Galwey.

93. AAC, Broussard papers, 6 Dec. 1772, Veuve de Galwey to Brousssard.

94. AAC, marriage contract.

95. AAC, Broussard papers, 15 Feb. 1767, Antoine de Galwey, La Rochelle, to Daniel Broussard.

96. AAC, copy letters in English 1768-1782, 30 March 1768, to Edward Galwey, Dungarvan.

97. AAC, Broussard papers, 5 Jan. 1769, Edward Galwey, Dungarvan, to Daniel Broussard; 14 March 1769, from a Galwey cousin, Waterford.

98. AAC, copy letters to English correspondents 1768-82, 29 Oct. 1770, to John Galwey, Carrick-on-Suir.

99. AAC, Broussard papers, 9 March 1769, Veuve Antoine de Galwey, La Rochelle, to Broussard.
100. AAC, Broussard papers, 2 April 1769.
101. HAC, 25 April 1770, John Saule, La Rochelle, to Richard Hennessy.
102. AAC, letter book 26 April 1765 to 26 Nov. 1766, letter to Antoine de Galwey, 18 Dec. 1765. This is a very badly mutilated letter book; its effective internal dates are 3 Dec. 1765 to 1 Nov. 1766.
103. MAC, letter book 1766-7, 29 Dec. 1766, to Didier.
104. HAC, letter book 1765-69, 11 or 16 June 1766, to Dominick Mahon, Dublin.
105. HAC, 25 Sept. Ayr; 13 Nov. 1766, London (?), Luke Bellew to Richard Hennessy. An undated letter to a James Hennessy which survives in the Hennessy archives would probably have been written to Richard's Ostend cousin, and would then have been written in or before 1760.
106. HAC, Archives départementales du Morbihan, Vannes, Warren papers, letters from Bellew to Richard Warren on various dates from 1757 to 1761, and some draft replies in Warren's hand, E1449^1; E 1451^1; E1452^1; E 1453^1.
107. HAC, 16 May 1766, Bouchard to Richard Hennessy. He seems to have dallied for while after the war in Bordeaux, which may account for the inference that he was a merchant there. K.J. Harvey, 'The family experience: the Bellews of Mount Bellew', in T.P. Power and K. Whelan, *Endurance and emergence: catholics in Ireland in the eighteenth century* (Dublin, 1990), p. 185, and note 30. His officer background is confirmed in correspondence from his brother-in-law. See K.J. Harvey, *The Bellews of Mountbellew* (Dublin, 1998), p. 124; and Archives départementales du Morbihan, Vannes, Warren papers, 8 Feb. 1767, Richard Wall to Richard Warren.
108. HAC, letter book 1771-5, 31 March 1772, to Francis Kiernan. See also K.J. Harvey, 'The family experience ...', p. 185.
109. MAC, letter book 1766-7, 1 Dec. 1766, to Didier.
110. HAC, letter book 1765-9, 6 June 1768, R. Hennessy to Isidore Lynch.
111. AAC, Broussard papers, 15 Feb. 1767, A. de Galwey, La Rochelle, to Broussard.
112. DAJ, 11 June 1784, Joseph C. Walker to William Delamain; 21 Nov. 1786, draft letter, Liverpool, William Delamain; HAJ, Delamain letter book, 1787-9 (no. 1), 3 Jan. 1788, to Jas Ireland, at the time in Montpellier.
113. HAC, 3 Nov. 1783, Samuel Turner to John Saule.
114. HAC, 14 Aug. 1787, John Saule, London, to Richard Hennessy.
115. DAJ, Cognac, 9 Nov. 1790, James Delamain, Bengal, lieut. 22nd battalion, to his father. As the writer's name is James, the addressee would appear to be an uncle of the brandy merchant.
116. The third, Guillaume Alexandre, was probably Protestant.
117. DAJ, 11 June 1784, Joseph Cooper Walker.
118. HAJ, Delamain letter book (no. 1), 1778-81, 10 Nov. 1778, to Alliane, Paris; 11 Nov., to Pineau, Angoulême.
119. MAC, letter book 1766-7, 6 April 1767, to Jean Pré D'Orvillez et fils.
120. HAC, 12 Aug. 1773, John Saule, La Rochelle, to Richard Hennessy.
121. HAJ, Delamain letter book, 1783-5 (no. 2), 20 Sept. 1783, to Val Jones, Belfast.

122. DAJ, letter book 1767-8, 16 April 1768, to Capt. Patrick Walsh.

123. Ibid., 23 Feb. 1768, to Capt. Arthur Turner.

124. Ibid., 10 May 1768, to James Rice.

125. HAC, 8 Aug. 1791, James Delamain, Jarnac, to Richard Hennessy.

126. HAJ, Delamain letter book, 1787-9 (no. 2), 31 Jan. 1789, to Thomas Gorman.

127. DAJ.

128. HAJ, Delamain letter book, 1778-81 (no. 2), 8 Dec. 1778, to de Mordieu.

129. R. Delamain, *Jarnac à travers les ages* (Angoulême, 2nd. ed.), pp. 163-4.

130. Ibid., p. 174.

131. HAJ, Delamain letter book, 1783-5 (no. 2), 17 April 1784, to Alley & Darby.

132. HAJ, Delamain letter book, 1787-9 (no. 2), 7 March 1789, to Necker.

133. HAJ, Delamain letter book, 1789-90, 27 Feb. 1790, to MacCarthy Bros.

134. HAJ, Delamain letter book, 1789-93, 13 April 1790, to Theodore Martell.

135. HAJ, Delamain letter book, 1787-9 (no. 1), 6 Sept. 1788, to Mallet *père et fils*.

136. Ibid., 27 July 1789, to Knowsley, Hull, and Ewback, Hull.

137. Ibid., 12 Sept. 1789, to Knowsley, Hull.

138. DAJ, letter book 1767-8, 12 July 1768, to Joseph Berry & Co., Hull.

139. Ibid., to Berry, 10 Sept. 1768. See also 9 July 1768, to Capt. Joseph Remington, Hull.

140. DAJ. An interesting run of letters documents this connection.

141. HAJ, Delamain letter book, 1783-5 (no. 2), 11 Nov. 1783, to Alley & Darby.

142. Ibid., 30 April 1785.

143. DAJ, letter book 1767-8, letter of 23 Aug. 1768.

144. HAJ, Delamain letter book, 1781-3 (no. 2), 20 Aug. 1782.

145. HAJ, Delamain letter book, 1797-1801 (no. 2), 22 Sept. 1799, to Yeats.

146. MAC, letter book, 1766-7 23 Aug. 1766, to Jean Gast Lallemand.

147. HAC, Contract of 28 December 1765.

5: THE HENNESSYS AT HOME AND ABROAD

1. Some Hennessy genealogical details are inaccurate. The marriage, in Burke's *Irish family records*, for instance, of a daugher of Charles Hennessy, brother to James, to Henry Goold in 1719, is impossible; a marriage of James Hennessy's sister is clearly implied. The Ulster background and recollections of the family are set out in an unsigned note dated Cork 1784. This is probably an extract from a document which is described in a letter from Sylvester O'Halloran of Limerick, dated 6 October of the same year, 'as some months past … a paper put into my hands on this subject'. The intermediaries in the contacts with O'Halloran were the Hennessys' Cork relatives, the Goolds.

2. The earliest surviving title is an 1862 fee farm, held by Ormsby & Co., solicitors, Dublin. That the pre-1704 lease was itself a three-life lease, and therefore for Catholics a lease that could have been issued only before 1704, is confirmed in a memorial in the Registry of Deeds, dated 22 July 1748 (130/302/89169). The subletting of Shanballyduff to Garret Nagle existed from at least 1719 (Registry of Deeds, 2 Nov. 1719, 24/453/14338), and some further land in Ballyduff was in 1756 held under an earlier transaction creating a

trust from Bowen of Kilbolane for the benefit of Garret Nagle (Registry of Deeds, 25 Oct. 1756, 184/190/122570).

3. HAC, 5 May 1774, Stephen Winthrop Roche, Limerick. This connection, through later marriages, also linked the Roche family distantly with the family of the late Princess of Wales, Diana Spencer.

4. *Correspondence of Edmund Burke* (hereafter referred to as *Burke corr.*), ed. T.W. Copeland, vol. 1 (Cambridge, 1958), vol. 1, p. 217.

5. *Burke corr.*, vol. 1, p. 228.

6. Archives de la guerre, Paris, personal file of Lieut-Colonel Richard Hennessy; also letters in A¹ 2770, nos. 76-93, 6 Aug. to 28 Dec. 1730. The personal file hints at Hennessy's important missions.

7. L.M. Cullen, 'The Blackwater Catholics and County Cork society and politics in the eighteenth century', *Cork: history and society* (Dublin, 1993), ed. P. O'Flanagan and C.G. Buttimer, p. 560.

8. M.J. O'Connell, *Last colonel of the Irish Brigade* (1892, Cork reprint, 1977).

9. James Roche, *Critical and miscellaneous essays by an octogenarian*, vol. 2 (Cork, 1851), p. 51.

10. *Burke corr.*, vol. viii, p. 99, 14 Dec. 1794, to Sir George Colebrooke.

11. HAC, Cork, 15 May 1772, Pat Nagle to Richard Hennessy.

12. HAC, 23 Feb. 1753, James Hennessy to Richard Hennessy, Ostend; 19 Nov. 1755, James Hennessy, Cork, to Richard Hennessy, Ostend.

13. HAC, letter book 1771-7, 22 Aug. 1772, to Connelly & Arthur; 18 Sept., Henry Galwey, Cork, to Richard Hennessy.

14. Later information reported that 'Captain George', Richard Hennessy's nephew, had married a daughter of Phil Stackpole with a dowry of £1200, and had 'gone very extensively in the wine business and failed shortly after for £7500 sterling'. HAC, 10 Sept. 1797, James Woods, Bordeaux. There is a hint of weakness of character in an earlier and boastful letter in 1789 that he had 'spent the last six months in Cork, gloriously, and at the rate of a man of large portions'. HAC, 17 Nov. 1789, George Hennessy, Bordeaux, to Richard Hennessy. His vicissitudes are recorded briefly in the *Burke corr.*, vol. 9, pp. 51-2, 51n., 109-11; vol. 10, p. 127. On the other Hennessy, Athanasius, see *Burke corr.*, vol. 3, p. 370.

15. *Burke corr.*, vol. 1, p. 329.

16. HAC, 'Extrait du dictionnaire historique de Morei, article O'Brien'. The certificate is dated 31 July 1758, and the notary's declaration bears the same date.

17. HAC, 'A schedule of my bro. George's will'. George left five children (see Richard Hennessy to John Saule, 13 Jan. 1776). A daughter of George's in Cork in 1782 married Samuel Flanrey of the island of Tortola (*Finn's Leinster Journal*, 26-30 Oct. 1782). I am indebted to Dr Kevin Whelan for this reference.

18. *Burke corr.*, vol. 111, p. 438.

19. For example, Registry of Deeds, 309/260/205612, 28 April 1775.

20. S. Lewis, *Topographical dictionary of Ireland*, vol. 2, p. 341.

21. *Burke corr.*, vol. 1, p. 147-8n.

22. L.M. Cullen, 'Burke, Ireland, and Revolution', *Eighteenth-century life*, vol. 16, n.s., no. 1 (Feb. 1992), pp. 27-8.

23. Archives de la guerre, Paris, Yb 820, registre de l'infanterie, 1752-7, f. 169.

24. Archives de la guerre, Paris, IYC 258. I am indebted to Monsieur Maurice Richard Hennessy for this reference.

25. Archives départementales du Morbihan, Vannes, Warren papers, E 1452, Aug. (no day indicated, but endorsed 17 Aug.), 14 Oct. 1759. Hennessy's letters to Warren run from 1758 to 1762 (E1451 to E1454 1).

26. In 1768 his wife wrote in his absence that he was on his first visit home for 13 years. HAC, letter book, 1765-9, 23 May 1768, to McGuire.

27. Roche, op. cit., vol. 1, p. 51. The Roches were very close to the Hennessys, and the marriage of one of Richard's sisters confirmed the links. One of the Roches stayed with the Hennessys in 1774 (HAC, 5 May 1774, Stephen Winthrop Roche, Limerick). James Roche and others of the Roche family in Bordeaux frequently feature in the Hennessy correspondence after his return to Cognac in 1789. Richard's long stay in Bordeaux from 1776 to 1788 would also have ensured regularity of contact from the time that the Roches settled there around 1780, though the contact was less intimate than that with his Galwey relatives.

28. HAC, 15 April 1757, Charles O'Brien, comte de Thomond, vicomte de Clare, Paris.

29. HAC, 28 Feb. 1753, James Hennessy, Cork, to Richard Hennessy.

30. HAC, 15 April 1757, Charles O'Brien, comte de Thomond, vicomte de Clare, Paris.

31. HAC, 6 Dec. 1776, Richard Hennessy to John Saule. See also AAE, CPA, vol. 425, ff. 320-60, 1748. The contrôleur général recognized in 1747 that the legal position of Irishmen required clarification. The problem was that the concessions to Irishmen arose from exemption in specific circumstances granted by various royal declarations, and that, as the comte de Thomond recognized in 1756, though the *ordonnance* of 30 November 1715 (itself verified before the Parlement), which provided naturalization for soldiers and officers having served 10 years in French service remained valid, the issue of something expressly for the circumstances of Irishmen at large would be helpful. AAE, CPA, 440, ff. 189-95, mémoire by Lord Clare, May 1756. This does not seem to have been done – its issue was deemed desirable by Clare in the context of officers who had their home circumstances in Ireland in mind more than their French rights – but the 1715 order remained the valid basis, by the issue of a certificate, for establishing their French rights.

32. AAE, CPA, vol. 440, ff. 82-3, 99-100, 102, 104, 109, 115, 117-24, 131-5, 139, 140, 147, 148, 149-50, 163-5, 182; ADG, Bordeaux, C1073, 21 Feb. 1756, Tourny to Florentin; 'Etat des anglais, écossais et irlandais à qui les ordres du roy ont été notifiés par Monseigneur l'intendant le 19 Février 1756, Despian, ayde majeur de la ville', Bordeaux, 5 March 1756. See also ADG, Bordeaux, C1074 for details of exemptions granted and for other correspondence, and Paul Parfouru, 'Les irlandais en Bretagne aux xvii et xviii siècles, *Annales de Bretagne,* vol. ix (1893), pp. 524-34. Various letters in the Warren papers in the Archives départementales du Morbihan illustrate the application of the order in Brittany.

33. HAC, letter book 1771-5, 16 June 1773, to John Galwey, Bordeaux.

34. HAC, letter book 1769-71, 18 May 1771. There is a small carnet entitled, in

Richard's hand, 'Copys of letters and accounts brought from Ostend'. It contains a few letters on largely-non mercantile business, two accounts (of which one only is of interest and simply because it related to a balance for goods on the account of John Holker of Rouen), and 'a list of the cost of my houshold furniture', presumably on his arrival in France.

35. See Hennessy correspondence with Warren in Archives départementales du Morbihan, Vannes, Warren papers, E1449¹ to E1454², years 1757 to 1762. The letters of Andrew Kavanagh were especially informative, especially letters of 2 Nov. 1757 (E1449²) and 3 Aug. 1759 (E1451²). In addition to letters from Richard Hennessy, some drafts of Warren's letters to him are also in the collection.

36. Archives départementales du Morbihan, Vannes, Warren papers, E1458², Kavanagh & Blake, 3 Dec. 1766.

37. HAC, Inventory of Charles Hennessy 1759; inventory of James Hennessy 1760. Details can be traced in the two inventories. See also 'Answer to the remarks annexed to Richard Hennessy of Bordeaux's letter 1 May 1787 to Mr Thomas Blake junior Ostend'.

38. On the house, see also HAC, 31 Jan. 1784, Richard Hennessy, Bordeaux, to John Saule. On Charles' disappointed marriage plans in Martinique in 1785, see Richard Hennessy to Saule, 26 April 1785. The Murdochs were a Scottish family who, when the Isle of Man business ended in 1765, had opened a house first in Guernsey and then in Dunkirk to supply the smuggler with contraband. The Murdochs did much business with Irish and Scottish houses.

39. HAC, 30 May 1778, Hennessy, Bordeaux, to Saule. The house eventually moved to Brussels. On the death of Pat Hennessy in Brussels, see Bordeaux 27 Jan. 1784, Hennessy to Saule.

40. HAC, see correspondence in 1787, and also letter from Ostend, 17 Feb. 1785, Thomas Blake to Richard Hennessy.

41. HAC, 10 Sept. 1765, Articles of partnership of Richard Hennessy of Ostend and Connelly & Arthur of Dunkirk.

42. HAC, Connelly genealogy. The orthography is variable.

43. HAC, 16 July 1765, Edward Barrett, Cork, to Richard Hennessy; 2 Aug., 7 Nov. 1765, John Galwey, Bordeaux, to Richard Hennessy; draft dated 11 Dec. of letter to John Galwey.

44. See i.a. HAC, Edward Barrett's letter of 21 Aug. 1773.

45. HAC, 1765-9, 27 April 1767, to Isidore Lynch, London.

46. HAC, letter book 1769-71, 18 March 1771, to Barnewall, London, 1771.

47. HAC, Jean Denizet, 'La famille et la maison Hennessy au XVIII siècle' (typescript).

48. HAC, letter book 1765-9, 21 Sept. 1767, to Connelly & Arthur.

49. Ibid., 7 Nov. 1766, to Connelly & Arthur.

50. Ibid., 25 March 1769, to Connelly & Arthur.

51. HAC, letter book 1769-71, 21 Nov. 1768, 6 May 1771, to Connelly & Arthur.

52. Ibid, 6 May 1771, to Connelly & Arthur.

53. HAC, letter book 1771-5, 19 Oct. 1772, to George Goold.

54. Ibid, to Thomas Blake, 6 March, 8 April 1775.

55. HAC, letter book 1769-71, to Connelly & Arthur, 6 May 1771.

56. HAC, letter book 1771-5, 23 June 1773, to D. MacCarthy.

57. Ibid., 11 June 1773, John Galwey, Bordeaux, to R. Hennessy.

58. Ibid., 25 April 1772, to Connelly & Arthur.

59. HAC, 24 Aug. 1766, Edward Barrett, Cork, to Richard Hennessy.

60. HAC, 7 Nov. 1766, John Galwey, Bordeaux, to Richard Hennessy.

61. HAC, 24 Aug. 1766, Edward Barrett to Richard Hennessy.

62. *Burke corr.*, vol. 1, p. 216.

63. *Burke corr.*, vol. 1, p. 329.

64. HAC, letter book 1765-9, 8 June 1768, (Mrs Hennessy) to John Galwey.

65. HAC, letter dated 20 March 1772 from Bordeaux (last page torn, and end of letter missing).

66. HAC, 4 March 1766, Edward Barrett, Cork, to Richard Hennessy.

67. HAC, 1 Sept. 1772, Edward Barrett, Cork, to Richard Hennessy.

68. HAC, 2 Oct. 1772, John Galwey, Bordeaux, to Richard Hennessy.

69. HAC, 10 Nov. 1772, Edward Barrett to Richard Hennessy.

70. HAC, 15 May 1773, John Galwey, Bordeaux, to Richard Hennessy. See also for Burke's interest in advancing him, *Burke corr.*, vol. 2, p. 305.

71. AAC, Broussard papers.

72. HAC, 6 June 1768, John Power, Bordeaux, to Richard Hennessy.

73. HAC, 22 Dec. 1766, John Galwey, Bordeaux, to Richard Hennessy.

74. HAC, letter book 1771-5, 16 Nov. 1771, to Murphy Byrne & Co., Bordeaux.

75. HAC, Thomas Egan to Thomas Egan junior c/o Laurence Saule, date not clear but apparently between 1763 and 1765.

76. HAC, 7 Feb. 1773, John Saule, La Rochelle, to Richard Hennessy.

77. HAC, 19 Sept. 1772, Thomas Egan, Dublin, to Richard Hennessy.

78. HAC, 'Saule's correspondents in1768', a paper enclosed with James Tuke's letter of 7 Nov. 1776, Dublin. As the list was drawn up in 1776, it is more likely to refer to a post-1768 marriage alliance with Tallon than to one which existed in 1768.

79. HAC, La Rochelle, 20 July 1775, Saule to Richard Hennessy.

80. HAC, 30 Sept. 1775 circular re Martell, Geoghegan and Co. The background to the association is described in MAC, letter book 1775-6, 19 June, 24 July, Lallemand to Anthony [Mc]Dermott; 24 July, to Garrett Geoghegan, Dublin.

6: A DECADE OF CRISES: THE 1770S

1. AAC, Broussard papers, 13 June 1769.

2. HAC, 19 Nov. 1771, John Saule, La Rochelle, to Richard Hennessy. Except where otherwise indicated, all correspondence in this chapter is in the Hennessy archives, and consists of letters exchanged between Saule and Hennessy. If the date of letter is indicated in the text, the letter is not usually identified in the notes.

3. 19 Sept. 1771, La Rochelle.

4. 18 July 1771, La Rochelle.

5. The uncertain relationship was a constant theme of the correspondence; see in particular letter of 21 July 1771.

6. 22 Sept. 1771, La Rochelle.

7. 6 July 1773, La Rochelle.
8. 12 April 1772, La Rochelle.
9. 30 April 1772, La Rochelle.
10. 30 April 1772, La Rochelle.
11 26 April 1772, La Rochelle.
12. 17 May 1772, La Rochelle.
13. 30 April 1772, La Rochelle.
14. 30 April 1772, La Rochelle.
15. 29 March 1772, La Rochelle.
16. 10 Nov. 1774, La Rochelle.
17. 30 June 1779, Cognac.
18. 20 Nov. 1774, La Rochelle.
19. 31 Jan. 1779, Cognac.
20. 26 Oct. 1774, Gothenburg, Mrs Erskine.
21. On Mehigan, see especially his letter of 10 March to Richard Hennessy, Brest, 10 March 1773.
22. 14 Oct. 1774, Brest, John Mehigan to Richard Hennessy.
23. 20 March 1773, La Rochelle.
24. 25 April 1773, La Rochelle.
25. 29 July 1773, La Rochelle.
26. 29 Feb. 1776 , La Rochelle.
27. 7 March 1776, La Rochelle.
28. 8 May 1777. Signed as uncle without indicating name. The uncle's name can be identified from a draft letter by Victoire to him, dated 14 May 1777, which survives. In it she defended Saule, saying, among many other things, that 'il m'a avoué quelque peu d'inconduite qu'il a eu pendant son séjour à La Rochelle', and denying that he had frequented prostitutes.
29. 3 Nov. 1774, La Rochelle.
30. 23 March 1775, La Rochelle.
31. 2 April 1775, La Rochelle.
32 9 April 1775, La Rochelle.
33. 20 March 1775, La Rochelle.
34. 25 May 1775, La Rochelle.
35. 9 April 1775, La Rochelle.
36. 1 June 1775, La Rochelle.
37. 29 Feb. 1775, La Rochelle.
38. 12 Oct. 1775, La Rochelle.
39. 19 Oct. 1775, La Rochelle.
40. 12 Nov. 1775, La Rochelle.
41. 30 Nov. 1775, La Rochelle.
42. 10 March 1776, La Rochelle.
43. 18 June 1776, La Rochelle.
44. ADC, Angoulême, *Contrôle des actes*, C1471, act dated Dublin 19 March 1778, registered Cognac, 7 Oct. 1778.
45. ADC, Angoulême, notaire Lauchère, 2E14416, procuration of 30 Sept., and first requisition of 30 Sept. 1778, notary Lauchère, registered 2 Oct; notarial act by Saule and Victoire, notary Lauchère, dated 7 Oct. with preceding docu-

ments dated 29 and 30 Sept.; second and third requistions of 3 and 7 Oct. respectively (registered 6 and 7 Oct., *Controle des actes*, C1471); marriage contract, dated 7 Oct. 1778, notary Lauchère.

46. 1 April 1781, Cognac.
47. 13 March 1779, Cognac.
48. 2 May 1779, Cognac.
49. 6 July 1779, Cognac.
50 11 Nov. 1778, Cognac.
51. 13 July 1781, Bordeaux, Mary Saule.
52. 16 June 1781, Bordeaux, Hennessy.
53. On her return Mary Saule sent 'two hampers of potatoes' for Saule, which were received in Bordeaux in late October. See 23 October 1781, Bordeaux, Richard Hennessy.
54. 24 Aug., 30 Nov. 1775, La Rochelle.
55. 1 Feb. 1776, Cognac.
56. AAC, copy letters to English correspondents 1768-82, 18 Dec. 1769, to Smith and Harrison, London.
57. HAC, letter book 1775-81, 18 Sept, 1776, to Paul Walshe, La Rochelle.
58. See 4 July 1776, La Rochelle.
59. 9 July 1776, La Rochelle.
60. 27 Jan. 1778, Bordeaux.
61. 13 Feb. 1781, Bordeaux.
62. 4 Jan. 1777, Bordeaux, William Coppinger.
63. 27 Jan. 1778, Bordeaux.
64. 8 April 1777, Bordeaux.
65. 10 June 1777, Bordeaux.
66. 18 May 1779, Bordeaux.
67. 6 Dec. 1779, Bordeaux. See also later letter of 13 July 1781.
68. 1 or 7 April 1780, Bordeaux.
69. 1 Sept. 1780, Bordeaux.
70. 29 May 1780, Bordeaux.
71. L.M. Cullen, 'Ireland and Irishmen in eighteenth-century privateering', in *Course et piraterie: études presentées à la Commission Internationale d'histoire maritime à l'occasion de son XVe colloque international pendant le 14e congrès international des sciences historiques (San Francisco, aout 1975)* (Paris, 1975), vol. 1, pp. 473-6, 480.
72. 10 Sept. 1781, Bordeaux.
73. 10 Oct. 1781, Dublin, Mary Saule.
74. 7 Nov., 8, 15 Dec., Bordeaux.
75. 8 Dec. 1780, Bordeaux.
76. 23 March 1781, Bordeaux.
77. 8 Dec. 1780, Bordeaux.
78. 13 July 1781, Bordeaux.
79. 3 July 1781, Bordeaux.
80. 23 Oct. 1781, Bordeaux.
81. 8 Feb. 1782, Bordeaux.
82. 2 Nov. 1781, Bordeaux.

83. 13 Nov. 1781, Bordeaux.
84. 2 Oct. 1781, Bordeaux.
85. *Burke corr.*, vol. 3, pp. 283-4; vol. IV, p. 371.
86. See Hennessy's letters of 5 April, 28 May, Bordeaux; 28 June 1782, Angoulême.
87. 28 Aug., 3 Sept. 1782, Bordeaux.
88. 3 Sept. 1782, Henry Galwey, Bordeaux.
89. 20 Aug. 1782, Bordeaux.
90. 31 Dec. 1782, Bordeaux.
91. *Burke corr.*, vol. V, p. 62, 62n. The *Burke corr.* refers to Barrett as Edmund, but this should be Edward.
92. 2 Oct. 1781, Bordeaux.
93. 30 Jan. 1781, Bordeaux.
94. 10 Feb. 1781, Richard Hennessy, Bordeaux, to James Hennessy, Douai.
95. 3 July 1781, Bordeaux.
96. 13 Jan. 1778, Bordeaux.
97. HAC, letter book 1775-81, 16 Sept, 1778, 18 May 1779, to Hennessy, Bordeaux. '
98. Ibid., 5 June 1779.
99. 29 June 1779, Bordeaux; 30 June 1779, Cognac.
100. HAC, letter book 1775-81, 15 Jan. 1780.
101. HAC, 1 June 1780, Connelly and Co., Flushing.
102. HAC, invoice book.

7: BORDEAUX AND COGNAC: BRANDY BUSINESS IN TWO CENTRES IN THE 1780S

1. HAC, 13 Nov. 1784, Hennessy, Bordeaux, to Saule.
2. HAC, 9 Jan. 1784, Hennessy, Bordeaux.
3. HAC, 16 April 1784, Hennessy, Bordeaux.
4. HAC, 7 Dec. 1784, Hennessy, Bordeaux.
5. HAC, 4 Jan. 1785, Hennessy, Bordeaux.
6. HAC, 13 Sept. 1785, Hennessy, Bordeaux, to Saule.
7. ADG, Bordeaux, livre journal 1788, 7B 1172; letter book of George Boyd and Co. of Royan 1785-8 and of Bordeaux 1788-9, 7B 1171; invoices 1788-9, 7B 1173; acquits, 7B 1174. While not involved in the humdrum business of supplying the regular brandy trade, Skinner occasionally gave very large orders: Boyd's books reveal some quite large commissions from Skinner & Fenwick.
8. MAC, 18 Nov., 6 Dec. 1786, Théodore Martell, Bordeaux.
9. ADG, Bordeaux, 7B 1171, letter book of George Boyd and Co. of Royan 1785-8 and of Bordeaux 1788-9. See especially letter of 11 Oct. 1787, to Boyd.
10. HAC, 6 July 1785, Hennessy, Bordeaux, to Saule.
11. See HAC, 27 Aug. 1784, George Boyd, Bordeaux, to Saule.
12. HAC, 14 Sept. 1784, Hennessy, Bordeaux, to Saule.
13. HAC, 29 June 1787, Hennessy, Bordeaux, to Saule.
14. HAC, 17 July 1787, Saule, Paris, to Hennessy.

15. HAC, 5 Jan. 1788, Saule, Cognac, to Hennessy.
16. HAC, 27 July 1787, Saule, London, to James Hennessy.
17. HAC, 17 July 1787, Saule, Paris, to Hennessy.
18. HAC, 4 Aug. 1787, Delamain, Jarnac, to Hennessy. See also Delamain's letter of 9 July 1787.
19. HAC, 16 Aug. 1787, Delamain, Jarnac, to Hennessy.
20. HAC, 17 July 1787, Saule, Paris, to Hennessy.
21. HAC, 18 August 1787, Saule, London, to Hennessy.
22. HAC, 28 June 1787, Hennessy, Bordeaux, to Saule.
23. HAC, 17 July 1787, Saule to Hennessy.
24. HAC, 5 Jan. 1788, Saule to Hennessy.
25. HAC, letter book, 1787-9, 24 Nov. 1787, to Boyd.
26. HAC, letter book 1787-9, 27 Feb. 1788, to Boyd.
27. HAC, 23 April, 28 May 1788, Saule, Cognac, to Hennessy; Bordeaux; 30 April 1788, Boyd to Saule. See also letter book 1787-8 for the months of April and May 1788.
28. HAC, 9 July 1787, Delamain, Jarnac.
29. HAC, 28 June 1788, Hennessy to Saule.
30. HAC, 28 June 1787, Hennessy, Bordeaux, to Saule.
31. HAC, 29 June 1787, Hennessy, Bordeaux, to Saule
32. HAC, 23 April 1788, Saule to Hennessy.
33. HAC, 2 April 1788, George Boyd, Bordeaux, to Saule.
34. HAC, letter book 1787-8, 27 February 1788, to George Boyd.
35 ADG, Bordeaux, 7B 1172, Journal for 1788.
36. HAC, letter book 1787-8, 12 April 1788, to Gastinel, Paris.
37. HAC, 15 Aug. 1788, James Hennessy to Saule.
38. HAC, letter book 1787-8, 12 April 1788, to Gastinel, Paris.
39. HAC, 6 Nov. 1787, Hennessy, Bordeaux, to Saule.
40. ADG, Bordeaux, 7B 538, Guiliory.
41. HAC, 20 Oct. 1789, James Hennessy, Dunkirk, to Turner.
42. HAC, 29 Sept. 1789, James Hennessy, London, to Richard Hennessy.
43. HAC, 23 Sept. 1789, Thomas Knight, Bordeaux, to Richard Hennessy.
44. HAC, 1 May 1790, Richard Hennessy, Bordeaux, to James Hennessy.
45. HAC, 13 Jan. 1790, Thomas Knight, Bordeaux, to Richard Hennessy.
46. HAC, 27/8 April, 1 May 1790, Richard Hennessy, Bordeaux, to James Hennessy.
47. HAC, 27 Nov. 1792, V.&P. French & Nephew, Bordeaux.
48. HAC, 14 Aug. 1787, Saule, London, to Hennessy.
49. See HAC, 5 Jan. 1788, Saule to Richard Hennessy.
50. HAC, 28 May 1788. The Broussards of Pons had many Irish associations; the first was their close working relationship with Galwey of La Rochelle in the 1760s, and the latest was a partnership from at least as early as 1778 with one of the Gernons which had been dissolved in 1784 because of Gernon's health (HAC, 20 July 1784, Saule, London, to Hennessy). In 1778 Broussard and Gernon's buying had been said to have driven the price in Cognac to 210 livres (HAC, 7 March 1778, Hennessy to Saule).
51. HAC, letter book 1788-90, 6 Oct. 1788, to Tim Brown, London.

52. HAC, 19 Nov. 1788, James Hennessy, Cognac, to Richard Hennessy.
53. HAC, letter book 1788-90, 20 Oct. 1788, to John Mors, London; 3 Nov. 1788, Murdoch, Dunkirk, to James Hennessy.
54. Ibid., 6 Dec. 1788 to Clancy & Parrant.
55. Ibid., 9 May 1789, to MacCarthy *frères*. See also letter of 27 May 1789, Richard Hennessy, Bordeaux, to James Hennessy.
56. HAC, 18 June 1784, Saule, Paris, to Hennessy.
57. HAC, I8 June 1784, Saule to Hennessy.
58. MAC, 7 Jan 1785, Yeats and Brown, London, to Martell.
59. HAC, 5 July 1788, Tim Brown, London, to Saule.
60. See chapter 2.
61. HAC, 19 Sept. 1786, Tallon, Dublin, to Saule.
62. HAC, 9 Oct. 1786., John Saule Kennedy, Dublin, to Saule. See also letter of 26 Oct. 1786.
63. Collins letters in R.B. McDowell, ed., 'The proceedings of the Dublin society of United Irishmen', in *Analecta hibernica*, vol. XVII (1949), pp. 1-143.
64. HAC, 25 Feb. 1786, Hennessy, Bordeaux, to Saule.
65. HAC, 15 July 1786, John Saule Kennedy, Dublin, to Saule.
66. HAC, 26 Aug. 1786, Saule Kennedy, Dublin, to Saule.
67. HAC, 30 July 1785, White, St. Martin's.
68. See HAC, 19 Sept. 1786, Tallon.
69. HAC, 24 Jan., 25 Feb. 1786, Richard Hennessy, Bordeaux, to Saule.
70. HAC, letter book, 1784-6, 1 May 1786, to Tallon.
71. HAC, 13 Nov. 1786, John Saule Kennedy, Dublin, to Saule. Moncks is described as 'Monaghan' in this letter, but the fact that Moncks was the man is made clear by a later letter.
72. HAC, 26 Aug. 1786, Collins, Dublin; letter book, 1786-7, 21 Oct. 1786, to White.
73. HAC, 25 July 1786, Richard Hennessy, Bordeaux.
74. HAC, 15 April, 26 July 1786, John Saule Kennedy, Dublin.
75. HAC, 13 Nov. 1786, John Saule Kennedy, Dublin.
76. HAC, 17 Aug. 1786, Tallon, Dublin.
77. HAC, 26 Oct. 1786, Saule Kennedy, Dublin.
78. HAC, letter book 1786-7, 22 Jan. 1787, Saule.
79. HAC, 1787 undated, Hennessy, Bordeaux, to Saule.
80. HAC, 7 Sept. 1786, Hennessy, Bordeaux.
81. HAC, 17 Aug. 1786, Dublin.
82. HAC, 22 November 1786, Hennessy, Bordeaux.
83. HAC, 2 November 1786, Hennessy, Bordeaux.
84. HAC, letter book 1786-7, 21 Oct. 1786, to Saule Kennedy.
85. HAC, ibid., 22 Jan. 1787, to Saule Kennedy.
86. HAC, 26 Aug. 1786, John Saule Kennedy, Dublin; 20 Sept., Knight, Bordeaux.
87. HAC, letter book 1786-7, 19 March 1787, to White.
88. Ibid., 7 April 1787, to White.
89. HAC, 26 Oct., Dublin; London. 20 Nov. 1786, Saule Kennedy.
90. HAC, 20 Feb. 1787, White.
91. HAC, 23 June 1788, Saule, Cognac, to Hennessy.

92. HAC, Richard Hennessy, 3 Jan. 1787, Bordeaux.
93. HAC, 24 June 1787, Edward Connelly, Barcelona.
94. HAC, letter book 1787-8, 16 June 1787, to Saule Kennedy.
95. HAC, letter book 1786-7, 19 March 1787, to White.
96. HAC, letter book 1787-8, 23 June 1787, to White.
97. HAC, 1 June 1780, Connelly and Co., Flushing.
98. HAC, 23 Jan. 1779, Saule, Cognac, to Hennessy. This is virtually the last reference to Louis-Gabriel Lallemand's active role in the Martell house. After a reference in a letter in MAC, letter book 1778-9, p. 30, there is little evidence in the Martell records themselves. Despite the fact that he lived till 1793 he and the widow Martell seem to have retired into the background from 1775.
99. HAC, 19 Dec. 1787, Saule.
100. HAC, letter book 1786-7, 19 Feb. 1787 to Bubbers; 19 Feb., 24 Feb. 1787, to Arthur.
101. HAC, Isaac Brown, 11 April 1787.
102. HAC, 28 March 1787, Isaac Brown.
103. HAC, 5 Jan. 1788, Saule, Cognac.
104. HAC, 21 Nov. 1787, Saule, Cognac.
105. HAC, 28 May 1788, Saule, Cognac.
106. HAC, Saule, letter of 28 May 1788.
107. MAC, 4 May 1787, Bevan, London.
108. HAC, 13 Aug., Saule to Hennessy *fils*; 3 Sept. 1788, to Hennessy *père*.
109. HAC, 3 Sept. 1788, Yeats & Brown, London.
110. MAC, 29 Aug 1788, Bevan, London.
111. HAC, 10 Sept. 1788, Saule, Cognac.
112. HAC, 3 Sept. 1788, Saule, Cognac.
113. HAC, April 23, 1785, Saule, Cognac.
114. HAC, letter book 1787-8, 6 October 1788.
115. HAJ, Delamain letter book, 1787-9 (no. 2), 6 Oct. 1788. to Yeats & Brown. See also HAC, letter book, 1788-90, 5 Oct. 1788, to Tim Brown.
116. HAC, letter book 1788-90, 20 Oct. 1788, to John Mors, London.
117. HAJ, Delamain letter book, 1787-9 (no. 2), 10 Nov. 1788, to Yeats & Brown.
118. HAJ, Delamain letter book, 1787-9 (no. 2), 20 Oct. 1788, to Yeats & Brown; 1787-9 (no. 1), 21 Oct. 1788, to Mallet, Paris.
119. HAJ, Delamain letter book 1787-9 (no. 2), 10 Nov. 1788, to John and Walker Gray. One of these houses was Brown's, the other J.W. Gray, whose brandy amounted to 100 puncheons.
120. Ibid., 8 Nov. 1788, to Yeats & Brown.
121. HAC, letter book 1788-90, 27 Oct. 1788, to Tim Brown.
122. HAJ, Delamain letter book 1787-9 (no. 2), 20 Oct. 1788, to Yeats & Brown.
123. HAC, letter book 1788-90, to Tim Brown, 27 Oct. 1788.
124. Ibid., to Tim Brown, 27 Oct. 1788.
125. HAJ, Delamain letter book 1787-9 (no. 2), 10 Nov. 1788, to Yeats and Brown.
126. MAC, letter book, 1788-9, 20 Oct. 1788, to Lallemand Lambert & Co., Charente.
127. MAC, letter book 1788-9 B. 29 Dec. 1788, to Yeats & Brown.
128. HAJ, Delamain letter book 1787-9 (no. 1), 8 Nov. 1788, to Mallet.

129. Ibid., 18 Nov. 1788, to Mallet.
130. Ibid., circular letter of 6 Dec. 1788. Saule's remaining parcels, amounting to 450 puncheons, realized prices of between 116 and 121 livres, ibid., 29 Nov. 1788, to Knowsley, Hull.
131. MAC, letter book 1788/9 B, 29 Dec. 1788, to Yeats & Brown.
132. ADC, Angoulême, *contrôle des actes*, 11C 1481, f. 60 recto. The act was *sous seign privé*, hence a copy does not survive in the notarial archives. Protests by James Hennessy on behalf of three houses, Brown, Henshaw and John & Walker Gray, relating to 120 puncheons of brandy, are in ADC, Angoulême, 1E 14272, *étude* Imbaud.
133. For details of the estate, see ADC, Angoulême, *étude* Imbaud, 2E 14272, inventaire; 11C 1481, *contrôle des actes*.
134. J. Jezequel, *Grands notables du premier empire* (Paris, 1986), p. 25. I am indebted also to Madame M.G. Jouannet, Messrs Hennessy, for information of Victoire's marriage.
135. HAC, 23 March 1795, Thomas Shoolbred to Richard Hennessy.
136. HAC, 28 June 1785, Hennessy, Bordeaux, to Saule.
137. HAC, 4 Nov. 1785, Hennessy, Bordeaux, to Saule.
138. HAC, 19 Dec. 1787, Saule to Hennessy.
139. HAC, Cognac, 5 Jan. 1788, Saule to Hennessy.
140. HAC, 1 Dec. 1789, James Hennessy, London.
141. HAC, Richard Hennessy, 18 Nov. 1788.
142. HAC, 18 Dec. 1789, James Hennessy, London.
143. HAC, 20 Nov. 1789, James Hennessy, London.
144. HAC, 20, 27 Nov. 1789, James Hennessy. She was a daughter of George, Hennessy's elder brother who had died in 1776. She had married in 1782. See chapter 5, note 17.
145. HAC, 17 Nov. 1789, James Hennessy.
146. HAC, 27 Dec. 1789, James Hennessy, Boulogne.
147. HAC, 1 July 1776, James Nagle, Libourne.
148. HAC, 3 June 1789, James Hennessy, Cognac.

8: BUSINESS UNDER THE REVOLUTION

1. HAJ, Delamain no. 1 letter book 1787-9, 22 Dec. 1788, to Crosthwaite.
2. Ibid. See especially letter to D'Assy, Meaux, 10 Feb. 1789.
3. MAC, letter book (B) 1788-9, 2 February 1789, to Yeats & Brown.
4. HAJ, Delamain no. 1 letter book 1787-9, 8 Aug. 1789, to Haworth & Bateman, Hull.
5. HAC, Richard Hennessy, Bordeaux, letters in February and March 1789.
6. HAC, 11 Nov. 1789, MacCarthy *frères*.
7. HAJ, Delamain no. 1 letter book, 1787-9, 27 Oct. 1789, to MacCarthy frères; letter from MacCarthy *frères*, 11 Nov. 1789.
8. HAJ, Delamain no. 2 letter book 1787-9, 19 Jan. 1789, to Yeats & Brown.
9. HAC, 17 May 1790, Jas. Woods, by procuration for John Galwey, Bordeaux.
10. HAJ, Delamain no. 2 letter book 1780-1793, 27 June 1791, to Gorman.

11. HAC, Knight, 14, 28 Feb. 1790.
12. HAC, Turner, 4 Feb. 1791.
13. HAC, undated letter by Richard. It is included in a packet of letters for 1798: however it is not consistent with this year. Richard's infirmity at this time and the large assembly firmly put the occasion into the early 1790s.
14. HAC, as reported in a letter from Richard Hennessy, London, 15 Nov. 1791.
15. HAC, Forster *frères,* 23 Aug. 1791.
16. HAC, Richard Hennessy, 15 Nov. 1791.
17. HAC, Veuve Fiquois, 24 Feb. 1792.
18. HAC, Richard Hennessy, 27 Sept. 1791.
19. HAC, 25 Dec. 1791.
20. HAC, 13 Jan. 1792.
21. HAC, John Aug[s]. Byrne, to Richard Hennessy, 17 June 1791, Bordeaux.
22. HAC, James Barrett, 19 Dec. 1791.
23. HAC, James Hennessy, Cognac, 31 Jan. 1792.
24. HAC, London, 17 Feb. 1792.
25. HAC, Woods, 27 Aug. 1793; 30 Germinal an 3 (19 April 1795); 5 Feb. 1797.
26. HAC, 15 June 1792.
27. HAC, James Barrett, 19 Dec. 1791, reporting news from Woods.
28. HAC, Richard Hennessy, London, 23 Dec. 1791.
29. HAC, 27 Nov. 1792.
30. HAC, Delamain no. 2 letter book 1793-8, 23 March 1793, to MacCarthy. Delamain's youngest son went to Paris in June 1794 for military training: 'Mon petit Victor est parti de ce matin pour Paris dans le dessein de profiter de l'éducation militaire dans l'établissement nouvellement creé, vous voyez qu'il veut courir la meme carrière de ses frères. C'est un brave garçon'. Delamain No. 2 letter book 1793-8, 14 June 1794, to Dupuy.
31. HAC, letter book D 1792-3, 15 March 1793, to Forster Bros.
32. Ibid., to Murdock, 28 Aug. 1793. Brandy was only one of a number of commodities which as prime necessities were prohibited. See F. Crouzet, *La grande inflation: la monnaie en France de Louis XVI à Napoleon* (Paris, 1993), p. 280.
33   F. Aftalion, *The French Revolution: an economic interpretation* (Cambridge, 1990), pp. 130, 157; Crouzet, op. cit., p. 143.
34. On the monetary events of the year, see Aftalion, op. cit., pp. 134, 149; Crouzet, op. cit., p. 143.
35. HAJ, Delamain no. 2 letter book 1793-8, 11 Nov. 1793, to Dupuy; 28 Nov. 1793, to Corneille, Paris.
36. Ibid., 11 Jan. 1794, to Réoger.
37. Ibid., 27 Aug. 1793, to Dardillouze & *neveu.* See also letter to MacCarthy *frères,* same date.
38. See R. Firino-Martell, *La famille Martell* (Paris, 1924).
39. HAC, 25 Nov. 1793 (5 Frimaire an 2), Jas Mayne. See also HAJ, no. 2 letter book 1793-8, 23 Nov. 1793, to Mérat. The name is mentioned as Mayne in a letter to Obry *l'ainé* on the same date.
40. HAJ, Delamain no. 2 letter book 1793-8, 26 Pluviôse, an 4 (18 Feb. 1796, *recte* 14 Feb.), to Edward Gayner at Caduques.

41. HAC, letter book F 1793-6, 12 Feb. 1795 (24 Pluviôse an 3), to Murdoch.
42. Firino-Martell, op. cit., pp. 48-61.
43. Elsewhere, according to report from Dunkirk, 'we live here like prisoners on parole, I mean the British and Irish settled here'. HAC, 8 July 1793.
44. HAC, 9 June 1793. The Woods' employment by Galwey suggests a Co. Cork background. The Woods family seems to be referred to in a letter of Burke's in 1776 (*Burke corr.*, vol. IX, p. 412). Reference to 'the Woods' in this letter makes more sense than reference to 'the woods' in the same letter as reprinted elsewhere in the *Burke Corr.*, vol. 3, pp. 283-4.
45. HAC, 26 Brumaire an 2 (26 Nov., *recte* 16 Nov. 1793).
46. HAC, 24 Germinal an 2 (13 April 1794), Woods.
47. HAC, 9 Frimaire an 2 (29 Nov. 1793), John Aug. Byrne; and 10 Frimaire an 2 (30 Nov. 1793), Woods.
48. HAC, Germinal an 2 (13 April), Woods.
49. HAC, 5 Vendémiaire an 3 (26 Sept. 1794), Woods.
50. HAC, 18 Nov. 1796, Woods.
51. HAC, 5 Nov. 1794 (15 Frimaire an 3).
52. HAC, 20 Floréal an 2 (9 May 1794), Woods.
53. HAC, 23 May 1794 (4 Prairial an 2), Woods.
54. See HAC, James Woods, 12 June 1794 (24 Prairial) an 2.
55. HAJ, Delamain no. 2 letter book 1793-8, 6 Nov. 1794 (16 Brumaire), to Holtman, Gothenburg.
56. Ibid., 4 Dec. 1794 (14 Frimaire an 3), to Richer *l'aîné*.
57. Aftalion, op. cit., p. 167; Crouzet, op. cit., p. 336.
58. HAJ, Delamain, letter book 1793-8, no. 2, 9 April 1795 (20 Germinal an 3), to Dupuy, Paris.
59. HAC, 13 Feb. 1795 (25 Pluviôse an 3), T. Martell, Bordeaux, to James Hennessy.
60. HAC, 25 July 1795 (7 Thermidor an 3), James Hennessy, Bordeaux.
61. HAC, 30 July 1795 (12 Thermidor an 3), James Hennessy.
62. HAC, 30 July 1795 (12 Thermidor an 3), Bagnères.
63. HAC, 8 Oct 1795, James Hennessy, Bordeaux.
64. HAC, 13 Oct 1795 (21 Vendémiaire an 4), James Hennessy.
65. HAC, 24 Oct 1795 (2 Brumaire an 4), James Hennessy, Bordeaux.
66. HAJ, Delamain no. 2 letter book 1793-8, 14 June 1795 (26 Prairial an 3), to Baco, Paris.
67. Ibid., 18 June 1795 (30 Prairial an 3), to Truxton, Philadelphia.
68. Ibid., 17 July 1795 (29 Messidor an 3).
69. HAC, letter book E 1793-96, 15 October 1795, to Thomas Blake.
70. HAC, 4 Dec. 1796, Woods.
71. HAC, 28 June 1795 (10 Messidor an 3), Woods. On Woods see HAC, 19, 20 Sept. 1797, Woods. Knight died in September 1797. He had married a widow late in life, and rented a house of Dowling's for his married life ('which he unthinkingly fitted up in a magnificent style'). The marriage did not work out, the widow breaking his heart, according to Woods, who related how he 'nearly lost himself by constantly tippling brandy etc even in the forenoon, in so much that he was frequently affected thereby on 'Change [*i.e. the Exchange*] ... With

an intention of *washing away grief*, as few men were more unhappy in their marriage than he was, but on the other hand, I never believe his amiable spouse could not boast much of her having made a good acquaintance in him' (HAC, 19 Sept., Woods; see also 22 Sept., Woods).

72. HAC, 26 Sept. 1794 (5 Vendémiaire an 3), Woods.
73. HAC, 19 April 1795 (30 Germinal an 3), Woods.
74. HAC, 28 June 1795 (10 Messidor an 3), Woods.
75. HAC, 25 Jan. 1795 (6 Ventôse an 3), Woods.
76. HAC, 26 Sept. 1795 (5 Vendémiaire an 3), Woods.
77. HAC, 17 March 1795 (27 Ventôse an 3), Woods.
78. HAC, 23 Oct 1795 (2 Brumaire an 4), James Hennessy, Bordeaux.
79. HAC, 25 July 1795 (7 Thermidor an 3), James Hennessy, Langon.
80. HAC, 28 Aug. 1795 (11 Fructidor an 3), James Hennessy, St Sauveur, to Sam Turner and Richard Hennessy.
81. HAC, 19 Oct. 1795 (28 Vend. an 3), James Hennessy.
82. HAC, 8 Oct. 1795, James Hennessy to Hennessy & Turner. Between January and September 1795, according to the Hennessy letter books E and F, the price per barrique in Cognac rose from 1200 livres to 8500 livres.
83. HAJ, Delamain no. 2 letter book 1793-8, to Mallet, 30 Sept. 1795 (8 Vendémaire, an 4).
84. Ibid., to Favry, Bordeaux, 22 Oct. 1795 (30 Vendémaire an 4).
85. HAC, 18 Nov. 1796, Woods, Bordeaux.
86. HAC, 22 Dec. 1795 (1 Nivôse an 4), James Hennessy, Bordeaux.
87. On the shortage of cash, see HAJ, Delamain no. 2 letter book 1793-8, to Hutchinson, 20 Pluviôse an 4 (9 Feb. 1796). On the currency changes, see also Aftalion, p. 175. On the culmination of the preceding inflation, see Crouzet, op. cit., pp. 338-42.
88. HAC, Woods, 5 February 1797.
89. MAC, 25 April 1796 (6 Floréal an 4), Théodore Martell, Bordeaux, to Martell Lallemand.
90. MAC, 20 Dec. 1796 (30 Frimaire an 5), T. Martell, Bordeaux, to Martell Lallemand. On the weather, see E. Le Roy Ladurie, *Histoire du climat depuis l'an mille* (Paris, 1983), vol. 2, p. 180.
91. OAC, letter book, 19 Germinal an 5 – 16 Pluviôse an 6, 1 Jan. 1797 (12 Nivôse an 6), 25 Jan. 1797 (6 Pluviôse an 6).
92. HAJ, Delamain no. 2 letter book 1793-8, 28 Aug. 1797 (11 Fructidor an 5), to Corneille; 7 Nov. 1797 (17 Brumaire an 6), to Cellier.
93. MAC, 19 June 1798 (1 Messidor an 6), Théodore Martell, Bordeaux, to Martell Lallemand.
94. MAC, 1 Feb. 1797, Théodore Martell, Bordeaux, to Martell Lallemand.
95. HAJ, Delamain letter book 1793-8 (no. 2), 28 May 1797, to John Shoolbred.
96. OAC, letter book 26 Floréal an 7 – 18 Pluviôse an 8., circular of 27 Aug. 1799 (10 Fructidor an 7).
97. HAC, 11 July 1799 (23 Messidor an 7), Murdock to Hennessy & Turner.
98. OAC, letter book 13 Nivôse an 7 – Floréal an 7, 25 Jan 1798 (6 Pluviôse an 7), to Emeric, Paris.
99. OAC, Copie de lettres aux associés 1 Germinal an 8 – 9 Prairial an 8, 26 May

1800 to John Wells, Hamburg.

100. HAC, 29 Oct. 1798, Turner, Hamburg.

101. HAC, 24 Feb. 1793, Jean-Auguste Fatou, Poitiers, to Samuel Turner.

102. HAC, 13 April 1789, Turner.

103. Registre des protestants, Segonzac. I am grateful to Madame Adol, a direct descendant, for this information.

104. Bruno Sepulchre, *Notes pour servir à l'histoire de la commune de Segonzac*, pp. 80, 84, 91, 92.

105. HAC, 23 Dec. 1791, Richard Hennessy, London, to James Hennessy.

106. HAC, 17 March 1800, Turner, Hamburg, to Richard Hennessy.

107. HAC, 21 March 1798, Johnson, Hamburg, to James Hennessy. Endorsed Turner, 21 March 1798.

108. HAC, 17 April 1798, Hamburg.

109. Woods on 14 March after he was released had reported that the remaining prisoners 'consist now of John Barton, Richard Galwey, Henry Martin, John Woods and partner, Dr Langhorn, Smith clerk to Fenwick, Gille a former clerk to MacCarthy, Segain, and poor Forster. The two latter have hopes to be out to-day'. HAC, 14 March 1798, Woods, Bordeaux. See also Woods' letter of 5 April 1798.

110. Firino-Martell, op. cit., pp. 125-6.

111. HAC, 26 March 1798, Hamburg.

112. See HAC, 17 Jan. 1798, Turner, Hamburg, to Hennessy.

113. HAC, 23 Sept. 1798, Turner.

114. HAC, 27 April 1798, Shoolbred.

115. HAC, 27 April 1798, John Shoolbred, London, to Turner.

116. An intercepted letter of the French minister, Reinhard, in Hamburg, surviving in the Castlereagh papers, refers in July 1798 to the departure from Dublin for Hamburg of a Mr Williams (Charles Vane, marquess of Londonderry, *Memoirs and correspondence of Visount Castlereagh* [London, 1848], vol. 1, p. 291. Reinhard to Talleyrand, 30 July 1798).

117. Public Record Office of Northern Ireland, Downshire papers, D607/F/ 432, 'A sincere convert', Hamburg, to J. Richardson.

118. The Downshire papers contain several letters regarding Richardson. Public Record Office of Northern Ireland, D607/F/79, 153, 4 March 1798, and late March – early May.

119. NA, Dublin, 620/1/4/3, 12 Aug. 1797, Joseph Nugent to Marquis of Hertford. I am grateful to my former student Mr Paul Weber for information which dates Turner's recruitment into his new role to an earlier date than generally assumed.

120. NA, Dublin, 620/10/118/10, 18 March 1801, Higgins; 620/3/51/33, Lt-Col Dunbarr (?), Newry, reporting information.

121. NA, Dublin, OP/132/2 Turner to Cooke, endorsed secret Hamburg, 18 May 1802. I am grateful to Miss Ann Neery, National Archives, for turning up this letter for me.

122. HAC, 30 Sept. 1768, Shoolbred, London, to Hennessy; 2 July 1784, Saule, London, to Hennessy.

123. HAC, 8 Feb. 1785, Shoolbred to Richard Hennessy.

124. HAC, 19 June 1792, John Shoolbred jnr to R. Hennessy. There was also another son, Thomas, who was in Cognac in 1795.
125. HAC, 2 Feb. 1797, James Delamain, Jarnac, to Richard Hennessy.
126. HAC, 4 May 1798, London, Shoolbred.
127. HAC, 6 April 1798, Turner.
128. HAC, 29 Oct. 1798, Turner, Hamburg.
129. HAC, 12 April 1798, Turner, Hamburg.
130. HAC, 30 Dec. 1799, Turner, Hamburg.
131. There was an intensive exchange on the subject in April and May 1798.
132. HAC, 1 Oct. 1795 (9 Vendémiaire an 4), James Hennessy.
133. HAC, 21 Feb. 1797, 28 May 1797, Delamain.
134. HAC, Madame Byrne, 30 July 1797.
135. HAC, 21 April 1798, Turner, Hamburg, to James Hennessy.
136. HAC, letter book N 1800-1801, 8 Oct. 1800, to Béhic.
137. Ibid., 10 Oct, 1800, to Haspais Gelot and Co., Paris.
138. HAJ, Delamain letter book 1799-1801, no. 2, 17 May 1800, to Hutchinson, Altona.
139. HAC, 15 Sept. 1790, Knight, Bordeaux.
140. HAC, 28 Jan 1789, Bordeaux.
141. HAC, 19 Nov. 1800 (28 Brumaire an 9), James Woods, Bordeaux.
142. P. Butel, 'Quelques leçons sur le dynamisme commercial: Cognac à la fin du XVIIIe siècle', in *Eaux-de-vie et spiritueux*, ed. A. Huetz de Lemps et Philippe Roudié (Paris, 1985), p. 35.
143. HAJ, Delamain no. 2 letter book 1793-8, 27 July 1797.
144. HAJ, Delamain no. 2 letter book 1778-81, 24 July 1781, to Alley.
145. HAJ, Delamain no. 1 letter book 1787-9, 19 Aug. 1788, to Knowsley.
146. HAJ, 9 June 1787, James Delamain.
147. HAJ, Delamain no. 1 letter book 1787-9, 12 Sept. 1789, to Knowsley.
148. HAJ, Delamain no. 2 letter book 1787-9, 2 Aug. 1788, to Huntingdon; letter book 1789-93 (torn volume), 17 April 1790, to Gorman.
149. HAJ, Delamain no. 1 letter book 1787-9, 19 Aug. 1788, to Knowsley.
150. Ibid., 26 Jan. 1789, to William Huntingdon.
151. Ibid., 10 Feb. 1789, 12 Sept. 1789.
152. HAJ, Delamain no. 2 letter book 1787-9, 30 Oct. 1789.
153. For example, HAJ, Delamain letter book 1793-8 (no. 2), 14 Nov. 1793.
154. HAJ, Delamain letter book 1798-1802, 27 Floréal an 9.
155. HAC, 20 April 1798, London.
156. HAC, 9 Oct. 1798, Shoolbred, London; 28 Jan. 1800, Shoolbred and Williams to Turner.
157. See property transaction of 19 June 1800 (30 Prairial an 8) in the possession of Messrs Hine's notary. I am indebted to M. Bernard Hine for a copy.
158. There is a reference to Hine handling accounts in 1793. HAJ, Delamain no. 2 letter book 1793-8, 31 Aug. 1793, to Jacques Dupuy, Paris.
159. HAJ, Draft of letter to father of Thomas Hine, 29 June 1795.
160. HAJ, 23 Sept. 1800 (1 Vendémiaire an 9), draft of articles of new partnership.
161. HAJ, Delamain letter book 1799-1801 (no. 2), 17 Jan. 1801, to Thomas Gorman.

162. HAJ, Delamain letter book 1802-06, 1 June 1805, to James Delamain.
163. Ibid., 14 May, 11 June 1806.
164. Ibid., 15 Oct. 1806.
165. Ibid., 23 July 1806. See also 4 July.
166. HAJ, circular 12 May 1817, act of 2 Nov. 1817.
167. Anne Phillipe Henri Delamain, son of Jean Isaac, placed in Ranson & Delamain as a clerk in 1812, should not be confused with Paul-Marie-Henri-Ferdinand.
168. J. Jezequel, *Grands notables du Premier Empire* (Paris, 1986), p. 19.
169. I am indebted to Madame Adol for this information.
170. HAC, 18 Nov. 1813, Turner, Vinade.
171. J. Jezequel, op. cit., p. 101.
172. P. Butel, *Les dynasties bordelaises de Colbert à Chaban* (Paris, 1991), p. 192.

Note on sources

The brandy trade is rich in business collections, mostly held in private possession or in commercial firms, though some items also survive in legal records, and a Martell letter book for 1742–3 is in the Archives Départementales de la Charente in Angoulême. The business records of six firms survived in company and family custody (and were held in eight locations); and two public archives in the region, in Angoulême and Bordeaux, also held material). They relate to the business of what were in business terms fourteen or so distinct enterprises, and in the narrowest legal terms to a rough twenty businesses or partnerships. The Hennessy archives are the richest, containing in- and out-correspondence from 1765. In particular they contain the correspondence of 1769–76 from John Saule in La Rochelle to Richard Hennessy in Cognac (with some although not all of his later correspondence to Bordeaux) and from Richard Hennessy during his residence in Bordeaux with a gap for a single year in the period from 1776 to 1788: at times therefore the correspondence, or some of it, survives simultaneously on both sides.

The Martell archives is next in scale, starting much earlier (from 1718), but with many gaps in the letter books before 1778; there is no incoming correspondence before 1784, from which date a variable portion, at times minute, at times substantial, survives. A full run of Ranson & Delamain letter books from 1778 is in the modern house of Hine, and Otard has its letter books from 1795. The house of Augier, while having little material for later decades, has a run of business letter books for the late 1710s and 1720s, and for the early 1720s the extraordinarily rich correspondence between the partners, surviving for both sides (and backed up by further letter books), in the traumatic economic difficulties occasioned by their reckless speculation under John Law's system. A number of letters for 1758-62 from Richard Hennessy in Ostend survive in the papers of the Irish army officer Richard Warren in Vannes. For a fuller account of the records, see the note on sources in Cullen, *The brandy trade under the Ancien Régime: regional specialisation in the Charente*. That book also contains a more complete bibliography; the bibliography below is confined to sources bearing directly on brandy and on brandy merchants.

The administrative framework of the trade is not well documented. The richest source is the archives of the Chambre de Commerce in La Rochelle, but smaller, though significant collections are in the *Intendance* papers in the Archives Départementales in Angoulême and in La Rochelle. The brandy trade also crops up in the *Correspondence Politique Angleterre* in the Archives du Ministère des Affaires Etrangères. The statistical sources are the usual ones but of special interest is F^{12} 1666 for its remarkably full trade figures for all French ports in 1789. Port books – or more accurately the *amirauté* documents on the regular arrival or departure of ships – do not survive for the ports in the *généralité* of La Rochelle, though there is an incomplete run for Bordeaux. The *congés* series in the Archives Nationales makes up in the 1780s for some of the deficiencies.

The legal records in the notarial archives are rewarding in the case of the *étude* of Cherpentier (Cherpantier) of Tonnay-Charente, held in the Archives départementales de la Charente Maritime in La Rochelle; the *études* for Rochefort are not very informative on the brandy trade, but the notarial records of Cognac together with the *Controle des actes*, held in the Archives départementales de la Charente in Angoulême, are illuminating on the marriage of Saule and, after his death, on his estate. Before the 1790s, while the notarial records of Cognac town are informative on families and property, merchants left the making of notarial acts about shipping and trade problems in the hands of their agents in Tonnay-Charente

In contrast to the large literature on Bordeaux wine, the brandy trade is poorly covered in books and articles. They draw scarcely at all on primary sources, repeating what is said in earlier works; and even works on local history have rather sparse elements on the trade or on the families.

Portraits present a fascinating and at times baffling scenario. Merchant portraiture in the eighteenth century usually exists only for great houses, and by no means for all or even most of them. As the brandy houses were small houses, with a few becoming large only in the second half of the century, portraits appear late. The two Martell sons in business in the second half of the century (together with their wives), and James Delamain and his spouse, the two families who represented the pinnacle of success on the Charente, are the first privately prompted instances. The portrait of Etienne Augier dates from his election as delegate to the States General of 1789, and the portrait of Richard Hennessy from his holding of office in the Garde Nationale in Cognac in the early 1790s.

The Hennessy portrait illustrates graphically some of the problems. Until recently the assumption in the modern house was that no such portrait existed, and the portrait, now presiding over the *Salle du courrier*, had been entirely lost sight of. It has never been reproduced, and is for instance neither presented nor mentioned in *Cognac à l'heure de la révolution de 1789*, the guide to the exhibition held in the Musée Municipal de Cognac in 1989, for which it would have been of particular relevance. Of its authenticity there seems no doubt, and the artistic evidence is confirmed by the fact that the diary of the Cognac Garde Nationale has survived among the archives of the house, illustrating how close was the identification between the house and Garde. The fact that a very early copy of part of the painting seems to have been made further confirms the standing of the portrait within the house contemporaneously or early in the nineteenth century.

A problem with portraits, as with other heirlooms, is that French inheritance laws give siblings more rights than Irish or British inheritance practice, which markedly favours the eldest inheriting son, with the consequence that portraits become dispersed within branches of the family, and can quickly become untraceable. Thus for instance the original authentic Martell portraits (reproduced in Firino-Martell's book in 1924) are now known in the house only in photographic form and are reproduced only from that source. The two Delamain portraits are not within the family of the inheriting branch of the business (though their location at least is known and they are for that reason accessible). On the other hand a portrait of Delamain in national guard uniform survives only in a very elderly photograph, and the location of the original is unknown.

A recently located portrait is said to be of James Hennessy, probably from 1816–17. There is also a portrait said to be of a Hennessy, allegedly the founder of the Ostend branch of the family, which is said to have been later sold by that branch and finally purchased back in modern times by a member of the Cognac family. It is rather grand for a portrait of a merchant family (man in background, two ladies, one seated in foreground, one with a dog): while the portrait is unquestionably of the style of the early eighteenth century, it is by no means certain that it is a portrait of a merchant family, or of Charles Hennessy or family, and is more likely to have been simply a portrait that came into the possession of the family and about which later family legend grew.

Success also created an urge to make good missing ancestors. Thus there is a Martell portrait, said variously in sources in or about Cognac to have been of the first or second Jean Martell. It is not convincing on artistic grounds – *a fortiori* in the case of the first Jean – and is a later painting. The portrait of Jean-Baptiste-Antoine Otard, representing him at the height of his economic and political success, at the time he received the *légion d'honneur* in 1821, would have held him up to ridicule if it had been painted in his lifetime. The face is young for his fifty-eight years, and its lack of character further points to a patently mechanical artistic quality. It is likely to be a production, later, though not necessarily much later, by a family or business basking in his repute or success. For a long time, within the house of Hennessy, the well-known painting of Hennessy in army uniform was held to be the only known representation of a member of the first two generations of the family (this is the painting referred to in Cullen, *The Brandy Trade under the Ancien Régime*, p. 185). Its history is not well known, and it is as likely, perhaps more so, to be twentieth-century than nineteenth-century: at any rate its use seems to have become widespread only from the 1930s, the decade in which the packing of brandy in cartons became widespread.

There is no portrait of John Saule, though there is one of the second husband of his widow, De Caminade.

Bibliography

PRIMARY SOURCES

BUSINESS RECORDS (ABROAD)

Bordeaux	*Archives départementales de la Gironde*
	7B1169-1176, Boyd-Guiliory partnership (George Boyd & Cie), 1780s
	7B 537-538, new Boyd-Guiliory partnership, 1787-9
Cognac	*Augier archives*
	Augier, Veuve Augier et Cie (various styles)
	Broussard
	Veuve Guerinet & cie, Charente
	Hennessy archives
	Hennessy & Cie, Saule & Cie, Hennessy & Turner
	Régnier, Charente
	Martell archives
	Martell; Veuve Martell, Lallemand & Cie (1742-3 letter book in *Archives départementales de la Charente*, J215)
	Martell, Fiott & Cie, Bordeaux
	Otard archives
	Otard & Dupuy
Guernsey	*Priaulx Library*
	Carteret Priaulx papers
Jarnac	*Delamain archives*
	Ranson & Delamain
	Hine archives
	Isaac Ranson & Cie
	Ranson & Delamain (and later styles)
	Hine

Jerez	Garvey & Co.
Lorient	*Service historique de la marine: Archives du port* (second) French East India Company
Vannes	*Archives départementales du Morbihan* Lamaignère & Delaye papers E2340-E2445 Warren papers E1435-1468

BUSINESS RECORDS (IN IRELAND)

Cork	*Archives Council* Hewitt papers (Irish Distillers deposit)
Belfast	*Public Record Office of Northern Ireland* Black papers
Dublin	*National Library of Ireland* Hutchins papers *National University, Dublin* O'Connell papers

ADMINISTRATIVE RECORDS

Angouleme	*Archives départementales de la Charente* Correspondence with Intendant, La Rochelle, 1782-4, 5C5, 5C6 Notarial minutes: Imbaud, Lauchère Contrôle des actes
Bordeaux	*Archives departementales de la Gironde* Intendant's correspondence about 'Anglais' in Bordeaux, 1756-8, C1072-1074 *Balance du commerce,* C4268-4271, 4385-4390 Notarial minutes: Guy, Guy fils Passports for passengers, 1727-1750, 6B 47, 48, 49, 50
Brest	*Service historique de la marine: archives du port* Intendant de la marine's letter books (outgoing)
Nantes	*Archives départementales de la Loire Atlantique* Declarations by masters of outward vessels 1738, Amirauté B4694[1] *Balance du commerce* for Nantes and for Brittany, Série C
Paris	*Archives nationales* Congés for outward bound vessels, Charente and Bordeaux, G[5] 47*, 48*, 50*, 51*, 62 lettres de naturalité and lettres de reconnaissance de noblesse, Série O[i] *Archives du ministère des affaires étrangères* Correspondance politique Angleterre *Archives de la guerre, Paris* Personal file of Lieut-Colonel Richard Hennessy Registre de l'infanterie 1752-7 Yb 820

Officer registre, IYC 258

Richard Hennessy's mission, AI 2770, nos. 76-93, 6 Aug. – 28 Dec. 1730

Rennes   *Archives départementales d'Ille-et-Vilaine*

Bourde de la Rogerie papers, 5 J 74, notes on Warren correspondence

La Rochelle   *Archives départementales de la Charente Maritime*

Letter book of an unidentifed Irish merchant, La Rochelle 1699-1707, 4J 2283

Notarial minutes, Tonnay-Charente: Cherpentier

Notarial minutes, La Rochelle: Teuleron (1645–1681), 3E 1294–1319; De la Vergne

Bibliothèque municipale

Ms 2703, Claude Claveau,' Le monde rochelais de l'Ancien Regime' (contains summary statistics of brandy exports drawn from *balance du commerce* records, p. 767)

Chambre de Commerce

Correspondence and *balance du commerce* documents

PRINTED SOURCES

E. Aerts, L.M. Cullen and R.G. Wilson, eds, *Production, marketing and consumption of alcoholic beverages since the late middle ages* (Leuven, 1990)

F. Aftalion, *The French Revolution: an economic interpretation* (Cambridge, 1990)

P. Butel, 'Quelques leçons sur le dynamisme commercial: Cognac à la fin du XVIIIe siècle', in *Eaux-de-vie et spiritueux*, ed. A. Huetz de Lemps and Philippe Roudié (Paris, 1985)

—, *Les dynasties bordelaises de Colbert à Chaban* (Paris, 1991)

—, *L'économie française au xviiie siècle* (Paris, 1993)

J.G. Clark, *La Rochelle and the Atlantic economy during the eighteenth century* (Baltimore and London, 1981)

T.W. Copeland, ed., *Correspondence of Edmund Burke,* 10 vols (Cambridge, 1958-78)

F. Crouzet, *La grande inflation: la monnaie en France de Louis XVI à Napoleon* (Paris, 1993)

L.M. Cullen, 'The Blackwater Catholics and County Cork society and politics in the eighteenth century', *Cork: history and society* (Dublin, 1993), ed. P. O'Flanagan and C.G. Buttimer, pp. 535-84

—, *The brandy trade under the Ancien Régime: regional specialisation in the Charente* (Cambridge, 1998)

—, 'Comparative aspects of Irish diet 1550-1850', in Hans J. Teuteberg, ed., *European food history* (Leicester, 1992), pp. 45-55

—, 'Galway merchants in the outside world 1660-1800', in D. O Cearbhaill, ed., *Galway: town and gown* (Dublin, 1984), pp. 63-89

—, 'The Huguenots from the perspective of the merchant networks of W. Europe (1680-1720)', in *The Huguenots and Ireland: anatomy of an emigration*

(Dublin, 1987), ed. C.J. Caldicott, G. Gough and J.P. Pittion, pp. 129-49

—, 'Ireland and Irishmen in eighteenth-century privateering', in *Course et piraterie: etudes presentees a la Commission Internationale d'histoire maritime a l'occasion de son XVe colloque international pendant le 14e congres international des sciences historiques (San Francisco, aout 1975)* (Paris, 1975), vol. 1, pp. 469–86

—, 'Le réseau commercial du negoce du cognac dans les années 1760', in *Le négoce international xiiie-xxe siècles*, ed. Francois M. Crouzet (Paris, 1989), pp. 153-68

—, 'Smugglers in the Irish Sea in the eighteenth century', in *The Irish Sea: aspects of maritime history*, ed. M. McCaughan and J. Appleby (Belfast, 1989), p. 85-99

—, *Smuggling and the Ayrshire economic boom of the 1760s and 1770s*, Ayrshire Archaeological and Natural History Society, Ayrshire monographs (Sept. 1994).

—, 'The smuggling trade in Ireland in the eighteenth century', *Proceedings of the Royal Irish Academy*, section C, vol. 67, no. 5 (1969), pp. 149-75.

R. Delamain, *Histoire du cognac* (Paris, 1935)

—, *Jarnac à travers les ages* (Angoulême, 2nd. ed., 1954)

Delaye, G., *L'Angoumois au temps des marchands flamands (17e siècle)* (Paris, 1990)

L. Dermigny, *Sète de 1666 à 1880, Esquisse de l'histoire d'un port* (Montpellier, 1955)

R. Dion, *Histoire de la vigne et du vin en France des origines aux xixᵉ siècle* (Paris, 1959)

R. Firino-Martell, *La famille Martell* (Paris, 1924)

A. Guimera Ravina, *Burguesia extranjera y comercio atlántico: la empresa comercial irlandesa en Canarias 1703-1771* (Tenerife, 1985)

K.J. Harvey, 'The family experience: the Bellews of Mount Bellew', in T.P. Power and K. Whelan, *Endurance and Emergence: Catholics in Ireland in the Eighteenth Century* (Dublin, 1990)

—, *The Bellews of Mount Bellew: A Catholic Gentry Family in Eighteenth-Century Ireland* (Dublin, 1998)

W. Henry, rector of Urney, *An earnest address to the people of Ireland against the drinking of spirituous liquors* (Dublin, 1753).

A. Huetz de Lemps and P. Roudié, eds, *Eaux de vie et spiritueux* (Paris, 1985)

A.G. Jamieson, *A people of the sea: the maritime history of the Channel Islands* (London, 1986)

J. Jezequel, *Grands notables du premier empire* (Paris, 1986)

—, *La Charente révolutionnaire 1789-99* (Poitiers, 1992)

W. Minchinton, 'The Canaries in the British Trade World of the Eighteenth Century', in Francisco Morales Padron, ed., *IX Coloquio de historia Canario-Americana* (Las Palmas, Canary Islands, 1990)

P. Reverchon, ed., *Cognac à l'heure de la révolution de 1789* (Cognac, 1989)

Jerome Royr, *Histoire de la franc-maçonnerie en Charente* (Paris, 1994)

Bruno Sepulchre, *Notes pour servir à l'histoire de la commune de Segonzac* ([Jarnac], 1984)

Index